KU-235-443

ECOCRITICISM

Ecocriticism explores the ways in which we imagine and portray the relationship between humans and the environment in all areas of cultural production, from Wordsworth and Thoreau to Disney and BBC nature documentaries. It is inspired by, but also critical of, modern environmental movements. Greg Garrard's accessible volume traces the development of the movement and explores the concepts that have most occupied ecocritics, including:

- Pollution
- Wilderness
- Apocalypse
- Dwelling
- Animals
- The Earth

Featuring a glossary of terms and suggestions for further reading, this is an invaluable introduction to one of the most exciting recent developments in literary and cultural studies.

Greg Garrard is a Lecturer in English at Bath Spa University College.

THE NEW CRITICAL IDIOM

SERIES EDITOR: JOHN DRAKAKIS, UNIVERSITY OF STIRLING

The New Critical Idiom is an invaluable series of introductory guides to today's critical terminology. Each book:

- provides a handy, explanatory guide to the use (and abuse) of the term
- offers an original and distinctive overview by a leading literary and cultural critic
- relates the term to the larger field of cultural representation.

With a strong emphasis on clarity, lively debate and the widest possible breadth of examples, *The New Critical Idiom* is an indispensable approach to key topics in literary studies.

Also available in this series:

Autobiography
by Linda Anderson

Class by Gary Day

Colonialism/Postcolonialism
by Ania Loomba

Culture/Metaculture
by Francis Mulhern

Discourse by Sara Mills

Dramatic Monologue
by Glennis Byron

Genders by David Glover and
Cora Kaplan

Gothic by Fred Botting

Historicism by Paul Hamilton

Humanism by Tony Davies

Ideology by David Hawkes

Interdisciplinarity by Joe Moran

Intertextuality by Graham Allen

Irony by Claire Colebrook

Literature by Peter Widdowson

Metre, Rhythm and Verse Form
by Philip Hobsbaum

Modernism by Peter Childs

Myth by Laurence Coupe

Narrative by Paul Cobley

Parody by Simon Dentith

Pastoral by Terry Gifford

Realism by Pam Morris

Romanticism by Aidan Day

Science Fiction by Adam Roberts

Sexuality by Joseph Bristow

Stylistics by Richard Bradford

Subjectivity by Donald E. Hall

The Unconscious
by Antony Easthope

ECOCRITICISM

Greg Garrard

Routledge
Taylor & Francis Group

LONDON AND NEW YORK

First published 2004
by Routledge
2 Park Square, Milton Park, Abingdon, Oxfordshire OX14 4RN

Simultaneously published in the USA and Canada
by Routledge
29 West 35th Street, New York, NY 10001

Routledge is an imprint of the Taylor & Francis Group

© 2004 Greg Garrard

Typeset in Adobe Garamond and Scala Sans by Keystroke,
Jacaranda Lodge, Wolverhampton
Printed and bound in Great Britain by TJ International Ltd,
Padstow, Cornwall

All rights reserved. No part of this book may be reprinted or
reproduced or utilised in any form or by any electronic,
mechanical, or other means, now known or hereafter invented,
including photocopying and recording, or in any information
storage or retrieval system, without permission in writing from
the publishers.

British Library Cataloguing in Publication Data
A catalogue record for this book is available from the British Library

Library of Congress Cataloging in Publication Data
Garrard, Greg.
    Ecocriticism / Greg Garrard.
        p. cm. — (New critical idiom)
    Includes bibliographical references and index.
        1. English literature—History and criticism—Theory, etc.
    2. Nature in literature. 3. American literature—History and
    criticism—Theory, etc. 4. Conservation of natural resources in
    literature. 5. Environmental protection in literature. 6. Philosophy
    of nature in literature. 7. Forests and forestry in literature.
    8. Wilderness areas in literature. 9. Outdoor life in literature.
    10. Criticism—Great Britain. 11. Criticism—United States.
    12. Landscape in literature. 13. Ecology in literature.
    14. Ecocriticism. I. Title. II. Series.
    PR143.G37 2004
    820.9'36–dc22   2004003429

ISBN 0–415–19691–4 (hbk)
ISBN 0–415–19692–2 (pbk)

For Holly

CONTENTS

SERIES EDITOR'S PREFACE

The New Critical Idiom is a series of introductory books which seeks to extend the lexicon of literary terms, in order to address the radical changes which have taken place in the study of literature during the last decades of the twentieth century. The aim is to provide clear, well-illustrated accounts of the full range of terminology currently in use, and to evolve histories of its changing usage.

The current state of the discipline of literary studies is one where there is considerable debate concerning basic questions of terminology. This involves, among other things, the boundaries which distinguish the literary from the non-literary; the position of literature within the larger sphere of culture; the relationship between literatures of different cultures; and questions concerning the relation of literary to other cultural forms within the context of interdisciplinary structures.

It is clear that the field of literary criticism and theory is a dynamic and heterogeneous one. The present need is for individual volumes on terms which combine clarity of exposition with an adventurousness of perspective and a breadth of application. Each volume will contain as part of its apparatus some indication of the direction in which the definition of particular terms is likely to move, as well as expanding the disciplinary boundaries within which some of these terms have been traditionally contained. This will involve some re-situation of terms within the larger field of cultural representation, and will introduce examples from the area of film and the modern media in addition to examples from a variety of literary texts.

ACKNOWLEDGMENTS

My first and foremost acknowledgment is to all my splendid and unusual family, for their support and encouragement, especially during the long years of PhD study. Specifically, Mum and Dad rushed in where the British Academy feared to fund, Pa provoked my interest in environmental issues and gave me someone to argue with, and Fliss shared my gardening obsession and sent Michael Pollan books to give it intellectual weight. And I am blessed with brilliant brothers and sisters.

Jon Bate was an exemplary supervisor, and suggested my name to Routledge for this series. I am deeply grateful for the practical consequences of his faith in me, such as having a job that I love immoderately. Amongst my many excellent colleagues at Bath Spa University College, Richard Kerridge has given me the benefit of his intelligence and insight in many a long argument, Tracey Hill has tried to save me from myself, and Paul Edwards has supported my research and commented on a first draft. Moreover, I have learned a great deal from our students, especially those on 'Writing and Environmental Crisis', 'Reading Texts' and 'Utopias'. In particular, John Gaskin read and commented on an early draft. The College has also provided me with some vital teaching relief. Beyond Bath, the members of ASLE have been an inspiration to me, especially Molly Westling and Terry Gifford.

John Drakakis was an extremely thorough and challenging editor, whose debates with me over successive versions greatly improved the eventual outcome. Liz Thompson was patient and supportive even when the manuscript was late for its late, revised deadline, and undertook further crucial editing.

Closest to home, much love and thanks must go to Caroline, who read most of the drafts and provided invaluable intellectual and stylistic comments. The discussion of the feminine sublime in Chapter 3 is specifically indebted to her. Thanks also, although they'll never know it, to Bryn, Hamish and P'ars'ley, whose seemingly constant demands for food, walks and games provided an ironic counterpoint to the writing of the 'Animals' chapter.

NOTE ON TERMINOLOGY

While it is usual in academic writing to refer to 'Native Americans' rather than 'American Indians', I have used both terms interchangeably in this book. Neither is wholly satisfactory, and my understanding is that many Native Americans prefer the traditional term.

1

BEGINNINGS: POLLUTION

It is generally agreed that modern environmentalism begins with 'A Fable for Tomorrow', in Rachel Carson's *Silent Spring* (1962). Carson's fairy tale opens with the words, 'There was once a town in the heart of America where all life seemed to live in harmony with its surroundings' and, invoking the ancient tradition of the pastoral, goes on to paint a picture of 'prosperous farms', 'green fields', foxes barking in the hills, silent deer, ferns and wildflowers, 'countless birds' and trout lying in clear, cold streams, all delighted in by those who pass through the town (1999: 21). Concentrating on images of natural beauty and emphasising the 'harmony' of humanity and nature that 'once' existed, the fable at first presents us with a picture of essential changelessness, which human activity scarcely disturbs, and which the annual round of seasons only reinforces. However, pastoral peace rapidly gives way to catastrophic destruction:

> Then a strange blight crept over the area and everything began to change. Some evil spell had settled on the community: mysterious maladies swept the flocks of chickens; the cattle and sheep sickened and died. Everywhere was a shadow of death.

In the ensuing paragraphs, every element of the rural idyll is torn apart by some agent of change, the mystery of which is emphasised by the use of both natural and supernatural terminology of 'malady' and 'spell'. The most impassioned passage concerns the collapse in bird populations: 'On the mornings that had once throbbed with the dawn chorus of robins, catbirds, doves, jays, wrens, and scores of other bird voices there was now no sound; only silence lay over the fields and woods and marsh' (1999: 22). The 'silent spring' of the title alludes, on one level, to this loss of birdsong, although it also comes to function as a synecdoche for a more general environmental apocalypse.

So the founding text of modern environmentalism not only begins with a decidedly poetic parable, but also relies on the literary genres of pastoral and apocalypse, pre-existing ways of imagining the place of humans in nature that may be traced back to such sources as Genesis and Revelation, the first and last books of the Bible. *Silent Spring* initially suggests that the mythical eco-catastrophe of the fable might be supernatural, and emphasises this by including an epigram from Keats' poem 'La Belle Dame Sans Merci', in which the magical power of a beautiful woman blights the environment: 'The sedge is wither'd from the lake, / And no birds sing.' But then the fable concludes: 'No witchcraft, no enemy action had silenced the rebirth of new life in this stricken world. The people had done it themselves.' The rest of the book sets out to prove that such an apocalypse was already going on in a fragmentary way all over America, so that the doom befalling this mythical town of the future could be seen as a composite of lesser tragedies already known, and scientifically validated, in 1962.

The real culprits, according to Carson, were the new organic pesticides such as DDT, aldrin and dieldrin that had been introduced after the Second World War and had already proven highly successful in controlling pest insects. *Silent Spring* marshalled an impressive array of scientific evidence to show that this very success constituted a serious threat both to wildlife and to human health, confronting the utopian claims of agricultural scientists on their own ground. Carson's scientific claims have since been largely confirmed (although there is still no evidence that DDT is harmful to humans), leading to increased public awareness of pesticide pollution, firmer state regulation and development of less persistent agricultural chemicals.

Environmentalist claims like these make crucial contributions to modern politics and culture, and many of us respond to them to some degree, yet for the student of the humanities they can be difficult to assess on their own terms. Academia has been organised into relatively autonomous 'disciplines' and scientific problems seem to require scientific expertise. Nevertheless, the rhetorical strategies, use of pastoral and apocalyptic imagery and literary allusions with which Carson shapes her scientific material may well be amenable to a more 'literary' or 'cultural' analysis. Such analysis is what we will call 'ecocriticism'. This book is a critical introduction to the field of ecocriticism today.

Let us look, then, at some provisional definitions of the subject. The first is from the 'Introduction' to *The Ecocriticism Reader* (1996), an important anthology of American ecocriticism:

> What then *is* ecocriticism? Simply put, ecocriticism is the study of the relationship between literature and the physical environment. Just as feminist criticism examines language and literature from a gender-conscious perspective, and Marxist criticism brings an awareness of modes of production and economic class to its reading of texts, ecocriticism takes an earth-centred approach to literary studies.
>
> (Glotfelty 1996: xix)

Glotfelty goes on to specify some of the questions ecocritics ask, ranging from 'How is nature represented in this sonnet?' through 'How has the concept of wilderness changed over time?' to 'How is science itself open to literary analysis?' and finally 'What cross-fertilization is possible between literary studies and environmental discourse in related disciplines such as history, philosophy, psychology, art history, and ethics?'

Ecocriticism is, then, an avowedly political mode of analysis, as the comparison with feminism and Marxism suggests. Ecocritics generally tie their cultural analyses explicitly to a 'green' moral and political agenda. In this respect, ecocriticism is closely related to environmentally oriented developments in philosophy and political theory. Developing the insights of earlier critical movements, ecofeminists, social ecologists and environmental justice advocates seek a synthesis of environmental and social concerns.

It is worth noting also that the questions posed by ecocriticism in Glotfelty's account follow a clear trajectory: the first question, for example, is very narrow and literary, tending to favour the student of

Romantic verse. Thus, two of the most important works of ecocriticism in the 1990s were studies of Wordsworth and Shelley (Bate 1991 and Kroeber 1994). The questions grow in scope as the list continues, with several of the later ones suggesting gargantuan interdisciplinary studies such as Simon Schama's *Landscape and Memory* (1995).

Richard Kerridge's definition in the mainly British *Writing the Environment* (1998) suggests, like Glotfelty's, a broad cultural ecocriticism:

> The ecocritic wants to track environmental ideas and representations wherever they appear, to see more clearly a debate which seems to be taking place, often part-concealed, in a great many cultural spaces. Most of all, ecocriticism seeks to evaluate texts and ideas in terms of their coherence and usefulness as responses to environmental crisis.
>
> (1998: 5)

We will have reason to question the monolithic conception of 'environmental crisis' implied here, and perhaps to resist the evaluation of 'texts and ideas' against a seemingly secure ecological yardstick: both as a science and as a socio-political movement, 'ecology' itself is shifting and contested. However, the emphasis on the moral and political orientation of the ecocritic and the broad specification of the field of study are essential.

From the point of view of academics, ecocriticism is dominated by the Association for the Study of Literature and the Environment (ASLE), a professional association that started in America but now has significant branches in the UK and Japan. It organises regular conferences and publishes a journal that includes literary analysis, creative writing and articles on environmental education and activism. Many early works of ecocriticism were characterised by an exclusive interest in Romantic poetry, wilderness narrative and nature writing, but in the last few years ASLE has turned towards a more general cultural ecocriticism, with studies of popular scientific writing, film, TV, art, architecture and other cultural artefacts such as theme parks, zoos and shopping malls. As ecocritics seek to offer a truly transformative discourse, enabling us to analyse and criticise the world in which we live, attention is increasingly given to the broad range of cultural processes and products in which, and through which, the complex negotiations of nature and culture take place.

Indeed, the widest definition of the subject of ecocriticism is the study of the relationship of the human and the non-human, throughout human cultural history and entailing critical analysis of the term 'human' itself. This book will reflect these trends by giving space to both literary and cultural ecocriticism. However, at this point there is a caveat: I will be dealing principally with British and North American literature and culture, although the principles of ecocriticism would of course admit of more general application.

Ecocriticism is unique amongst contemporary literary and cultural theories because of its close relationship with the science of ecology. Ecocritics may not be qualified to contribute to debates about problems in ecology, but they must nevertheless transgress disciplinary boundaries and develop their own 'ecological literacy' as far as possible. I therefore provide brief discussions of some important environmental threats faced by the world today. To consider these in detail is beyond the scope of this book, but it is essential for ecocritics to recognise that there are serious arguments about the existence of the problems, their extent, the nature of the threat and the possible solutions to them. So, for example, in Chapter 5, I consider the problem of 'over-population' from a demographic point of view, before going on to explain how the issue has been refracted through apocalyptic rhetoric.

It may seem obvious that ecological problems are scientific problems rather than objects of cultural analysis. Indeed, when *Silent Spring* was published the agro-chemical industry reacted by criticising the book for its literary qualities, which, they implied, could not coexist with the appropriate scientific rigour. Would we not be recapitulating the propaganda published by the pesticide producers if we read Carson's book using literary-critical tools? John Passmore has proposed a distinction that may help to negotiate the problem. 'Problems in ecology', he maintains, are properly scientific issues, to be resolved by the formulation and testing of hypotheses in ecological experiments, while 'ecological problems' are 'features of our society, arising out of our dealings with nature, from which we should like to free ourselves, and which we do not regard as inevitable consequences of what is good in that society' (1974: 44). To describe something as an ecological problem is to make a normative claim about how we would wish things to be, and while this arises out of the claims of ecological scientists, it is not defined by them. A 'weed' is not a kind of plant, only the wrong kind in the wrong place. Eliminating weeds is obviously a 'problem in gardening', but defining weeds in the first place requires a cultural, not horticultural, analysis. Likewise 'pollution' is an ecological problem because it does not name a substance or class of substances, but rather represents an implicit normative claim that too much of something is present in the environment, usually in the wrong place. Carson had to investigate a problem in ecology, with the help of wildlife biologists and environmental toxicologists, in order to show that DDT was present in the environment in amounts toxic to wildlife, but *Silent Spring* undertook cultural not scientific work when it strove to argue the moral case that it *ought* not to be. The great achievement of the book was to turn a (scientific) problem in ecology into a widely perceived ecological problem that was then contested politically, legally and in the media and popular culture. Thus ecocriticism cannot contribute much to debates about problems in ecology, but it can help to define, explore and even resolve ecological problems in this wider sense.

One 'ecocritical' way of reading is to see contributions to environmental debate as examples of rhetoric. I have already suggested that Carson deploys both pastoral imagery and apocalyptic rhetoric, and will return to these subjects, but there are many other applications of formal rhetorical analysis. For example, Ralph Lutts has attempted to account for the impact of *Silent Spring* by drawing attention to the underlying analogy Carson uses between pesticide pollution and another kind of pollution that was strong in popular consciousness in 1962:

> She was sounding an alarm about a kind of pollution that was invisible to the senses; could be transported great distances, perhaps globally; could accumulate over time in body tissues; could produce chronic, as well as acute, poisoning; and could result in cancer, birth defects, and genetic mutations that may not become evident until years or decades after exposure. Government officials, she also argued, were not taking the steps necessary to control this pollution and protect the public. Chemical pesticides were not the only form of pollution fitting this description. Another form, far better known to the public at the time, was radioactive fallout. Pesticides could be understood as another form of fallout.

> (2000:19)

So Carson combined ancient ways of imagining nature with contemporary ways of imagining a threat derived from 'fallout hysteria', with a view to establishing particular normative claims about pollution. Detailed rhetorical analysis shows how *Silent Spring* is constructed in order to achieve certain political results: not only the concrete measures described in the final chapter, but also a subtle revision of the concept of 'pollution' itself.

Reading *Silent Spring* as rhetoric has a number of advantages for an overtly politicised critical practice, some of which are set out by Marxist critic Terry Eagleton:

> What would be specific to the kind of study I have in mind . . . would be the kinds of *effects* which discourses produce, and how they produce them. Reading a zoology textbook to find out about giraffes is part of studying zoology, but reading it to see how its discourse is structured and organised, and examining what kind of effects these forms and devices produce in particular readers in actual situations, is a different kind of project. It is, in fact, probably the oldest form of literary criticism in the world, known as rhetoric.
>
> (1996: 205)

I will be reading culture as rhetoric, although not in the strict sense understood by rhetoricians, but as the production, reproduction and transformation of large-scale metaphors. Each of my chapters will examine one such metaphor, thought to have specific – though sometimes ambivalent – political effects or to serve particular social interests. Some, like 'pastoral', are established literary tropes, whilst others name more heterogenous materials that one can provisionally unify under a single title. Since all are, in some sense, ways of imagining, constructing or presenting nature in a figure, I will call my chapter headings 'tropes'. Each trope will gather together permutations of creative imagination: metaphor, genre, narrative, image. This introduction explores the trope of 'pollution' as an example. The basis upon which each trope is defined and limited is worked out in each chapter, with the constant proviso that, as ecocritics like to say, 'the map is not the terrain'. My tropology is not definitive or exhaustive; it is intended to be enabling, not limiting.

Rhetorical analysis suggests that the meaning of tropes is closely related to their wider social context. They are therefore not fixed entities but develop and change historically. 'Pollution', for example, derives from the Latin 'polluere' meaning 'to defile', and its early English usage reflects its theologico-moral origins: until the seventeenth century it denoted moral contamination of a person, or acts (such as masturbation) thought to promote such contamination. This essentially interior or subjective definition was gradually transformed into an exterior or objective – in fact, specifically environmental – definition between the seventeenth and nineteenth centuries, to the point where today only its later definition is widely known. The process is exemplary in that it highlights how people had to learn to hate their detritus, as well as indicating the deep cultural roots of the fear attaching to such immoral emissions. Most of the tropes in the book are traced to ancient origins before I explore their modern inflection.

The first citation of the modern sense of 'pollution' in the *Oxford English Dictionary* is from Francis Bacon's *The Advancement of Learning* (1605), a founding text of modern scientific methodology: 'The Sunne . . . passeth through pollutions, and it selfe remaines as pure as before.' Bacon seems here to be writing about a material, not a moral, phenomenon, which constitutes a crucial shift in meaning, and the very birth of a new way of seeing and thinking. Yet a key text in ecocritical history, Carolyn Merchant's *The Death of Nature* (1980), ascribes to Bacon a pivotal role in the construction of an environmentally destructive world view where 'the image of an organic cosmos with a living female earth at its center gave way to a mechanistic world view in which nature was reconstituted as dead and passive, to be dominated and controlled by humans' (1990: xvi). Thus the trope of 'pollution' is historically implicated in both environmental destruction and salvation since Bacon both 'discovered' pollution in the modern sense and, according to Merchant, helped make much more of it. From an ecocritical perspective this reflects the ambivalent role of science as both a producer of environmental hazards and a critical analyst of them. All the tropes examined in this book show some such ambivalence.

Another crucial feature of rhetoric is that tropes are assumed to take part in wider social struggles between genders, classes and ethnic groups. Cultures are not shaped equally by all their participants, nor are the many world cultures equally powerful, and we must remain aware that even tropes that might potentially confront or subvert environmentally damaging practices may be appropriated. So although wilderness might seem to form a bulwark against an industrialised, materially progressive world view and social order, elements of that order such as manufacturers of four-wheel-drive Sports Utility Vehicles have still been able to appropriate the wild as the 'natural home' of their products in their advertisements (see Campbell 1998). Since these vehicles virtually require their own oil well to feed their huge engines, the irony of the juxtaposition might suggest to us that 'wilderness' has an ideological function in this case, helping to legitimise the conspicuous consumption of a privileged class and nation.

In ordinary usage, 'rhetoric' suggests language that substitutes for literal truth: it is all 'hot air'. The sense intended in this book, however, is emphatically interested in literal meaning. This would be a negligible point were there not important trends in literary and cultural theory that would seem to marginalise the role of literal truth in literature and culture, even in science itself. Structuralism and post-structuralism, for example, have emphasised the linguistic function of signs that relate to each other rather than refer to real things. Developments in other areas have reinforced this separation of language from reality; post-colonial and feminist literary theorists have shown that apparently real or 'natural' categories such as race and sex are better understood as 'cultural constructions' that covertly substitute normative claims about how, for example, women ought to be for how women actually or necessarily are. Feminist critics have distinguished between sex, which is a biological category, and gender, which is a social construction, and shown how a male-centred world view and social order have tried to legitimise changing gender constructions by referring them back to a supposedly fixed 'natural' sexual identity. 'Femininity' is not, according to many feminist theorists, a natural or necessary consequence of being genetically 'female', but rather a set of culturally prescribed behaviours. This argument largely or wholly detaches the female sex from a 'constructed' feminine gender identity that lives only in language and culture. Whilst this strategy provides opportunities for women to escape repressive stereotypes, it also represents a marked prioritisation of the claims of culture over those of nature.

'Constructionism' is a powerful tool for cultural analysis, and indeed, I have relied on it above in my discussion of the construction of 'pollution'. But it does suggest that 'nature' is only ever a cover for the interests of some social group. The challenge for ecocritics is to keep one eye on the ways in which 'nature' is always in some ways culturally constructed, and the other on the fact that nature really exists, both the object and, albeit distantly, the origin of our discourse. Lawrence Buell calls this 'a myth of mutual constructionism: of physical environment (both natural and human-built) shaping in some measure the cultures that in some measure continually refashion it' (2001: 6) The imprecision of that phrase 'in some measure' is entirely necessary since such reciprocal 'shaping' networks of nature and culture are bound to be complex to the attentive eye. Throughout this book, the aim is to balance a constructionist perspective with the privileged claims to literal truth made by ecology. Ecocritics remain suspicious of the idea of science as wholly objective and value-free, but they are in the unusual position as cultural critics of having to defer, in the last analysis, to a scientific understanding of the world.

Buell's phrase is certainly neat and useful, but part of the problem lies in the metaphor of 'construction' itself, which even in his revised version suggests an artefact like a building or machine, an autonomous work of minds and hands. I doubt many readers would automatically imagine a natural construction such as a termite mound. But if any building or machine, however technologically advanced, must be made by evolved animals (*Homo sapiens*) of materials of natural origin in accordance with natural 'laws' of mechanical physics, then it follows that all our vaunted cultural constructions are, in a sense, natural constructions. Perhaps the architectural metaphor obscures, or mystifies, the natural basis of all human culture and exalts only our own powers as a species. The excessively culturalistic implications of 'construction' are not easily avoided by a substitution of terms, but I tend to use 'shaping', 'elaboration' or 'inflection' to describe the complex transformations and negotiations between nature and culture, or between real and imagined versions of nature.

Returning to pollution with this in mind, we might observe that the rhetorical history of the term has been very closely aligned with the truth claims of ecologists and environmental toxicologists. Techniques of chemical analysis have developed to the point where unimaginably small amounts of chemicals can be detected in the environment:

> In dealing with environmental reports or policies or regulations we must always keep in mind that what was zero today will no longer be zero tomorrow. We have already moved from measuring micrograms in the 1950s to measuring picograms in the 1980s and 1990s. . . . At the same time, we must keep in mind that there is no relationship between toxic effects and our ability to detect a chemical. Small amounts only matter if they do effect living organisms.
>
> (Baarschers 1996: 46–7)

Baarschers is highly critical of environmentalist 'hysteria' surrounding the presence in the environment of amounts of chemicals far below levels of observable toxicity. His frustration at widespread misunderstanding and ignorance of environmental science is reasonable, given that people regularly accept the very high risks involved in, say, smoking, whilst demanding the elimination of infinitesimal risks associated with high-anxiety technologies. Environmental pressure groups may also promote ignorant paranoia rather than educated critique (see Chapter 5).

At the same time, Baarschers does not account for the possibility that public anxiety is a response to precisely the extent and degree of environmental surveillance that he describes. Rather than simply divorcing the 'real risk' as defined by toxicologists from the 'perceived risk' felt by the public, then criticising people for not trusting the experts, we ought to see perceived risk as, paradoxically, a consequence of increasingly sophisticated surveillance. The more accurately the expert measures hazards, the greater the disjunction between official estimates of risk and any conceivable lay assessment based on personal experience, a process of alienation sociologist Ulrich Beck describes as 'expropriation of the senses' (1999: 55). Furthermore, nuclear, biological and chemical 'megahazards' undermine the traditional guarantors of industrial safety such as private insurance, compensation and State regulation of measurable and calculable risks precisely insofar as the threat revealed by environmental surveillance dwindles below the point of statistical determinability. We cannot, by ourselves, assess risks, and industrial safety scientists actually render risks less knowable and more fearful the more they minimise them.

The result, Beck argues, is that security claims produced by mega-hazard industries themselves produce public insecurity. Carson's reconstruction of 'pollution' to include minute quantities of pesticides as well as the gross, observable pollution of traditional industrial production was the continuation of an historical process of redefinition that continues in contemporary culture. The proliferation of types and sources of 'pollution' means that artificial light and noise may now be considered pollutants and carbon dioxide defined as a climatological pollutant even though it occurs naturally in vast quantities. Baarschers's attempt to rationalise and minimise this continual extension cannot reckon with the political and media culture that Beck's constructionist analysis illuminates.

This generalisation and, from an ordinary sensory perspective, dematerialisation of pollution has significant ramifications in our culture, constituting a 'world risk society' of impalpable, ubiquitous material threats that are often in practice indissociable from their cultural elaborations. 'Pollution' has seeped into our culture in many areas and on various levels of representation, from the implicit environmental concern of Sylvia Plath's poetry (Brain 1998) to explicit environmental thrillers such as Hollywood 'green thriller' *On Deadly Ground* (1994) (Kerridge 2000; Ingram 2000). Buell has set out four criteria of such 'toxic discourse' as a cultural genre: a 'mythography of betrayed Edens' (2001: 37) based, like Carson's parable above, in pastoral; horrified, 'totalizing images of a world without refuge from toxic penetration' (p. 38) founded most probably in the postwar fear of radioactive miasma from nuclear weapons; 'the threat of hegemonic oppression' (p. 41) from powerful corporations or governments as contrasted with threatened communities; and the 'gothicization' of squalor and pollution characteristic of the environmental exposé. These criteria, and the genealogy of 'pollution' set out above, enable a vital modern ecocritical trope to be identified in slum gothic such as Dickens' *Hard Times* (1854), environmental lawsuit dramas like *Erin Brockovich* (2000), and the exploration of contamination of place and family in Terry Tempest Williams' *Refuge* (1991). Andrew Ross identifies New York as Hollywood's perfect toxic landscape: 'On the other side of authority lies a city teeming with biological perils. Surely no other city has had such a fantastic bestiary of historical residents – from alligators to ninja turtles – in its sewage tunnels' (1994: 135).

However, in the postmodern world of media saturation, the modern trope of 'pollution' can become dangerously separated from its referent in ways that Baarschers would not recognise. In Don DeLillo's *White Noise* (1986) the protagonist and narrator Jack Gladney strives to come to terms with the proximity of an unexpected 'toxic airborne event':

> Smoke drifted from red beams of light into darkness and then into the breadth of scenic white floods. The men in Mylex suits moved with a lunar caution. Each step was the exercise of some anxiety not provided for by instinct. Fire and explosion were not the inherent dangers here. This death would penetrate, seep into the genes, show itself in bodies not yet born.
>
> (1986: 116)

In one way this seems to confirm Beck's argument that the risk anxiety cannot be relieved or even addressed by 'instinct', the lack of definite threat itself making it all the more pervasive. Even so, the narrative struggles to characterise the 'event' in terms of other, pre-existing narratives, such as the 'conquest of space' with its spectacular imagery and military-industrial brand names. Pollution has become a spectacle that is almost detached from any real sense of threat thanks to the ubiquity of such images: 'the cloud resembled a national promotion for death, a multi-million dollar campaign backed by radio spots, heavy print and billboard, TV saturation' (p. 158). People living close to the emission rely on the media for its definition: at first, 'a feathery plume', then 'a black billowing cloud' and finally 'the airborne toxic event'. Reversing Baarschers's priority of fact over representation, the symptoms of victims change as the media risk reports are updated. The radical disproportion between saturation of imagery and paucity of fact marks the toxic event out as the kind of postmodern crisis with which ecocriticism must increasingly engage. Environmentalism and ecocriticism both rely on and produce exactly the sort of univeralising truth claims or 'grand narratives' that postmodernists such as Jean Baudrillard regard as untenable. As historian Peter Coates argues:

> According to universally disempowering postmodernist logic, the belief in the existence of a global environmental crisis is just another grand

narrative, for cultural theory insists that environmental threats (like everything else) are socially constructed and culturally defined: there are no shared, universal threats – different groups privilege those confronting their own particular interests.

(1998: 185–6)

Nevertheless, appeals to scientific truth claims as a counter to post-modernism are complicated by the fact that the science of ecology is itself undergoing transformation. Long-cherished notions of nature's inherent harmony are challenged by postmodern ecology, as set out in Chapter 3. We need to distinguish between postmodernist theory, which is mainly inimical to ecocriticism, and postmodern ecology, which will increasingly become its scientific reference point.

So these are the basic propositions of this book: environmental problems require analysis in cultural as well as scientific terms, because they are the outcome of an interaction between ecological knowledge of nature and its cultural inflection. This will involve interdiscipli-nary scholarship that draws on literary and cultural theory, philosophy, sociology, psychology and environmental history, as well as ecology. The study of rhetoric supplies us with a model of a cultural reading practice tied to moral and political concerns, and one which is alert to both the real or literal and the figural or constructed interpretations of 'nature' and 'the environment'. Breaking these monolithic concepts down into key structuring metaphors, or tropes, enables attention to be paid to the thematic, historical and geographical particularities of environmental discourse, and reveals that any environmental trope is susceptible to appropriation and deployment in the service of a variety of potentially conflicting interests. Ecocriticism makes it possible to analyse critically the tropes brought into play in environmental debate, and, more tentatively, to predict which will have a desired effect on a specific audience at a given historical juncture. To confront the vast, complex, multifarious agglomeration of ecological crises with the apparently flimsy tools of cultural analysis must be seen by the ecocritic as a moral and political necessity, even though the problems seem perpetually to dwarf the solutions.

The next chapter gives a brief account of the various political and philosophical orientations within the broad spectrum of environmentalism, in part to make clear that no single or simple perspective unites all ecocritics. From Chapter 3 onwards, the analysis is arranged under the names of important ecocritical tropes, starting with 'Pastoral', the most deeply entrenched, and concluding with the construction of the 'Earth' as a unified whole. Within each chapter, the development of the trope is traced historically and, in some cases, geographically, and I mix discussion of canonical texts and critics with more marginal materials in order to indicate the depth and breadth that the field has already assumed. The chapters follow a rough trajectory from traditional concerns with the local to contemporary concepts of the global: from place to space, from earth to Earth. Throughout the book I will return to the implications of postmodern ecology for ecocriticism.

Chapters 3 to 5 examine a linked series of tropes that are heavily indebted to the Euro-American Judaeo-Christian narrative of a fallen, exiled humanity seeking redemption, but fearing apocalyptic judgement – 'Pastoral', 'Wilderness', 'Apocalypse' – and assess the significance of the shapes these tropes have acquired in the modern world. Chapter 6 compares two quite distinct conceptions of 'dwelling' upon the Earth: the European 'georgic' tradition of writing about working on the land, and the more recent identification of indigenous ways of life as potential models for a harmonious existence. To discuss these constructions of humanity's relationship with the natural world, however, takes for granted the problematic distinction between our species and other animals. Therefore Chapter 7 looks at the different ways in which animals, wild and domestic, are represented and conceptualised. I argue that reconsideration of the idea of 'the human' is a key task for ecocriticism, tending to drag it away from pastoral and nature writing towards postmodern concerns such as globalisation and 'cyborg' interfaces of humans with technology. In the final chapter, I explore the meanings that have clustered around the extraordinary images of the whole Earth from space, ranging from global marketplace to precious super-organism.

2

POSITIONS

'Environmentalism' is relatively young as a social, political and philosophical movement, but already a number of distinct eco-philosophies
have emerged that seem as likely to compete with each other as to
combine in any revolutionary synthesis. Each approach understands
environmental crisis in its own way, emphasising aspects that are either
amenable to solution in terms that it supplies or threatening to values it
holds most dear, thus suggesting a range of political possibilities. Each
one, moreover, might provide the basis for a distinct ecocritical approach
with specific literary or cultural affinities and aversions.

CORNUCOPIA

Despite the remarkable degree of consensus that exists amongst scientists
about the environmental threats posed by modern civilisation, there are
nevertheless some who argue that most, if not all, such dangers are illusory
or exaggerated. This 'cornucopian' position is therefore, in an important sense, not environmentalist at all, and is in some cases financially
supported and disseminated by anti-environmentalist industrial pressure
groups. Free-market economists and demographers are amongst its
most outspoken intellectual proponents, arguing that the dynamism of
capitalist economies will generate solutions to environmental problems as

they arise, and that increases in population eventually produce the wealth needed to pay for environmental improvements.

The key positive claim put forward by cornucopians is that human welfare, as measured by statistics such as life expectancy or local pollution, has demonstrably increased along with population, economic growth and technological progress. They point out that, in the long run, the supposed scarcity of natural resources is belied by falling prices of food, minerals and commodities relative to wages; as a specific resource becomes harder to obtain, the price increases, leading capitalist entrepreneurs to search for substitute sources, processes or materials. The discovery of alternatives leads to a fall in price of the original material, such as the drop in real copper prices brought about by the widespread substitution of fibre-optic cables for copper wires. 'Scarcity' is therefore an economic, not an eco-logical, phenomenon, and will be remedied by capitalist entrepreneurs, not the reductions in consumption urged by environmentalists: 'The fact is that the concept of resources itself is a dynamic one; many things become resources over time. Each century has seen new resources emerge' (Beckerman 1995: 60). More people on the planet means more resource-ful brains, more productive hands, more consumption and therefore more economic growth. The confidence of economist Julian Simon in the 'virtuous circle' of economic and demographic growth was such that he issued a standing bet:

> You pick (a) any measure of human welfare – such as life expectancy, the price of aluminum or gasoline, the amount of education per cohort of young people, the rate of ownership of television sets, you name it; (b) a country (or a region such as the developing countries); (c) any future year, and I'll bet a week's or a month's pay that that indicator shows improvement relative to the present while you bet that it shows deterioration.
>
> (Myers and Simon 1994: 21)

Simon won one bet, with ecologist Paul Ehrlich, over the scarcity of mineral resources as measured by prices during the 1980s. Ehrlich in turn has attacked Simon for 'brownwashing', which he describes as the use of spurious science to attack environmentalism (Ehrlich and Ehrlich 1998).

Alongside the claims of an endless cornucopia of wealth, growth and commodity production, Beckerman, Simon and others bring criticisms of environmental 'scare-mongering', pointing to inaccurate projections of global cooling and worldwide famine made by ecologists in the 1970s. They point to the acknowledged uncertainty in, for example, species extinction rates or global climatic modelling, and argue on this basis for inaction or, at best, further research.

It is certainly important to remember the vast improvements in measurable human welfare brought about in both developed and developing countries, albeit terribly inequitably, by economic growth and technological progress. Capitalism mobilises problem-solving capacities in humans that it would be wise not to underestimate. However, this position suffers from a major inconsistency: many of the environmental improvements enjoyed by post-industrial nations have not only been achieved by moving damaging industries to developing countries, but have been driven by the political agitation of the environmental campaigners cornucopians now claim are obstructing economic and technological progress. It is not capitalism alone that produces the solutions cornucopians identify, but entrepreneurs responding to morally motivated consumers and government regulations.

A more serious objection is that cornucopians take little or no account of the non-human environment except insofar as it impacts upon human wealth or welfare. Nature is only valued in terms of its usefulness to us. Many environmentalists argue that we need to develop a value system which takes the intrinsic or inherent value of nature as its starting point. This fundamental distinction is evident in the debate between Simon and conservation biologist Norman Myers, from which I have quoted above.

ENVIRONMENTALISM

The very broad range of people who are concerned about environmental issues such as global warming and pollution, but who wish to maintain or improve their standard of living as conventionally defined, and who would not welcome radical social change, will be described hereinafter as 'environmentalists'. Many value rural ways of life, hiking or camping, or are members of one of the mainstream environmental organisations such as the Sierra Club, Nature Conservancy and Audubon Society in the USA, or the Royal Society for the Protection of Birds and the Council for the Protection of Rural England in the UK. They may be concerned about natural resource scarcity or pollution but would look to governments or non-governmental organisations such as charities to provide solutions, usually technological ones. Their hopes for curbing population growth, mainly seen as a problem for developing countries, would lie in family-planning campaigns rather than, say, State-sponsored sterilisation. Activism may range from recycling bottles and buying organic food to major commitment to conservation activity. In terms of philosophical and religious orientation, environmentalists still regard Western traditions such as liberal democracy, human rights, Christianity and notions of historical or scientific progress as valuable, to a greater or lesser degree, even in the light of environmental crisis. So characterised, a substantial proportion of the populations of developed countries would count as environmentalists. Political and consumer pressures wielded by environmentalists are responsible for many concrete improvements such as the rapid expansion in organic agriculture in recent years.

Environmentalism, then, is widespread and, in certain respects, very powerful. Political parties must at least pay lip service to it, and industries respond in ways that range from costly modifications to production processes to merely cosmetic 'greenwashing' to appeal to or appease it. At the same time, environmentalism, or 'shallow environmentalism' as it has been called, has been attacked by radical critics for the compromises it makes with the ruling socio-economic order. Each of the following approaches accuses environmentalists of failing to address the allegedly more fundamental malaise it has identified.

Many of the most prominent scientific proponents of environmental protection, such as Rachel Carson, Paul and Anne Ehrlich, E.O. Wilson and Stephen Schneider, espouse this position for the most part, although in terms of environmental philosophy and criticism, environmentalism has found few systematic defenders. Martin Lewis's *Green Delusions* (1994) combines a vigorous attack on radical environmentalism with a reformist programme that emphasises the role of science, technology and government policy change. Against the 'Arcadian' approach of radicals advocating de-urbanisation, use of non-synthetic products and low-technology solutions, Lewis's 'Promethean' environmentalism promotes the 'decoupling' of human economy and natural ecology as far as possible, in order to protect nature. He points out that cities are not only centres of cultural vitality, but less environmentally costly than suburban sprawl or exurban flight, and argues that capitalism guided by educated voters and consumers can provide technological solutions to many problems of resources and pollution. The anti-interventionist, 'nature knows best' approach that Lewis ascribes to eco-radicals is inadequate: 'Prometheans maintain . . . that for the forseeable future we must *actively manage* the planet to ensure the survival of as much biological diversity as possible. No less is necessary if we are to begin atoning for our very real environmental sins' (1994: 251). Richard North's *Life on a Modern Planet* (1995) adopts a similar position, setting out a moderate 'manifesto for progress'.

It may be said that this technocratic, managerial approach has already failed if we accept both the long-standing popularity of the cause and the continuing pace of environmental destruction. At the same time, the mainstream environmental movement not only has significant successes on specific issues such as ozone-depleting CFC emissions to its credit, but also represents the constituency to which radicals must appeal either for conversion or coalition. Successful radical organisations, such as Greenpeace, have attempted to maintain their reputation for radical activism whilst simultaneously promoting recycling and 'green consumerism'. The future of any of the more radical positions outlined here will probably depend upon a similar balancing act. Moreover, since most ecocritics espouse radical views, they will likewise seek to exploit environmentalism amongst readers whilst tempting them towards a politics or philosophy more adequate to the environmental crisis as they perceive it.

DEEP ECOLOGY

Of the four radical forms of environmentalism, deep ecology is the most influential beyond academic circles, inspiring many activists in organisations such as Friends of the Earth, Earth First! and Sea Shepherd. This position, and its variants, will recur most often in this book as the explicit or implicit perspective of ecocritics, and aspects of it will be discussed further in several chapters. The 'poet laureate' of deep ecology is Gary

Snyder (b. 1930; see Chapter 4) and its philosophical guru is Arne Naess. Naess sets out eight key points of the deep ecology platform in George Sessions's definitive anthology *Deep Ecology for the 21st Century* (1995). The crucial ones are as follows:

1. The well-being and flourishing of human and non-human life on Earth have value in themselves (synonyms: intrinsic value, inherent worth). These values are independent of the usefulness of the non-human world for human purposes.

4. The flourishing of human life and cultures is compatible with a substantially smaller human population. The flourishing of non-human life *requires* a smaller human population.

(Sessions 1995: 68)

The second of these points refers not only to developing but also to developed countries, whose populations consume far more per capita. Deep ecologists argue for long-term population reduction throughout the world. The lethal combination is that of rapid population growth in developing countries, which exacerbates environmental problems associated with poverty such as land pressure and deforestation, accompanied by rapid economic growth in developed countries, which exacerbates problems associated with wealth, such as domestic waste disposal and greenhouse gas emissions.

Many deep ecologists see the first point as distinguishing their position from environmentalism; whereas 'shallow' approaches take an instrumental approach to nature, arguing for preservation of natural resources only for the sake of humans, deep ecology demands recognition of intrinsic value in nature. It identifies the dualistic separation of humans from nature promoted by Western philosophy and culture as the origin of environmental crisis, and demands a return to a monistic, primal identification of humans and the ecosphere. The shift from a human-centred to a nature-centred system of values is the core of the radicalism attributed to deep ecology, bringing it into opposition with almost the entirety of Western philosophy and religion:

Deep ecology is concerned with encouraging an egalitarian attitude on the part of humans not only toward all *members* of the ecosphere, but even toward all identifiable *entities* or *forms* in the ecosphere. Thus, this attitude is intended to extend, for example, to such entities (or forms) as rivers, landscapes, and even species and social systems considered in their own right.

(Sessions 1995: 270)

This remarkable even-handedness might well seem to empty deep ecology of any substantive content: if value resides everywhere, it resides nowhere, as it ceases to be a basis for making distinctions and decisions. It is not being alive or being sentient that qualifies an entity or form for intrinsic value, but rather, it would seem, whatever kind of purposive organisation one could claim to find equally in a single bird, a river, an entire species, a distinct ecosystem or an ethnic group. The considerable debates about the concept of intrinsic value may be traced in the influential journal *Environmental Ethics* or in one of several anthologies (Elliot and Gare 1983; Cooper and Palmer 1992; Elliot 1995).

One major, recurrent objection to deep ecology is that ecocentrism is misanthropic, and indeed certain advocates such as Dave Foreman and Christopher Manes have made inhumane and ill-informed statements about population control, for example. But alongside this 'hard' wing is the 'soft' mainstream for whom ecocentrism is merely an 'orientation' within which major differences of opinion will always subsist. It is specifically allowed by Naess, for example, that 'vital' human needs may take priority over the good of any other thing, thus ruling out difficult conflicts between the interests of humans and the interests of a man-eating tiger or a bubonic plague bacillus. In fact, when it comes down to specifics, deep ecologists often reaffirm the conventional priorities they criticise in environmentalists, not least because they risk the charge of misanthropy if they do not. Moreover, it seems likely that any given concerned individual will probably have both eco- and anthropocentric attitudes at different times, under different conditions. At the same time, it is important to distinguish both perspectives from the animal rights philosophy that argues for the extension of the moral consideration accorded humans to certain higher mammals (see Chapter 7).

The notion of ecocentrism has proceeded from, and fed back into, related belief systems derived from Eastern religions, such as Taoism and Buddhism, from heterodox figures in Christianity such as St Francis of

Assisi (1182–1286) and Teilhard de Chardin (1881–1955), and from modern reconstructions of American Indian, pre-Christian Wiccan, shamanistic and other 'primal' religions. Alongside this strongly spiritualistic dimension subsists, somewhat uneasily at times, the scientific ecology from which the movement takes its name. In fact, not one of the essays in the substantial Sessions anthology is written by an ecologist, and 'ecology' appears there, if at all, as a laudable background activity that need never be discussed directly, but can rather be used to validate existing 'intuitions'. Where intuition and science clash, the former typically wins out, so that scientifically informed attempts to manage ecosystems, for example, are seen as part of the 'problem'. Ecologists can be accused of being 'anti-ecological', not because their projects might accidentally inflict damage, but because the undertaking of such projects betrays an anthropocentric managerialism at odds with the true, ecocentric promise of the discipline. In fact, developments in postmodern ecology would seem fatally to undermine deep ecology, if it would only attend to them. It would be absurd if 'deep ecology' were in the end not only to question but indeed to contradict the science of ecology from which it must ultimately derive.

ECOFEMINISM

Deep ecology identifies the anthropocentric dualism humanity/nature as the ultimate source of anti-ecological beliefs and practices, but ecofeminism also blames the *andro*centric dualism man/woman. The first distinguishes humans from nature on the grounds of some alleged quality such as possession of an immortal soul or rationality, and then assumes that this distinction confers superiority upon humans. The second distinguishes men from women on the grounds of some alleged quality such as larger brain size, and then assumes that this distinction confers superiority upon men. Ecofeminism involves the recognition that these two arguments share a common 'logic of domination' (Warren 1994: 129) or underlying 'master model', that 'women have been associated with nature, the material, the emotional, and the particular, while men have been associated with culture, the nonmaterial, the rational, and the abstract' (Davion 1994: 9), and that this should suggest common cause between feminists and ecologists.

If women have been associated with nature, and each denigrated with reference to the other, it may seem worthwhile to attack the hierarchy by reversing the terms, exalting nature, irrationality, emotion and the human or non-human body as against culture, reason and the mind. Some ecofeminists, especially those promoting 'radical ecofeminism' and goddess worship, have adopted this approach. Thus, for example, Sharon Doubiago asserts that 'ecology consciousness is traditional woman consciousness'; 'Women have always thought like mountains, to allude to Aldo Leopold's paradigm for ecological thinking. (There's nothing like the experience of one's belly growing into a mountain to teach you this.)' (1989: 41, 42). Charlene Spretnak similarly grounds a kind of women's spirituality in female biology and acculturation that is 'comprised of the truths of naturalism and the holistic proclivities of women' (1989: 128–9).

Yet, as suggested earlier, feminists have long argued against the acceptance of some 'feminine essence' grounded in biological sex, showing instead how gender is culturally constructed. Because this applies regardless of whether the essence is construed negatively or positively, radical ecofeminism would then appear to present us with a mirror-image of patriarchal constructions of femininity that is just as limited and limiting. Even a positive valuation of femininity as 'closer to nature' thanks to female biology or social experience neglects the reality that all the gender distinctions we know have been constructed within patriarchal societies. Radical ecofeminist essentialism has been rightly criticised by ecofeminists with a philosophical or sociological orientation (Warren 1994; Biehl 1991), who point out that 'a truly feminist perspective cannot embrace either the feminine or the masculine uncritically, [but] requires a critique of gender roles, and this critique must include masculinity *and* femininity' (Davion 1994: 9). This objection now seems to have been generally accepted by ecofeminists.

If radical ecofeminism is questionable in terms of its feminism, it is even more so in terms of ecology. The desire to reverse the androcentric priority of reason over emotion leads to a striking anti-scientism (e.g. Kheel 1989; Griffin 1978). Mary Daly's *Gyn/Ecology* (1979) frankly appropriates a vaguely 'green' rhetoric in the service of a sententious, sustained and unqualified assault on the 'phallic myth and language' of science, especially medical science. Yet, as Val Plumwood's brilliant analysis shows, merely differentiating men from women, humans from nature, or reason from emotion, does not itself constitute problematic anthropo- or androcentrism. Rather, the underlying model of mastery shared by these forms of oppression is based upon *alienated* differentiation and denied dependency: in the dominant Euro-American culture, humans are not only *distinguished* from nature, but *opposed* to it in ways that make humans radically alienated from and superior to it. This polarisation, or 'hyperseparation', often involves a denial of the real relationship of the superior term to the inferior (Plumwood 1993: 47–55). So, for example, Plumwood shows how philosopher René Descartes (1596–1650) proposed an influential account of the difference between mind and body that struggled to eliminate all traces of the corporeal from the mental domain of reason. He had to

> reinterpret the notion of 'thinking' in such a way that those mental activities which involve the body, such as sense perception, and which appear to bridge the mind/body and human/animal division, become instead, via their reinterpretation in terms of 'consciousness', purely mental operations.
>
> (1993: 115)

Descartes hyperseparated mind and body, and denied to animals not only the faculty of reason, but the whole range of feelings and sensations that he had associated with thought. As a result, he saw animals as radically different from, and inferior to, humans. They were bodies without minds, effectively machines.

Plumwood's most important contribution is a critique of the gendered reason/nature dualism. She presents it as 'the overarching, most general, basic and connecting form' of a historically varied series of dualisms. It can serve this general analytical function because 'reason' has so often been called upon to hyperseparate both men from women and humans from animals, and so can stand in for both dominant terms. She does not argue for a rejection of either science or reason, but rather a qualification of the philosophies that would polarise reason and nature in opposition: whereas scientific 'objectivity' decrees that any talk of intention or purpose in nature constitutes unscientific anthropomorphism, Plumwood advocates a recognition of both similarity and difference in the human–nature continuum. We can continue to distinguish reason and emotion, man and woman, human and animal, but without the neurotic obsessiveness of the mainstream philosophical tradition. In doing so, the mastery model that legitimates anthropo- and androcentrism is undermined (see also Plumwood 2001).

Reason, once rescued from its idealisation by androcentric philosophy, can acknowledge and respect 'earth others', afflicted by neither ultra-rationalistic alienation nor animistic assimilation: 'We need to understand and affirm both otherness and our community in the earth' (Plumwood 1993: 137). This position rejects both cornucopian dualism, privileging the rational economic subject above all else, and simplistic ecofeminist and deep ecological monism, in which the distinctive capacities and needs of the human species are in danger of being submerged in an undifferentiated, apolitical ecosphere. Unfortunately, it may nevertheless lead to the position espoused by Caroline Merchant in her influential historical critique of 'mechanistic' science, *The Death of Nature*: a somewhat pious recommendation of 'holistic' or 'vitalist' science based on its moral, rather than its methodological or pragmatic, superiority over 'reductive' conventional science. The place of science in the two major forms of radical ecology, then, remains vexed.

Ecofeminism emphasises environmental justice to a far greater degree than deep ecology. The logic of domination is implicated in discrimination and oppression on grounds of race, sexual orientation and class as well as species and gender. Whereas the *Deep Ecology* anthology contains essays on 'dead white males' such as D.H. Lawrence, John Muir and Henry Thoreau, a recent anthology of *Ecofeminist Literary Criticism* (Gaard and Murphy 1998) includes work on East German, French, Native American, Chicana and other writers, mainly but not exclusively women. This diversity is thought to derive necessarily from ecology, as argued here by Ynestra King:

> A healthy, balanced ecosystem, including human and nonhuman inhabitants, must maintain diversity. Ecologically, environmental simplification is as significant a problem as environmental pollution. Biological simplification, i.e., the wiping out of whole species, corresponds to reducing human diversity into faceless workers, or to the homogenization of taste and culture through mass consumer

ns

...ollow from systems of domination or exploit...
...r humans. Focusing on these intraspecies rela...
...uate, deep ecologists claim, the anthropocentr...
...target of any earth-centred critique. At the...
...and eco-Marxists lament the individualis...
...deep ecologists, which, they argue, re...
...thought and real political engagemen...
...are explicitly political, and have thei...
...thought: the anarchism of M...
...Kropotkin (1842–1921), the...
...Friedrich Engels (1820–95)...
...Social ecology and ec...
...cornucopian economi...
...that the notion of ec...
...of 'overshoot' of...
...and absorb wa...
...but this anal...
...of producti...
...and dem...
...initia...
...pro...

to c...

essentialism...

Plumwood, however, ...

give the position far greater dept..., ...

in the growing significance of ecofeminist litera...,

within the ecocritical field, and in the complex analyses ...

can make of, for example, population problems, which greatly exceed in

both diagnostic and prescriptive power the crude analyses of deep ecolo-

gists (Cuomo 1994). Ecofeminists have also provided sharp critiques of

globalisation, free trade and 'international development' that link their

project as much to the politically orientated positions associated with

social ecology and eco-Marxism as to ethically and spiritually orientated

deep ecology (Shiva 1989).

SOCIAL ECOLOGY AND ECO-MARXISM

Like ecofeminism, the positions discussed here do not suggest that
environmental problems are caused by anthropocentric attitudes alone,

...ation of humans by

...tionships, they perpet-

...ism that ought to be the

...same time, social ecologists

...and pervasive mysticism of

...present a retreat from rational

...t. Social ecology and eco-Marxism

...origins in nineteenth-century radical

...khail Bakunin (1814–76) and Pyotr

...ommunism of Karl Marx (1818–33) and

...o-Marxism share the crucial insight with the

...ts, whom they diametrically oppose politically,

...ological 'limits' is a kind of mystification. The fear

...he capacities of natural systems to provide resources

...te informs both deep ecology and environmentalism,

...sis obscures the way scarcity is created by capitalistic forms

...on that depend on the manipulation of the dynamic of supply

...and. Furthermore, technology modifies the dynamic, both by

...ng new demands, and, through changed extraction or production

...cesses, offsetting or exacerbating scarcity. In other words, 'scarcity' is

...ot simply an objective fact about the natural world, but a function of the will and means of capital: the purposes that guide production, and the technologies that facilitate it. Change the political structure of society so that production to meet real needs replaces production for the accumulation of wealth, it is argued, and the ecological problem of limits produced by capital's structural need for perpetual growth will disappear. It is worth noting that, whilst this argument is persuasive in relation to mineral resources, it is far less so when applied to non-substitutable and economically invisible resources such as freshwater aquifers or biodiversity.

Social ecologists, most of whom recognise political philosopher Murray Bookchin as their intellectual guru, share with eco-Marxists a distinctive view of the place of humans in nature. They claim the ecocentric monism enjoined by deep ecologists is disingenuous because, although humans are supposed to be 'part of nature', many of the things humans do are still portrayed as 'unnatural', thereby reintroducing the dualism they were trying to overcome. Opposing this false monism is a dialectical perspective that envisages the evolution of human culture, or 'second nature', from 'first nature', in an ongoing process in which each defines and transforms the other:

> Marx . . . recognised the priorness [*sic*] of an 'external' or 'first' nature, that gave birth to humankind. But humans then worked on this 'first' nature to produce a 'second' nature: the material creations of society plus its institutions, ideas and values. This process, as Bookchin . . . stresses, is part of a process of *natural* evolution of society.
>
> (Pepper 1993: 108)

Eco-Marxists and social ecologists are therefore neither monists nor dualists. One of the consequences of this view is that environmental problems cannot be clearly divorced from things more usually defined as social problems such as poor housing or lack of clean water. It gives these positions a clear affinity with environmental justice movements that protest the common association of acute environmental degradation and pollution with poverty.

In line with traditional Marxist thought, eco-Marxists argue that there is a structural conflict between workers and the owners of the means of production, in which the latter cream off the surplus value created by the labour of the proletariat. This objective exploitation is at the heart of all other forms of exploitation and oppression, as Pepper argues: 'The true, post-revolutionary, communist society will be classless, and when it is attained the state, environmental disruption, economic exploitation, war and patriarchy will all wither away, being no longer necessary' (1993: 207–8). Against this vision of a planned economy based on need rather than greed, social ecology promotes a decentralised society of non-hierarchical affiliations avowedly derived from an anarchistic political tradition:

> A fundamental unit will be the *commune*, a closely knit, small community based on love, friendship, shared values, and commitment to a common life. . . . cooperative institutions in all areas of social life will be formed: mutualistic associations for child care and education, for production and distribution, for cultural creation, for play and

enjoyment, for reflection and spiritual renewal. Organization will be based not on the demands of *power*, but rather on the *self-realization of persons* as free social beings.

(Clark 1990: 9)

If eco-Marxists identify class conflict as the key political issue, social ecologists oppose the power relations and hierarchy they see as afflicting all kinds of societies, be they capitalistic or centrally planned socialist. In place of a workers' revolution, social ecologists promote exemplary lifestyles and communities that prefigure a more general social transformation and give people practice in sustainable living and participatory democracy.

Eco-Marxism seems at present to be a marginal force in the green politics of rich nations, although its role in Third World environmental justice movements may be more significant. However, it suffers from association with the environmental horrors perpetrated by the former Soviet Union and its Eastern European satellites. On the other hand, social ecology and anarchism more generally, seem to be experiencing a resurgence in the anti-globalisation and bioregional movements. Anarchism has the advantage of not requiring an elusive revolutionary proletariat for its realisation, and is clearly amenable to a range of counter-cultural movements. Nevertheless, Marxists are right to emphasise the pervasive power and reach of global capital, and the probable futility of rebellious actions by individuals or small, loosely affiliated groups against a handful of its symbols but none of its essential structures. Despite these differences, in what follows, holders of both these positions will be called 'social ecologists'.

HEIDEGGERIAN ECOPHILOSOPHY

Whilst it is undoubtedly marginal to green political thought, the philosophy of Martin Heidegger (1889–1976) has inspired a number of ecocritics. It is apparently impenetrable to the beginner, but some critics argue that Heidegger's thought is among the most profound critiques of industrial modernity because it combines a poetic awe before the Earth's being with a savage deconstruction of the death-denying project of world mastery that we are taught to call 'progress' (see Foltz 1995; Garrard 1998; Zimmerman 1990 and 1993).

Heidegger's starting point is the fundamental difference between mere material existence and a revelation of 'being', or the thing-ness of things. To 'be' is not just to exist, but to 'show up' or be disclosed, which requires human consciousness as the space, or 'clearing' (*Lichtung*), in and through which it is disclosed: 'At bottom, the ordinary is not ordinary; it is extraordinary' (Heidegger 1993: 179). Once again, the problem of dualism is not so much resolved as displaced, as being only 'is' through this clearing, and human being is in turn properly realised in the letting be of beings in its 'space' of consciousness. The clearing and what shines forth there have a mutual need for one another, as the sheltering Earth provides the entities from which human being founds a world: 'A stone is worldless. Plant and animal likewise have no world; but they belong to the covert throng of a surrounding into which they are linked. The peasant woman, on the other hand, has a world because she dwells in the overtness of beings' (p. 170).

The relationship of being and clearing, or Earth and world, is not a simple one, however, because the responsiveness or attunement between them may be more or less responsible, and beings may or may not be 'let be' (i.e. be disclosed, show up, emerge). Thus responsible humans have an implicit duty to let things disclose themselves in their own inimitable way, rather than forcing them into meanings and identities that suit their own instrumental values. One of the crucial modes of proper letting be or unhindered disclosure of being is poetry: language, especially archaic or oblique poetic language, rightly understood discloses to us the act of disclosure itself. It enables showing-up itself to show up. On the other hand, Heidegger was dismissive of everyday chatter because it discloses both language and beings to us as mere instruments of our will; disposable words correspond to a world of disposable stuff. Worse still, things may emerge as mere resources on call for our use when required, so that a living forest may show up as merely a 'standing reserve' of timber (*Bestand*), no longer trees even but just lumber-in-waiting, and even the mighty Rhine may be disclosed as just a source of hydroelectric power. In meditation upon the poetic word, however, we discover that 'language is the house of Being in which man ek-sists by dwelling' (Heidegger 1993: 237), and Heidegger claims that the essence of beings, their autonomy and resistance to our purposes, is disclosed by a similarly resistant language. Through poetry, then, we learn that 'Man is not the lord of beings. Man

is the shepherd of Being' (p. 245). We learn resistance to the instrumentalism or en-framing (*Ge-stell*) that discloses beings always in its
narrow and reductive terms. We seek attunement to the demand beings
put on us to disclose them without constraint. We learn, that is, to let
beings be.

Thanks to the pivotal role he assigns to the work of art in what he
calls 'saving the earth', Heidegger's philosophy has obvious attractions
to ecocritics. Yet many philosophers argue that Heidegger's writings
are virulently anti-rational, besides being infuriatingly difficult to read.
Moreover, from 1934 to 1945, Heidegger was an enthusiastic Nazi,
believing that Hitler could lead Germany in saving the Earth. Some
philosophers consider that this has no bearing on his thought, whilst
others see a profound congruence between his philosophy and his politics.
The situation is complicated further by the claims of some historians that
early Nazism included environmentalist elements. The place of Heidegger
in ecocriticism is considered further in Chapter 7.

3

PASTORAL

Since the Romantic movement's poetic responses to the Industrial Revolution, pastoral has decisively shaped our constructions of nature. Even the science of ecology may have been shaped by pastoral in its early stages of development and we have seen that the founding text of ecocriticism, *Silent Spring*, drew on the pastoral tradition. No other trope is so deeply entrenched in Western culture, or so deeply problematic for environmentalism. With its roots in the classical period, pastoral has shown itself to be infinitely malleable for differing political ends, and potentially harmful in its tensions and evasions. However, its long history and cultural ubiquity mean that the pastoral trope must and will remain a key concern for ecocritics.

What then is this 'pastoral' tradition, and what is its significance for environmentalism? Terry Gifford distinguishes three kinds of pastoral: the specifically literary tradition, involving a retreat from the city to the countryside, that originates in ancient Alexandria and becomes a key poetic form in Europe during the Renaissance; more generally, 'any literature that describes the country with an implicit or explicit contrast to the urban' (1999: 2); and the pejorative sense in which 'pastoral' implies an idealisation of rural life that obscures the realities of labour and hardship. This chapter will explore these three manifestations of the trope.

The first of Gifford's 'kinds' I will call 'classical pastoral', which I take to include all pastoral literature up until the eighteenth century. Classical pastoral precedes the perception of a general crisis in human ecology by thousands of years, but it provides the pre-existing set of literary conventions and cultural assumptions that have been crucially transformed to provide a way for Europeans and Euro-Americans to construct their landscapes. Gifford's contrast of country and city comes to the fore in Romantic pastoral, at a time when mass urbanisation made these contrasts relevant to many more people than ever before. The later popularisation of Romantic poetry has provided the language, imagery and even locations for the subsequent generalisation of pastoral in such diverse cultural forms as the novel, TV or promotional materials for conservation organisations. Modern advertisements for wholewheat bread featuring idyllic, rolling fields of grain in the sunshine, populated by ruddy farmers and backed by classical music, would offer one example. Gifford's third, pejorative sense of the word emerges especially in Marxist critiques of Romanticism, which provide a useful ground for contrast of this tradition in cultural criticism with ecocriticism. Some ecocritics claim, for instance, that the emergent environmental sensibility of Romantic pastoral suggests a kind of radicalism not recognised by anthropocentric political critics. Derivations from the Romantic model of course depend on the contexts in which they have developed, and American pastoral has followed its own distinct trajectory as a response to an environmental and social history very different from that of Britain. At the end of the chapter I discuss how 'pastoral ecology' promoted notions of nature's essential harmony that are still prevalent in environmental discourse today.

CLASSICAL PASTORAL

The genre of pastoral emerged in poetry of the Hellenistic period. The *Idylls* of the Alexandrian poet Theocritus (*c.* 316–260), and the subsequent revisions, critiques and translations they engendered, enduringly associated three terms: the 'idyll' was originally the 'small picture' or poetic vignette, but came to mean the represented situation of rural escape or repose itself; 'bucolic', deriving from *boukolos* meaning 'cowherd', one of the typical singers of the idyll; and 'pastoral', a term of Latin origin retrospectively applied to Theocritus' work thanks to the shepherds (Latin *pastor*) who engaged in singing competitions with the cow- and goatherds therein. The emergence of the bucolic idyll correlates closely with large-scale urbanisation in the Hellenic period. There are two key contrasts from this period that run through the pastoral tradition: the spatial distinction of town (frenetic, corrupt, impersonal) and country (peaceful, abundant), and the temporal distinction of past (idyllic) and present ('fallen').

Many of Theocritus' *Idylls* in fact seem tangential to the later trajectory of pastoral poetry, but a few can provide us with initial bearings. From the outset, pastoral often used nature as a location or as a reflection of human predicaments, rather than sustaining an interest in nature in and for itself. What is perhaps surprising, given that 'pastoral' and 'idyll' have acquired such connotations of idealisation, is that the *Idylls* include both hard work and earthy humour. Idyll V includes references to bestiality and hetero- and homosexual lust, whilst 'Reapmaster Milton' of Idyll X counters Boucaeus' lovelorn song with some rather more pragmatic verses of his own: 'let the reapers rise with the rising lark, rest in the heat, and not leave off till dark' (1978: 100). At the same time, the joy and plenty of a good harvest comes through in Idyll VII with compelling immediacy. Chris Fitter's fascinating historical account of the aesthetics of 'landskip' (*sic*) has shown how Theocritus combines learned literary allusion and exact observation:

> Throughout antiquity landskip will never fully escape the condition of 'scaena', of elaborated backdrop, yet with Theocritus such specificity turns gain, as a 'poetry of place' is born. The Harvest Home (Idyll 7) borrows the device of the bird-catalogue from Homer's Calypso, and the nightingale singing from the thicket is directly Homeric; but the assiduous naturalism – the accurately reported positioning of the landmarks along the eight-kilometre walk to Phrasidimus' farm – and the correct natural history (the rare tomb-crested lark, and the other birds referred to, seem always to have been resident in Cos) embed a paradisal tonality in the closely mapped familiar world.
>
> (1996: 40–1)

So the *Idylls* also provide us with the first instance of a contrast of civilised poetic artifice and a 'naturalism' to which it is conventionally opposed.

Virgil (70–19 BC) alludes to Theocritus frequently in his *Eclogues*, but in some ways his is a more systematic and self-conscious approach, incorporating a pointed contrast of rural retreat and the harms consequent on civilisation. At several points, moreover, Virgil alludes to environmental problems associated with Roman civilisation, which have been blamed by some environmental historians for its eventual decline (Hughes 1996a). One of the key factors, it is widely agreed, was deforestation. Virgil's shepherd, Menalcas, notes that 'For gladness even the unshorn [*intonsi*] mountains fling their voices / Toward the stars' (1984: 65). Pastoral often suggests that nature responds to human emotions, a poetic conceit called 'pathetic fallacy' because it wrongly locates feeling (*pathos*) in, say, mountains or trees; in this respect, Menalcas' line is fairly typical. However, he is also drawing attention to the 'shorn' state of Mediterranean hillsides in his own time. Comparison might be made with comments in Plato's *Critias* (1920: 75) on the state of Attica's hillsides, where the connection between deforestation, erosion and loss of fertility is explicit. This process may be traced back to Sumeria, the earliest civilisation in the region, which left us the *Epic of Gilgamesh*, the earliest known literary work. Numerous historians and ecocritics have examined this work and, as Harrison notes: 'What interests us about the epic above all is the fact that the first antagonist of Gilgamesh is the forest' (Harrison 1992: 14; cf. Hughes 1996a; Oelschlager 1991; Westling 1996; Fitter 1996).

Virgil's importance is obvious as progenitor of later pastoral poetry, but it is also worth examining his significance for two major forerunners of ecocriticism, both of which dealt with the pastoral tradition. The first of these is Leo Marx's *The Machine in the Garden* (first published 1964), an analysis of pastoral in American literature. This key text does not mention ecology or environmentalism directly, but clearly situates its discussion in relation to the increasingly problematic place of technology in the American landscape. Virgil provides a crucial archetype in Eclogue I:

> Lucky old man, the land will then remain your own,
> And large enough for you, although bare rock and bog
> With muddy rushes covers all the pasturage:
> No unaccustomed feed will try your breeding ewes,
> And no infection harm them from a neighbour's flock.
>
> (1984: 33)

According to Marx, this is the 'middle landscape' that was eventually to form the American ideal: 'This ideal pasture has two vulnerable borders: one separates it from Rome, the other from the encroaching marshland. It is a place where Tityrus is spared the deprivations and anxieties associated with both the city and the wilderness' (1964: 22).

We will return to Marx's claim below. In terms of British criticism, Raymond Williams' *The Country and the City* (first published in 1973) profoundly influenced both Marxist readings of pastoral and the ecocritical responses that arrived later to qualify or contradict them. One of Williams' key insights is that pastoral has always been characterised by nostalgia, so that wherever we look into its history, we will see an 'escalator' taking us back further into a better past. At the same time, he argues, 'what seemed a single escalator, a perpetual recession into history, turns out, on reflection, to be a more complicated movement: Old England, settlement, the rural virtues – all these, in fact, mean different things at different times, and quite different values are being brought into question' (1993: 12). In addition to the elegy and the idyll in Virgil, we can also find a prophetic moment in Eclogue IV that suggests utopian possibilities:

> She-goats unshepherded will bring home udders plumped
> With milk, and cattle will not fear the lion's might.
> Your very cradle will pour forth caressing flowers.
>
> (1984: 57)

Williams argues that this 'includes within its celebration the consciousness of the very different present from which the restoration will be a release' (1993: 18). Pastoral, then, need not always be nostalgic, but may be utopian and proleptic. Both Leo Marx and Williams identify this progressive potential, and both critics later associated it with the emergence of environmental politics (see Williams 1989).

We can set out three orientations of pastoral in terms of time: the *elegy* looks back to a vanished past with a sense of nostalgia; the *idyll* celebrates a bountiful present; the *utopia* looks forward to a redeemed future. Once schematised like this, the relationship of pastoral and the Judaeo-Christian conception of time becomes clear: Genesis 3, the story of Man's fall, is essentially an elegy of lost pastoral bounty and innocence.

In Milton's *Paradise Lost*, an elaboration upon Biblical materials, pastoral Eden is influenced by Graeco-Roman models, and Man's Fall partakes in a shared elegiac mood: 'O unexpected stroke, worse than of death! / Must I leave thee Paradise?' (XI. 268–9). At the same time, the series of covenants between God and Man offer the possibility of present grace, as for example after the Flood, when God promises the continuance of nature as part of a renewed covenant. This must be taken into account alongside Lynn White Jr.'s claim, based mainly on Genesis, that 'Christianity, in absolute contrast to ancient paganism and Asia's religions (except, perhaps, Zoroastrianism), not only established a dualism of man and nature but also insisted that it is God's will that man exploit nature for his proper ends', and his conclusion that 'we shall continue to have a worsening ecologic crisis until we reject the Christian axiom that nature has no reason for existence save to serve man' (1996: 10, 14). These arguments will be considered in later chapters.

As Williams says, the meanings and values implied by pastoral elegy and idyll vary according to the historical context in which they appear, but we may nevertheless identify a marked tendency for the classical English pastorals influenced by Theocritus to present a vision of rural life so removed from the processes of labour and natural growth that they constitute a persistent mystification of human ecology. In the work of Williams, and later critics such as John Barrell and John Bull (1982) we see the emergence of Gifford's sense of 'pastoral' as a pejorative term for an evasive or mendacious depiction of rural life. Reading the verse they discuss makes it harder to dispute the case, because with few exceptions it betrays two preoccupations: an interest in the conventions of pastoral poetry themselves, and, with just as much self-regard and often syco-phancy too, the celebration of the landed estate or ordered, productive countryside generally. Thomas Carew's 'To Saxham' (1640) compliments a patron's bounty so extravagant that even the animals come to the slaughter joyfully, as in some butcher's Eden:

> The Pheasant, Partiridge, and the Larke,
> Flew to thy house, as to the Arke.
> The willing Oxe, of himselfe came
> Home to the slaughter, with the Lambe,
> And every beast did thither bring

Himselfe, to be an offering.
The scalie herd, more pleasure tooke,
Bath'd in thy dish, then in the brooke.
        (Barrell and Bull 1982: 173)

The obvious hyperbole is further exaggerated by the reference to Noah's Ark: after the Flood, a burnt 'offering' of fowl made by Noah induced God to rescind the curse placed on Adam's farming of the earth. Here, not only is Saxham the Ark, but the offering is to its owner rather than God, his beneficent rule seeming to represent a secular providence that has little need of divine assistance. The cornucopian conceit of self-sacrificing animals is, on one level, a piece of pure hypocrisy that denies the facts of both rural labour and animal suffering. On another level, though, Carew is representing the real distance between his patron and the things that sustain him, in that the ox could well have offered himself up for all the Lord might know. On yet another level, the conceit is so absurd that the text may seem a witty comment on pastoral idealisation. The pastoral poetry of the century after 'To Saxham' becomes even more self-involved and I will not discuss it here, but Williams, Halperin, Gifford and Alpers (1996) have conducted useful surveys.

Classical pastoral was disposed, then, to distort or mystify social and environmental history, whilst at the same time providing a locus, legitimated by tradition, for the feelings of loss and alienation from nature to be produced by the Industrial Revolution.

ROMANTIC PASTORAL: WORDSWORTH VERSUS CLARE

For Williams, the interaction of Romanticism with the Industrial Revolution brought about a decisive shift in the relations of the country and city of the imagination. He identifies a new sense of sympathetic interrelation of the creative human mind and the creative nature of which it is a part, but from which it seems curiously, painfully, apart (1993: 127). According to Keith Thomas, during the early modern period and the eighteenth century,

> there had gradually emerged attitudes to the natural world which
> were essentially incompatible with the direction in which English society

was moving. The growth in towns had led to a new longing for the countryside. The progress of cultivation had fostered a taste for weeds, mountains and unsubdued nature. The new-found security from wild animals had generated an increasing concern to protect birds and preserve wild creatures in their natural state. Economic independence of animal power and urban isolation from animal farming had nourished emotional attitudes which were hard, if not impossible, to reconcile with the exploitation of animals by which most people lived.

(1984: 301)

Pastoral, which is part of the long shift that Thomas traces, graduates in the Romantic period from a simple logic of compensation for progress to the possibility of confronting it.

Williams's work on pastoral did not produce Gifford's pejorative sense of the word by itself, but it did provide impetus for a succession of critics who identified various forms and locations of the pastoral mystification he so trenchantly exposed. Several important examples are collected in an anthology of Wordsworth criticism that exemplifies the approaches ecocritics initially set out to challenge (J. Williams 1993). For example, Roger Sales argues in 'Michael, A Pastoral Poem' that the depiction of the hardship suffered by the shepherd Michael and his wife without any specific allocation of blame or detailed socio-political diagnosis amounts to a blatant example of what one might call 'pastoral kitsch'. He compares Wordsworth's poem to cynical 'advertising boys' using images of a cheerful farmer's wife 'at work on an antique spinning-wheel' to sell us 'old-fashioned, hand-knitted socks' then asks 'What is Wordsworth trying to peddle in "Michael"?' (1993: 97–8). The answer to the rhetorical question is: a harmonious vision of rural independence and fortitude that hides a harsh world in which people are bought and sold at hiring fairs, and where customary tenure keeps Cumberland 'statesmen' like Michael in a state of feudal vassalage to local aristocrats who are nevertheless equally adept at capitalist, wage-based forms of exploitation. Sales's main evidence, apart from the complaint that Wordsworth's poem is not an economic treatise, is that things befall Michael or his environment without anyone apparently being responsible for them:

> The Cottage which was nam'd The Evening Star
> Is gone, the ploughshare has been through the ground
> On which it stood; great changes have been wrought
> In all the neighbourhood, yet the Oak is left
> That grew beside their door; and the remains
> Of the unfinished Sheep-fold may be seen
> Beside the boisterous brook of Green-head Gill.
>
> (Wordsworth 1969: 110)

Sales wants us to ask who drove the plough, who wrought the changes and for what reasons? By attributing 'change' to mysterious forces or 'Strangers', no doubt from the 'dissolute city', Wordsworth is deliberately obscuring the exploitation going on within his beloved Lakeland.

What is strikingly absent from Sales's essay is any serious consideration of either Michael's profound attunement to his natural environment or the poet's admiration for his necessary fortitude. The latter functions as a rebuke at the beginning of the poem, a reminder of the importance of 'the heart of man and human life' in addition to the 'power of Nature'. Sales's critique is wrong, as we can see from the poet's elaboration of Michael's practised sensitivity to the weather:

> Hence he had learn'd the meaning of all winds,
> Of blasts of every tone, and often-times
> When others heeded not, He heard the South
> Make subterraneous music, like the noise
> Of Bagpipers on distant Highland hills;
> The Shepherd, at such warning, of his flock
> Bethought him, and he to himself would say
> 'The winds are now devising work for me!'
>
> (Wordsworth 1969: 104)

This is far from manipulative pastoral kitsch. The simile that brings together wind and bagpipe in a 'subterraneous music' suggests the bass drone of the instrument and the gale with a vividness unimagined from Sales's account. Moreover, the shepherd's ability to take warning from the 'meaning' he derives from the 'music' of the weather suggests a responsiveness as sophisticated as it is crucial to the survival of his flock.

LIVERPOOL JOHN MOORES UNIVERSITY
LEARNING SERVICES

It is with this sort of objection in mind that Jonathan Bate promoted a return to the nineteenth-century conception of Wordsworth as a 'poet of nature' in *Romantic Ecology* (1991), rejecting the reflex that made Sales associate 'nature' with political obfuscation. Bate begins with the end of Soviet communism, emphasising the huge environmental problems which contributed to it and suggesting that, in this new era, the old political models of left versus right are no longer useful. This starting point has two functions. First, it establishes a concern for nature not, as Marxist critics other than Williams have assumed, as a refuge from politics but as a potential form of political engagement. Second, it suggests that, prominent as they are in anthologies of 'radical' readings of Wordsworth, Marxist and historicist critics are marginal in terms of modern politics and perhaps reactionary with respect to progressive environmental politics. Whereas Marxist critics see a concern with nature as a mystification of a 'reality' they define in socio-economic terms, ecocritics point out that economics ultimately depends on ecology, and so it is arguably Marxism that obscures reality by refusing to attend to the primary productivity of nature.

Wordsworth's poetry, Bate argues, can act as an initiation into a utopian promise as well as an elegiac commemoration, such as 'Michael'. For the poet, as for his educated, alienated, mainly urban readership, Michael's inarticulate, unconscious bond with the land has consciously to be sought out, which is accomplished, according to Bate, in the 'Poems on the Naming of Places' at the end of *Lyrical Ballads*. Wordsworth's sense of being 'at home' in the Lake District is articulated in these poems, producing 'a truly ecological poetry. The word "ecology" is ultimately derived from the Greek *oikos* and *logos*. What Wordsworth has produced here is a *logos* of the *oikos*, the home. Man has come home to nature and the place takes on a wholeness, a unity that is entire' (Bate 1991: 103). Just as important, Bate insists that, as the title of Book Eight of *The Prelude* suggests, 'Love of Nature [Leads] to Love of Mankind', rather than being opposed to it, as Marxist critics had often claimed; Wordsworth's vision of the Lake District is a working paradise of rural republicanism. Moreover, his fervent advocacy led, long after his death, to the creation of a National Park there.

However, this claim to 'ecological sainthood' needs to be strongly qualified. Bate's attempt to use green politics to rescue a particular reading of Wordsworth may be challenged on both political and ecocritical grounds. There are significant differences within the broad political spectrum of environmentalism which correspond to the familiar left–right continuum, even if they are not simply reducible to it, and in any case it seems clear that Wordsworth's enthusiasm for 'nature' does not correspond to modern ecological concern. Wordsworth is, on the whole, far more interested in the relationship of non-human nature to the human mind than he is in nature in and for itself. Most of 'Michael', for example, concerns the family relations and domestic affections of the human protagonists; Wordsworth spends rather little time describing nature, and rather a lot reflecting upon his own and other people's responses to it. This argument is acknowledged in Bate's second major book of ecocriticism, *The Song of the Earth* (2000), but appears as a virtue rather than a vice: in the convoluted reflexivity of 'Lines written a few miles above Tintern Abbey' the distinction between observing human subject and observed natural objects is systematically undermined, leading to a 'dissolution of the self from perceiving eye into ecologically connected organism' (Bate 2000: 145). A firmer sense of the contrast between ecocritical and other reading practices could be obtained by comparing Bate's reading of this poem with competing readings of particular force, such as John Barrell's essay 'The Uses of Dorothy' (J. Williams 1993) and Marjorie Levinson's reading in *Wordsworth's Great Period Poems* (1986).

Moreover, the 'nature' that Wordsworth valorises is not the nature that contemporary environmentalists seek to protect. Romantic nature is never seriously endangered, and may in its normal state be poor in biological diversity; rather, it is loved for its vastness, beauty and endurance. By focusing attention upon sublime landscapes, mainly mountainous, Wordsworthian Romanticism may have diverted it from places that are more important and under more severe pressure ecologically but less 'picturesque', such as fens, bogs and marshes. Indeed, as Rod Giblett shows in *Postmodern Wetlands* (1996), swamps have long been viewed with fear rather than admiration in Western culture, to be filled or drained where possible. On a practical level, drainage for agriculture and peat-digging have reduced these wetlands so that few examples survive intact. In the work of Irish poet Seamus Heaney, the bog at least seems to have found a poet to speak for it. But perhaps the most catastrophic changes in the British countryside have occurred in the ordinary agricultural landscapes of pasture, hay-meadow and arable field, as described in Graham Harvey's *The Killing of the Countryside* (1997). These quotidian landscapes, where economic and ecological values coincide or clash on the largest scale and with the greatest consequence, seem relegated by a Wordsworthian aesthetic to the realm of the merely pretty, and so lacking in the qualities which make for both beauty and fear. The relatively barren landscape of the Lake District could function as inspiration and education, in contrast to the fat, complacent but biologically diverse lowlands.

Compared to Wordsworth, John Clare (1793–1864) has a much better claim to be the true poet of nature. John Middleton Murry proclaimed that 'The intensity with which he adored the country which he knew is without a parallel in English literature; of him it seems hardly a metaphor to say he was an actual part of the countryside' (Coupe 2000: 42). In saying this, Murry was employing a distinction first proposed by Friedrich Schiller (1759–1805) in his essay 'On Naive and Sentimental [or 'Reflective'] Poetry', a prototype of ecocritical theory. Schiller argues that the ancients were so little alienated from nature that they treated it as an extension of the human world, full of analogous conflicts, loves and jealousies. They wrote with a naïve curiosity and joy that never differentiated between 'the scenes and characters of nature' and a 'description of a tunic, a shield, a suit of armour, some domestic article, or any mechanical object' (Schiller 1985: 189). Being, like Michael the shepherd, immersed in nature, the naïve poet did not need to celebrate or mourn it especially, whereas for the modern 'sentimental' poet, perceptions of nature must always be suffused with either irony or regret: 'Our feeling for nature is like the feeling of an invalid for health' (p. 190). Having such an alienated, or 'reflective', relation to nature is an ambiguous predicament, because by it we gain in freedom and perspective what we lose in spontaneous immediacy and feeling. Moreover, whilst a naïve poet may become, or be forced to become, reflective, the reverse trajectory could only be an affectation. When Schiller claims that poets 'will either *be* nature, or they will *seek* lost nature' (p. 191), he shows how deeply ecocritical concepts remain indebted to Romanticism: the state of the naïve poet might be redefined as biocentric, whilst the anxieties that might attend anthropocentrism could be seen as distinctively sentimental yearnings. Schiller's is a 'poetics of authenticity' in that he proposes that the relationship of the ancients to nature was more authentic, because it was intuitive, unalienated and inarticulate. Many ecocritics still adhere implicitly to Schiller's duality, and seek a naïve literature even as they mourn its impossibility.

Critics have continued to think of Clare's poetry as 'naïve', only each has valued this differently. A major reason for this is the distinctiveness of his poetic voice:

EMMONSAILS HEATH IN WINTER

I love to see the old heaths withered brake
Mingle its crimpled leaves with furze and ling
While the old Heron from the lonely lake
Starts slow and flaps his melancholly wing
And oddling crow in idle motions swing
On the half rotten ash trees topmost twig
Beside whose trunk the gipsey makes his bed
Up flies the bouncing wood cock from the brig
Where a black quagmire quakes beneath the tread
The field fare chatters in the whistling thorn
And for the awe round fields and closen rove
And coy bumbarrels twenty in a drove
Flit down the hedgerows in the frozen plain
And hang on little twigs and start again

(Clare 1986: 136)

This edition prints Clare's poem in its naïve, unpunctuated form, idio-syncratic in spelling ('brig' rather than 'bridge'), frequently grammatically incorrect and full of dialect words such as, here, 'oddling' (solitary), 'bumbarrel' (long-tailed tit), 'awe' (haw), 'closen' (small field). Yet we might also note that this is a sonnet, which ought to remind us that he was not the naïve, scarcely lettered 'peasant poet' his untidy verse and his earlier critics might imply. He was, in fact, skilled in the artifice of innocence, besides having a knowledge, based on agricultural labour and study of natural history, of his natural surroundings quite unparalleled in English poetry. Thus the hungry energy of the flock of tits, combing the hedges in a roving wave, is vivid and exact. We might note also the unobtrusive presence of the gypsy, not glamorised or demonised as in so much Romantic writing, merely present in this filthy, freezing, un-Romantic landscape. And finally, we might note the way the poem begins with unaffected love of a place treated as empty, wild or recalcitrant space by agrarian improvers, a love complemented by rage in poems such as 'The Mores', 'Helpstone' and 'To a Fallen Elm' at the destruction of this known landscape. Raymond Williams argues that:

> Clare shared many of the insights of the modern 'green movement', a name which would have pleased him. Like them, he insisted that man does not own the earth and is not entitled to do whatever he likes with it. Instead he must treat it as a responsible steward, for his own sake and that of the other species (rabbits, elms, cattle) which also have a right to exist.
>
> (Clare 1986: 212)

In the light of the first chapter, where ecocentric and anthropocentric approaches were contrasted, Williams' claim seems confused. The rhetoric of 'stewardship' belongs to the shallow, or environmentalist, approach, as does the appeal to human self-interest, yet alongside this is a more radical appeal to the 'rights' of nature. For example, 'The Lament of Swordy Well' ventriloquises a voice that is specifically inhuman:

> Though Im no man yet any wrong
> Some sort of right may seek
> And I am glad if een a song
> Gives me the room to speak
> (Clare 1986: 94)

Here we are to imagine an actual place, Swordy Well, speaking; elsewhere we hear the 'Lamentation of Round-Oak Waters', of which Bate asks, in *The Song of the Earth*:

> Is the voice of Round Oak Waters to be understood only as a metaphor, a traditional poetic figuration of the genius loci, or 'an extreme use of

the pathetic fallacy'? Or can we conceive the possibility that a brook
might really speak, a piece of land might really feel pain?

(Bate 2000: 165)

These questions are thrown out with something of a rhetorical flourish,
as Bate is clearly aware of the sceptical answers most readers will have
formed already.

Adopting the Heideggerian approach outlined above is one way
to circumvent the post-Romantic problem of a poetic voice which
is necessarily human and 'reflective' and yet almost naïvely open to
the natural 'other' in the way that Clare is always and Wordsworth
is sometimes. Whereas the 'nature-lover' tradition of Clare criticism had
claimed that he spoke a word (*logos*) for our natural home (*oikos*), some
more recent criticism has found in his poetry a fulfilment of Heidegger's
notion that we must 'let beings be' precisely in and through language.
Implicitly reversing the usual formulation, Robert Pogue Harrison argues
that '*logos* [language] is that which opens the human abode [*oikos*] on the
earth' (1992: 200). Somewhat at odds with the usual ecocritical emphasis
on the ways in which language refers to the world, Harrison is saying that
we dwell not on Earth but in language.

Although the philosopher gets a mention only in an endnote, *Forests*
is consistently Heideggerian, and Harrison's book appears to have been a
crucial factor in shifting Bate from the green humanism of *Romantic
Ecology* to the dialectic of Heidegger and Adorno that plays through the
pages of *The Song of the Earth*. In Clare's wonderful, copious poems on
birds' nests, Bate finds a 'clearing' (*Lichtung*) in which, poetically, such
fragile things are allowed to 'be'. Here Clare decidedly thought further
ahead of his fellow Romantics; in a fragile social and mental situation
himself, he was able to 'think fragility' with fewer of the tensions and
confusions engendered in the others by an abstract 'nature'.

The converse of Clare's sense of fragility is a kind of political resistance that still eludes simple classification. Williams sees him as an
environmentalist with some leftist inclinations, Bate as a deep ecologist
speaking for unenclosed nature, and yet neither provides direct evidence
that the enclosure of common land, which Clare protested, had damaging
ecological effects. Indeed, enclosure may even have been beneficial by
preventing a burgeoning population from overexploiting the commons.

It certainly did continue a process of economic rationalisation that was steadily converting the natural world into 'standing-reserve', and it is this process that Clare wanted to resist. There is a desperation in some of Clare's writing that is often echoed in modern environmentalist writing, and his occasional hopeless rage (see Bate 2000: 172) is reflected in uncompromising activism in radical movements such as the Sea Shepherd organisation. And yet this seems to occur at precisely the point where pastoral has gone beyond the jarring encounter with rural labour to a collision with a non-human nature no longer easeful, plentiful, pretty, instructive or enduring. Just when it comes closest to being 'ecological', answering most of the objections raised above, Romantic pastoral starts to seem both un-Romantic and post-pastoral. Of course, pastoral poetry and the more general phenomenon go on long after this, but in both popular and literary forms pastoral has tended to function in British culture in ways that are ecologically delusive; to the extent that environmental movements have succeeded, it is as a result of the admixture to the Romantic landscape ideal of scientific observations that are not, in a strict sense, aesthetic at all. An aesthetic construct that, like English pastoral, may be as good at exhorting men to go and fight in the trenches in the First World War on the pretext that they are saving threatened habitats must be treated with great caution by ecocritics, and may turn out to be amenable today only to the promotion of 'country' products, as the complex, conflicted pastoral of Romanticism descends over two centuries to the status of a generic logo for pastoral kitsch.

AMERICAN PASTORAL

Although British Romantic models dominated early Anglo-American literature, pastoral has a very different place in American literature, criticism and culture. Both contrasts and parallels are instructive: where British ecocriticism focused on Wordsworth in its early explorations, American ecocriticism identified Henry David Thoreau as a key figure. As Jonathan Bate re-opened the question of pastoral as posed, pre-eminently, by Raymond Williams, so Lawrence Buell interrogated the place of nature in an American canon shaped in part by the proto-ecocritical work of Leo Marx. However, British ecocritics have had to meet the Marxist challenge, whereas American readings of pastoral have responded to critique primarily by feminist and multicultural critics. It is not the ratification of an oppressive social order, identified with a landed aristocracy, that provides a pejorative edge to 'pastoral' for Americans, but its identification with masculine colonial aggression directed against women, indigenes and the land. Great differences of history and topography ensure differing meanings of pastoral on either side of the Atlantic.

Pastoral remains significant for an American ecocriticism, orientated towards the revaluation of non-fictional nature writing, because it continues to supply the underlying narrative structure in which the protagonist leaves civilisation for an encounter with non-human nature, then returns having experienced epiphany and renewal. Moreover, the more domesticated forms of pastoral seem in American literature and culture to emphasise agrarianism, a political ideology associated with Thomas Jefferson that promoted a land-owning farming citizenry as a means of ensuring a healthy democracy. As Chapter 6 suggests, American writing about the countryside emphasises a working rather than an aesthetic relationship with the land. At the same time, the British Romantics' more sublime versions of pastoral were sharpened into a distinctively New World obsession with wilderness.

Nevertheless such distinctions have only recently emerged. Whereas contemporary ecocriticism, driven by preservationist politics, sees the wild as the ultimate destination of American pastoral, Leo Marx argued that it seeks a neo-classical 'middle landscape' between civilisation and true wilderness. Here American literature, emerging in the nineteenth century in the midst of massive industrialisation, can attempt to mediate between competing values, 'the contradiction between rural myth and technological fact' (1964: 354). Marx focuses upon moments when pastoral peace is interrupted by an actual or metaphorical machine, as when the railroad impinges upon Thoreau's retreat in *Walden*:

> The whistle of the locomotive penetrates my woods summer and winter, sounding like the scream of a hawk sailing over some farmer's yard, informing me that many restless city merchants are arriving within the circle of the town, or adventurous country traders from the other side.
>
> (Thoreau 1992: 91)

When the cattle train passes, Thoreau comments wryly, 'So is your pastoral life whirled past and away' (p. 97) and the metaphor of penetration above might indicate his resistance to this incursion. The sojourn at Walden Pond is clearly designed to make possible a revaluation of modernity, if not its outright rejection, and Thoreau's intense concentration upon the virtues of silence and contemplation of nature, models for so much nature writing thereafter, suggests that the noisy passing of a train would be most unwelcome. However, as Marx points out, the quote above naturalises the sound of the train, comparing it to the call of a hawk, and throughout his meditation Thoreau betrays a profound ambivalence towards technology:

> The image of the railway on the shore of the pond figures an ambiguity at the heart of *Walden*. Man-made power, the machine with its fire, smoke and thunder, is juxtaposed to the waters of Walden, remarkable for depth and purity and a matchless, indescribable color – now light blue, now green, almost always pellucid. The iron horse moves across the surface of the earth; the pond invites the eye below the surface. The contrast embodies both the hope and the fear aroused by the impending climax of America's encounter with wild nature.
>
> (Marx 1992: 251)

In fact, Thoreau betrays a certain wondering delight in the presence of the railroad, even a cosmopolitanism at odds with the persona developed in most of *Walden*, that of an ornery sage retreating from the bustle of civilised life to rediscover the fundamental truths of human existence: 'I am refreshed and expanded when the freight train rattles past me, and I smell the stores which go dispensing their odours all the way from Long Wharf to Lake Champlain, reminding me of foreign parts, of coral reefs, and Indian oceans' (p. 97) (see Garrard 2000). Marx explains this apparent contradiction by arguing that its resolution is not to be sought in the reconciliation of nature and culture through social or political change, but in literature, specifically in the pages of *Walden* itself. In effect, Thoreau returns pastoral hope to its classical origins, as a witty and learned literary game. It can be nothing else, in Marx's view, for an 'intricately organized, urban, industrial, nuclear-armed society' (p. 354) where the machine is reality and the future, and pastoral merely a myth about history. Later ecocritics would find fault both with this reading of Thoreau and the confident simplicity of the analytical dichotomy applied to it.

The crucial gender implications of pastoral were first explored in Annette Kolodny's psycho-historical study *The Lay of the Land*, which argued that pastoral was more than an imaginary construct for American pioneers because

> at the deepest psychological level, the move to America was experienced as the daily reality of what has become its single dominating metaphor: regression from the cares of adult life and a return to the primal warmth of womb or breast in a feminine landscape. And when America finally produced a pastoral literature of her own, that literature hailed the essential femininity of the terrain in a way European pastoral never had . . . and . . . took its metaphors as literal truths.
>
> (1975: 6)

The gendered landscape that seemed to be the fulfilment of Old World fantasies of endless plenitude generated a fundamental ambivalence, however, with a kernel of irremediable guilt. As a nurturing maternal presence, the land could be the object of puerile but essentially harmless regressive fantasies. However, as a desirable Other of a self-consciously virile frontier society, the land might well become a lover to be subdued by aggression. In the conflict between these versions of the pastoral metaphor, between the idyllic world they found and the hard, brutal work required to win and to work it, American writers found a rich source of tension between 'the dream and its betrayal . . . [of] guilt and anger' (p. 8). Moreover, the seeming literalisation of the stale Old World pastoral convention was a promise perennially situated just the other side of a frontier that was always receding westwards. The closing of the frontier was therefore not the end of the impulse, but its final, irrevocable frustration: 'What appears today as the single-minded destruction and pollution of the continent is just one of the ways we have continued to express that anger' (p. 137). Without fundamental change, androcentric conceptions of pastoral are doomed to shuttle endlessly between the regressive and aggressive poles of an essentially adolescent masculine symbolic order.

Perhaps the most influential work in American ecocriticism to date, Lawrence Buell's *The Environmental Imagination* (1995) provides a thorough critique of pastoral ideology in American fiction, with an extended treatment of Thoreau that moves from the evaluation of *Walden*'s 'environmental projects' through an analysis of the author's canonisation in American literary history and, later, ecocriticism, to a reconsideration of the role and significance of nature writing in the literary canon. *Walden* is crucial to Buell's argument because it is a transitional work, at the midpoint of a movement from youthful anthropocentric transcendentalism to the mature, biocentric perspective revealed in the late essays on wilderness, the dispersion of seeds and the succession of forest trees. Thoreau's trajectory, and the polyvalence of his nature writing under prolonged critical scrutiny, makes him an exemplary figure whose posthumous career reveals much about the changing place of the environment in American culture and the literary academy. The 'ecological saint' is but one of his reincarnations:

> During one ten-year span from the mid-sixties through the mid-seventies . . . Thoreau was acclaimed as the first hippie by a nudist magazine, recommended as a model for disturbed teenagers, cited by the Viet Cong in broadcasts urging American GI's to desert, celebrated by environmental activists as 'one of our first preservationists,' and embraced by a contributor to the [extreme right-wing] John Birch Society magazine as 'our greatest reactionary.'
>
> (Thoreau 1992: 314)

This position as culture hero contrasts strongly with the vague piety and general indifference surrounding Britain's Wordsworth, and adds a certain urgency to Buell's argument. Moreover, although the Lake District suffers a massive annual influx of contemporary Romantic tourists of the picturesque, this has little of the distinctive character of the 'Thoreauvian pilgrimage' to the 'sacred' Walden Pond. More striking, albeit opposed to Thoreau's warning that he 'would not have any one adopt [his] mode of living on any account', is the tradition of 'home-steading experiments', both solitary and communal, that are often explicitly attributed to the inspiration of *Walden*.

Yet if Thoreau's flawed masterpiece can be reread without disturbance to the received canon of American literature, Buell argues further that an environmental crisis ought to prompt a re-evaluation of the very criteria by which such a list is drawn up. In particular, nature writing, which enjoys considerable popularity in the USA, has tended to be downgraded by academic prejudices favouring fiction over non-fiction, and human dramas over narratives of interaction of humanity and nature. Buell warns that ecocritical criteria are apt to seem either too broad, incorporating any of the vast array of literary works in which 'nature' figures at all, or far too narrow, excluding all but the most clearly ecologically orientated work. Nevertheless, he suggests the following four criteria:

1. The nonhuman environment is present not merely as a framing device but as a presence that begins to suggest that human history is implicated in natural history.
2. The human interest is not understood to be the only legitimate interest.
3. Human accountability to the environment is part of the text's ethical orientation.
4. Some sense of the environment as a process rather than as a constant or a given is at least implicit in the text.

(Buell 1995: 7–8)

Clearly pastoral would often struggle to fulfil several of these criteria, but arguably it would also fail the tests brought to the debate by eco-feminists. Buell gives some prominence to feminist arguments, but it is in Louise Westling's *The Green Breast of the New World* (1996) that they provide the basic theoretical framework. Taking her lead from Kolodny in some respects, Westling analyses 'the strange combination of eroticism and misogyny that has accompanied men's attitudes toward landscape and nature for thousands of years' (1996: 5). From a speculative account of attitudes to nature implied by Palaeolithic art, discussion moves rapidly through Sumerian and Biblical narratives to the central issue; Westling agrees that Emerson and Thoreau 'consolidate the imperialist nostalgia that has always been at the heart of American pastoral – a sentimental masculine gaze at a feminized landscape and its creatures that masked the conquest and destruction of the "wild" continent' (p. 52), then explores a number of twentieth-century novelists, including Ernest Hemingway,

Eudora Welty and William Faulkner, to see whether they 'find a way to project a more realistic and responsible sense of Americans in their land' (p. 53).

For example, Hemingway, whose fascination with such virile pursuits as big-game hunting and bull-fighting is well known, founds his narratives of masculine initiation and self-discovery very firmly in a destructive opposition between the feminised landscape and his 'narrow and primitive' male protagonists. On the other hand, Willa Cather in her early work grafted sturdy 'Amazon' heroines onto this androcentric stock, as in her story of the first farmers of the Nebraska prairies, *Oh Pioneers!* (2000). Alexandra Bergson's perspectives on the landscape she loves and exploits are shifting and contradictory. Here Cather carries out a pastoral mystification worthy of Carew:

> She had never known before how much the country meant to her. The chirping of the insects down in the long grass had been like the sweetest music. She had felt as if her heart were in hiding down there, somewhere, with the quail and the plover and all the little wild things that crooned or buzzed in the sun. Under the long shaggy ridges, she felt the future stirring.
>
> (2000: 71)

In one respect, this reflects a radical departure from the androcentric tradition, as Alexandra identifies herself with the land. Yet 'the future' she senses as immanent there is, in fact, the catastrophic destruction of the prairie ecosystem under her pragmatic and capable direction. Westling argues that Cather creates 'an exclusively female dynamic of erotic attraction and identification in which the Nebraska landscape and Alexandra Bergson are dual protagonists in a passionate interplay that move from strife to yearning, to ecstatic conjunction' (1996: 65) This lesbian eroticism, however, is overbalanced by the novel's participation in an androcentric pastoral tradition that 'encodes a benign version of the conquest of the Plains, erasing its violence' (p. 81).

Destructive 'hyper-separated' and hierarchical gender oppositions are fundamental to the pastoral vision, but it also has a highly problematic racial dimension. The indigenous American perspective is shaped by the fact that, whether as idealised 'noble savages' or as savages pure and simple, Indians have historically been reduced to a mere feature in the pastoral landscape or even eliminated from it. As Buell points out, colonised peoples in Australia and South Africa may have a similar ambivalence towards 'settler pastoral', while Francophone African writers developed the 'indigene pastoral' of the Négritude movement. For African Americans, the meanings of pastoral are different again, reflecting the historical experience of plantation slavery and, later, rural lynchings. As Michael Bennett shows in his study of Frederick Douglass's auto-biography:

> The kinds of spaces that most mainstream environmentalists and ecocritics validate – the pastoral and the wild – were not likely to be appreciated by Douglass and other slaves whose best hopes lay with negotiating an urban terrain. Slavery changed the nature of nature in African American culture, necessitating a break with the pastoral tradition developed within European American literature.
>
> (2001: 205)

Social ecology, with its analysis of the social and environmental injustices meted out to ethnic minorities, therefore seems a more promising theoretical model than deep ecology for multicultural critics.

Despite Bate's defence of Wordsworth, then, ecocritics have tended to be highly suspicious of pastoral, albeit unwilling to dispense entirely with the implicit critique of contemporary society it may offer. As ecocriticism has developed through collections on specific writers such as John Ruskin and Henry Thoreau, pastoral remains one of the tropes necessarily explored (Wheeler 1995; Schnieder 2000). The ambivalence of pastoral will not be eliminated but rather enhanced by ecocritical readings.

A thorough cultural critique of the contemporary meanings of pastoral in film, TV, popular fiction and advertising has yet to be written, but Alexander Wilson (1992) analyses its influence on the development of suburban housing, with its endless lawns requiring fantastic amounts of high-technology upkeep, and Michael Bunce shows how the pastoral landscape ideal has commodified and altered the rural environments onto which it has been projected:

> In the process of realising their own particular version of a country

retreat, the country gentry, exurbanites, weekend cottagers, even back-to-the-landers have profoundly altered the character and the meaning of the rural landscape. They have fabricated a landscape which has transformed both natural environments and productive spaces into areas which conform to the idealisation of countryside as a place of leisure, refuge and alternative living. For the most part it is an amenity landscape, designed to provide pleasure rather than economic sustenance. It is also a predominantly private landscape controlled by the power and exclusivity of property ownership.

(1994: 110)

The ways in which our cultures of nature might move beyond this core pastoral inflection will occupy the remainder of this book.

PASTORAL ECOLOGY

It may be that one contemporary pastoral refuge lies within the discourse of ecology itself. At the root of pastoral is the idea of nature as a stable, enduring counterpoint to the disruptive energy and change of human societies. Both Judaeo-Christian and Graeco-Roman traditions imagine a divinely ordained order of nature, and find proof in the remarkable fitness of the Earth as a habitat for its various species. Cicero (106–43 BCE), for example, observes how well suited the elephant's trunk is to its dietary needs, and how the bark of trees protects them from the elements. The Scientific Revolution of the seventeenth and eighteenth centuries accepted the pastoral conception of nature, but refracted it through a new view of the Universe as a great mechanism designed by God. This metaphor of Nature as a harmonious and stable machine remained at the heart of the new science of ecology as it emerged in the early twentieth century, and shaped the rhetoric of later environmental movements even as scientific ecologists became increasingly sceptical of the 'balance of nature'. In this instance we must use contemporary ecology to critique a supposedly 'ecological' rhetoric that draws on outmoded and poorly understood scientific models.

The plant ecologist Frederick Clements (1874–1945), for example, proposed that 'associations' of plant species would necessarily evolve together in a particular habitat towards a 'climax' stage. Clements developed the idea of 'succession', in which disturbed ecosystems would be quickly colonised by fast-growing, hardy 'pioneer' species, to be succeeded by slow-growing species with longer life-spans and sometimes a tolerance for the conditions produced by the pioneers (see Brewer 1994: 373–405). He argued that succession tended to lead from an immature state, with large numbers of a few pioneer species, towards a complex, highly organised state of balance and stability with more diverse species. The long transition from abandoned cropland through shrubby birch woods to a mature, climax deciduous woodland would be typical. Historian Peter Coates argues, 'Early twentieth century US ecologists such as Frederick Clements firmly believed in nature's original and intrinsic identity' (1998: 143). This identity was essentially a version of pastoral, since it postulated a stable, harmonious state of nature in the absence of human 'interference'.

Clementsian theory was rejected by ecologists in the 1940s, but its rhetoric continues to shape environmental discourse. The association between biological diversity, ecosystem stability and an ideal, mature state of nature is an article of faith for most ecocritics and philosophers, not least because it appears to provide an objective basis for criticising the impoverished, single-species ecosystems of modern agriculture. However, Colleen Clements has dismissed this 'fairy tale ideal of an ecosystem of achieved and unchanging harmony' (1995: 215), claiming that stasis is unusual in natural systems. She points out that succession is a continuous process over time, from which no static norm or ideal end-point of plant associations can be derived. Ecosystems do maintain a kind of equilibrium, but it is characterised as much by change as by stasis: 'Equilibrium, or balance, or stasis is not . . . a well-meshed, smoothly-working, serene system but one representing many stasis breakdowns compensated for by new inputs which keep the oscillations within certain critical limits' (p. 218). Richard Brewer is less dismissive, but points out that the evidence of a correlation between stability and biological diversity is mixed, since 'there are very simple communities that are apparently very stable, such as those of hot springs' (1994: 404). Moreover, some unstable ecosystems, such as wetlands with fluctuating water levels, seem to generate diversity precisely because of their change-ability.

Since ecocriticism has both to deploy and to critique scientific concepts, several of the succeeding chapters will employ the contrast between popular pastoral ecology, wedded to outmoded Clementsian models of harmony and balance, and the new postmodern ecology exemplified by the work of Daniel Botkin, who stresses 'that nature undisturbed is not constant in form, structure, or proportion, but changes at every scale of time and space' (1992: 62). Clearly, not all changes are desirable, but unlike Clements's climax concept, postmodern ecology looks to human values to discriminate between them, rather than appealing to the illusory objectivity of a supposedly authentic or pristine state of nature.

4

WILDERNESS

The idea of wilderness, signifying nature in a state uncontaminated by civilisation, is the most potent construction of nature available to New World environmentalism. It is a construction mobilised to protect particular habitats and species, and is seen as a place for the reinvigoration of those tired of the moral and material pollution of the city. Wilderness has an almost sacramental value: it holds out the promise of a renewed, authentic relation of humanity and the earth, a post-Christian covenant, found in a space of purity, founded in an attitude of reverence and humility. The wilderness question is also central to ecocriticism's challenge to the status quo of literary and cultural studies, in that it does not share the predominantly social concerns of the traditional humanities. Unlike pastoral, the concept of wilderness only came to cultural prominence in the eighteenth century, and the 'wilderness texts' discussed by ecocritics are mainly non-fictional nature writing, almost entirely neglected by other critics. Much work in this area might easily count as intellectual history or philosophy, thus stretching the bounds of traditional literary criticism.

Wilderness narratives share the motif of escape and return with the typical pastoral narrative, but the construction of nature they propose and reinforce is fundamentally different. If pastoral is the distinctive Old World construction of nature, suited to long-settled and domesticated landscapes, wilderness fits the settler experience in the New Worlds – particularly the United States, Canada and Australia – with their apparently untamed landscapes and the sharp distinction between the forces of culture and nature. Yet settler cultures crossed the oceans with their preconceptions intact, so the 'nature' they encountered was inevitably shaped by the histories they often sought to leave behind. To understand current conceptions of wilderness, then, we must explore the Old World history of 'wilderness'. Nor can we take for granted the politics of the wild: for many critics, after all, the 'wildness' we should seek is epitomised in the American West, which was assumed to be an untrammelled realm to which the Euro-American has a manifest right.

OLD WORLD WILDERNESS

If pastoral has a dual origin in Judaeo-Christian and Graeco-Roman cultures, the meanings with which wilderness was endowed at the beginning of the eighteenth century seem to be based almost entirely on Judaeo-Christian history and culture. The word 'wilderness' derives from the Anglo-Saxon 'wilddeoren', where 'deoren' or beasts existed beyond the boundaries of cultivation. So useful is the word 'wild' to designate the realms of the 'deoren' that neither its spelling nor its simple meaning have changed in a millennium and a half, although as the forests receded and the wilds were colonised the word attracted new connotations.

Wilderness is, in the history of our species, a recent notion. To designate a place apart from, and opposed to, human culture depends upon a set of distinctions that must be based upon a mainly agricultural economy: for the hunter-gatherer, concepts such as fields and crops, as opposed to weeds and wilderness, simply would not exist (see Oelschlaeger 1991: 28). If farming people define 'home' as opposed to the 'wilderness' and are inclined to view the fruits of their labour as the consequence of a struggle against nature rather than its blessings, the transition from Palaeolithic hunter-gatherer to Neolithic farmer is for many wilderness advocates a crucial turning point, marking a 'fall' from a primal ecological grace. Agriculture becomes both the cause and the symptom of an ancient alienation from the earth that monotheistic religion and modern science then completed. Certainly the Paleolithic ways of life of Eurasia deserve respect for sustaining human populations under extremely difficult climatic conditions for an almost inconceivable period, during which extraordinary spiritual, technological and artistic developments occurred. Snyder speaks of 'a 25000-year continuous artistic and cultural tradition' (1999: 391). However, it is worth noting some inevitable difficulties in the reliance of wilderness advocates on a notion of the 'primal mind', which they contrast with the alienated 'civilised mind'. In the absence of written records, Oelschlaeger's confident reconstruction of the 'Paleolithic mind', for example, is based on a highly contentious interpretation of European cave art.

Whatever might be argued about the Palaeolithic mind, the very earliest documents of Western Eurasian civilisation, such as *The Epic of Gilgamesh*, depict wilderness as a threat, and by the time the Judaic scriptures were written it is viewed with ambivalence at best. After the ejection from Eden, the wilderness is the place of exile. Yet, just as Abraham led his people into the wilderness to found a nation, Moses led the people of Israel through it to return home, finding it a more hospitable place than the civilised but enslaving Egypt. The wilderness is associated with Satan: 'Then was Jesus led up of the Spirit into the wilderness to be tempted of the devil' (Matthew 4:1). But it is also identified with early monastic traditions: to escape both persecution by Roman authorities and the temptations of the world early Christian hermits went to the deserts. The Judaeo-Christian conception of wilderness, then, combines connotations of trial and danger with freedom, redemption and purity, meanings that, in varying degrees, it still has.

For many ecocritics, the next crucial point in the fall from grace of Western Europeans is the advent of the scientific revolution. For both deep ecologists and ecofeminists, the view of the universe as a great machine put forward by, among others, Francis Bacon (1561–1626), René Descartes (1596–1650) and Isaac Newton (1642–1727) represents the decisive blow to the organic universe inhabited by our ancestors. If, as Westling claims, Palaeolithic people venerated a fecund Magna Mater or Great Mother figure, these men were to complete the process of her annihilation begun by the dominance of the male Judaeo-Christian sky god. In place of the Earth as nurturing mother, natural philosophers posited a universe reducible to an assemblage of parts functioning according to regular laws that men could, in principle, know in their entirety. Descartes, like Bacon, sought the basis for a new, practical philosophy, in which 'knowing the force and action of fire, water, air, the stars, the heavens, and all the other bodies that surround us' he and his contemporaries might become 'masters and possessors of nature' (Descartes 1986: 49). Reason became the means to achieving total mastery over nature, now conceived as an enormous, soulless mechanism that worked according to knowable natural laws.

Ecocritics attack this view as 'reductionist', claiming that it substitutes a fragmented, mechanical worldview for a holistic, organic one. Plumwood points out that once the human mind is seen as the sole source and locus of value besides God, nature ceases to have any worth or meaning beyond that assigned to it by reason and argues that 'It is no coincidence that this view of nature took hold most strongly with the rise of capitalism, which needed to turn nature into a market commodity and resource without significant moral or social constraint on availability' (Plumwood 1993: 111). Moreover, the critique of the scientific revolution has gender implications. Carolyn Merchant sees in the sixteenth and seventeenth centuries the feminine Magna Mater finally disenchanted and set upon by a rationalising, masculine reason, and perhaps her last followers, Europe's 'witches', being brutally rooted out (Merchant 1990: 172).

This critique also coincides with Heidegger's attack on 'en-framing' or instrumentalism, in which beings are made to show up as mere instruments of our will. The metaphor Heidegger uses to describe a world reduced to mere resources is a forestry term: *Bestand*, or 'standing timber'. Yet the scientific revolution literally affected forestry, as Harrison shows. Where forestry had traditionally concerned itself with protection of the legal domains called 'forests' as both sites of production and as habitats, the advent of scientific principles banished their traditional value and symbolic resonance:

> For this sort of enlightened humanism . . . there can be no question of the forest as a consecrated place of oracular disclosures; as a place of strange or monstrous or enchanting epiphanies; as the imaginary site of lyric nostalgias and erotic errancy; as a natural sanctuary where wild animals may dwell in security far from the havoc of humanity going about the business of looking after its 'interests.' There can be only the

claims of human mastery and possession of nature – the reduction of forests to utility.

(Harrison 1992: 121)

The ultimate extension of scientific forestry was the German *Forstgeometer*, or forest geometer, who 'enframed' the woods with mathematics, reducing them to calculable 'standing timber', eliminating the ancient, mysterious *Wald* or forest of German history and legend. Thus deep ecologists, ecofeminists and Heideggerian ecocritics identify the scientific revolution as an ecological disaster in and through which a primal authenticity was lost.

However, it is very doubtful whether the mechanistic world view has ever been as pervasive or as pernicious as these writers suggest. Keith Thomas and Simon Schama have shown that mixed, perhaps conflicting attitudes have persisted throughout modern times – even Bacon recommended including a bit of wilderness in one's garden – and we should not underestimate the attraction of the practical benefits wrought by science to people of any world view. In any case, even as the wild places were being disciplined by reason, an emergent Romantic sensibility was urging a revaluation, and in the eighteenth century wilderness was given a new inflection with the popularisation of the idea of the sublime.

THE SUBLIME

The ambivalence of the Judaeo-Christian tradition towards wilderness had been resolved in early modern philosophy and literature into something approaching outright hostility. Thomas Burnet's *Sacred Theory of the Earth* (1684) explained mountain ranges as being the physical outcome of God's displeasure with mankind, scars inflicted upon a previously unwrinkled globe by the 'Great Flood' that Noah and his family survived. The crust of the world had burst open, he argued, releasing a terrible deluge from within the planet that left the Edenic Earth battered and broken. However, Burnet's readers found the apocalyptic terror of this ruined world strangely appealing, including a young man later known for his *Reflections on the Revolution in France*, Edmund Burke (1729–97). His *Philosophical Enquiry into the Origin of our Ideas of the Sublime and the Beautiful* represents, Schama demonstrates, a counter-current in the philosophy of the 'Enlightenment', with Burke setting himself up as 'the priest of obscurity'. For Schama, Burke's sublime was found in 'shadow and darkness and dread and trembling, in cave and chasms, at the edge of the precipice, in the shroud of cloud, in the fissures of the earth' (Schama 1995: 450). Whereas the merely beautiful arouses feelings of pleasure, Burke claims that 'the passion caused by the great and sublime in nature . . . is Astonishment; and astonishment is that state of the soul, in which all its motions are suspended, with some degree of Horror' (Burke 1990: 53). The beautiful is loved for its smallness, softness, delicacy; the sublime admired for its vastness and overwhelming power. Feminist critics have shown that the qualities associated with the sublime and the beautiful are gendered, and concluded, perhaps with less justice, that 'the sublime moment is peculiarly male' (Day 1996: 188). Just as the feminine and beautiful is denigrated by comparison with the masculine sublime in Burke's definitions, it is argued, so women were excluded from encounters with the wild.

Burke's *Enquiry* was published in 1757, but it was in Romantic poetry that sublime wilderness found its literary apotheosis. The most familiar of Romantic landscapes such as the Scottish Highlands and the Lake District derive their fame from their resemblance to the archetypal locus of the European sublime, the Alps. William Wordsworth, for example, takes the climbing of English mountains as an apprenticeship in awe, although it is specifically a female who is addressed in 'To — on her first Ascent to the Summit of Helvellyn':

Lo! the dwindled woods and meadows;
What a vast abyss is there!
Lo! the clouds, the solemn shadows,
And the glistenings, heavenly fair!

And a record of commotion
Which a thousand ridges yield;
Ridge, and gulf, and distant ocean
Gleaming like a silver shield!
Maiden! now take flight; – inherit
Alps or Andes – they are thine!
(Wordsworth 1987: 173)

Nor had this awe left behind its religious dimensions, although Wordsworth's piety was not, in his early work at least, conventionally Christian. 'Lines Composed a Few Miles Above Tintern Abbey' finds the poet moved by a 'presence':

> . . . a sense sublime
> Of something far more deeply interfused,
> Whose dwelling is the light of setting suns,
> And the round ocean and the living air,
> And the blue sky, and in the mind of man:
> A motion and a spirit, that impels
> All thinking things, all objects of all thought.
>
> (1987: 164)

His sister, Dorothy, contributed sublime descriptions to William's *Guide to the Lakes*, and both the Wordsworths learned their appreciation in part from *A Short Residence in Sweden* (1796) by the feminist radical Mary Wollstonecraft (1759–97). She seems as moved by the 'wild beauties' of Sweden as her male contemporaries:

> The impetuous dashing of the rebounding torrent from the dark cavities which mocked the exploring eye, produced an equal activity in my mind: my thoughts darted from earth to heaven, and I asked myself why I was chained to life and its misery? Still the tumultuous emotions this sublime object excited, were pleasurable . . .
>
> (Wollstonecraft and Godwin 1987: 153)

The categories may be gendered, but the experience is circumscribed neither by gender nor by place. In Percy Shelley's 'Mont Blanc', the Alpine original inflames the imagination. For ecocritic Karl Kroeber, 'Shelley's poem intensifies the Wordsworthian literalized interactivity of mind and landscape' (Kroeber 1994: 127). It exploits the oxymoron of the mountain's 'silent voice', reflecting on its contrast with both the poet's mind 'which passively / Now renders and receives fast influencings' and the larger political world whose pettiness and deceits it exposes: 'Thou hast a voice, great Mountain, to repeal / Large codes of fraud and woe'.

However, if the sublime required a degree of terror to induce the requisite spiritual or even political be-wilderment, it would always be vulnerable to technological and cultural change. European civilisation largely mastered its mountains with trains, roads and ski-lifts, whilst the exploration of the American West brought news of the Grand Canyon and the Rocky Mountains, making the wildernesses of the Old World look decidedly tame.

NEW WORLD WILDERNESS

Thoreau's *Walden* can be regarded as the terminus of Old World pastoral in American literature, as it collides with both the technology and autonomous cultural confidence of the young republic. His *Maine Woods* (1864) can, with a similar degree of oversimplification, be highlighted as an early example of the wilderness tradition that borrows the ancient rhetoric of retreat and applies it to the endless miles of sublime landscape in America. After climbing Mount Ktaadn, Thoreau writes:

> It is difficult to conceive of a region uninhabited by man. We habitually presume his presence and influence everywhere. And yet we have not seen pure Nature, unless we have seen her thus vast, and drear, and inhuman . . . Nature was here something savage and awful, though beautiful. This was that Earth of which we have heard, made out of Chaos and Old Night.
>
> (1983: 71)

His insight is achieved while standing on a peak of just 5,300 feet. Yet it leaves him in awe of his own body, as well as the wilderness about him:

> this matter to which I am bound has become so strange to me. I fear not spirits, ghosts, of which I am one, – *that* my body might, – but I fear bodies, I tremble to meet them. What is this Titan that has possession of me? Talk of mysteries! Think of our life in nature, – daily to be shown matter, to come into contact with it, – rocks, trees, wind on our cheeks! the *solid* earth! the *actual* world! the *common sense! Contact! Contact! Who* are we? *where* are we?

The sublime provocation of the mountain scenery, and the near-hysteria at the moment of 'contact' it enables, tends to belie the permanently threatening proximity of that other wilderness, the human body. The anxieties attending the boundary of human intelligence and animal matter will be discussed in Chapter 8.

One of Thoreau's most enthusiastic disciples, the Scottish immigrant John Muir (1838–1914) contributed more than any other single writer to the establishment of wilderness as a touchstone of American cultural identity, and a basis for conservation activities. He is best known for hymning the virtues of California's Sierra Nevada mountains and for his political campaigns on behalf of wilderness. In *My First Summer in the Sierra*, Muir's journal entry for 15 July 1869 recounts a view of 'sublime domes and canyons, dark upsweeping forests, and glorious array of white peaks deep in the sky, every feature glowing, radiating beauty that pours into our flesh and bones like heat rays from fire' (Muir 1992: 232). Paul Brooks, in *Speaking for Nature*, positions Muir alongside John Burroughs as one of the two fathers of American conservation. Explaining how Muir chafed at his domestic responsibilities, he exclaims: 'How different his voice sounds when he is back in his beloved mountains!' (Brooks 1980: 21–2). Muir's extravagant prose is the mark of one of nature's spokesmen for Brooks, whose critical approach verges on worship. Yosemite Valley had already been the first place in America protected by an Act of Congress in 1864. Muir's writings and personal activism would lead to the creation of Yosemite National Park in 1890 and the formation of a wilderness protection organisation in 1892, the Sierra Club, which Brooks calls 'the most powerful conservation organization in the western hemisphere' (Brooks 1980: 23).

Daniel Payne claims that 'it is hard to overstate the importance of John Muir's contribution to the wilderness preservation movement' (1996: 85), citing his tireless lobbying, participation in Congressional debates and commissions, his prolific writing and even the camping trip he took with President Theodore Roosevelt. For Max Oelschlaeger, Muir also has a contemporary role assisting us in the development of a new 'Palaeolithic consciousness' that will supersede the mechanistic world view: 'his wilderness theology – a profoundly insightful evolutionary pantheism – is a complementary development that revivifies an archaic sense of the sacrality of all being' (p. 173). This would seem to be contradicted by the apparently conventional piety of Muir's experience of the sublime on North Dome, where he offers himself 'humbly prostrate before the vast display of God's power' (p. 238). Elsewhere, though, Muir asserts that 'when we try to pick out anything by itself, we find it hitched to everything else in the universe. One fancies a heart like our own must be beating in every crystal and cell, and we feel like stopping to speak to the plants and animals as friendly fellow mountaineers' (p. 248). He is an incisive and sardonic critic of anthropocentrism, as in a diary entry ridiculing the 'numerous class of men' who 'are painfully astonished whenever they find anything, living or dead, in all God's universe, which they cannot eat or render in some way what they call useful to themselves' (p. 160). Muir argues that alligators, lions, poisons and diseases are all ample proof that Creation is not prefabricated for human use and comfort, and that every living thing down to the 'smallest transmicro-scopic creature' has intrinsic value. He even avers that 'if a war of races should occur between the wild beasts and Lord Man, I would be tempted to sympathize with the bears' (p. 155). Such ecocentric piety nevertheless coexisted with a thorough scientific knowledge of botany and geology.

'THE TROUBLE WITH WILDERNESS'

Although Oelschlaeger draws attention to the ways in which Muir attacks the arrogance of 'Lord Man' and espouses a more inclusive spirituality, it might be argued that he does not succeed in showing the usefulness of such a pantheistic theology. He criticises playful, sceptical, fragmented 'postmodernism', as it is usually understood, as an indulgent extension of ecocidal, mechanistic modernism and offers as the only alternative to a solipsistic obsession with human sign systems his notion of a genuinely postmodern ecocentrism that would resanctify nature, unifying 'holistic' science and wilderness religion. In common with many deep ecological critics, he assumes that ecological problems stem from a single moral or spiritual source, and that the adoption of pantheism would therefore solve them. But if God is identical with the universe, arguably that eliminates the distinction, basic to traditional theology, between how things are and how divine providence would have them be: a pantheistic theology would have to worship not only the pure streams of Yosemite Valley but also toxic waste dumps, which would be quite at odds with Muir's rhetoric of the purity of wilderness and its essential opposition to the filthy realms of 'Lord Man'. For the literary critic, a further objection is that Muir's prose alternates between tedious enumeration of species and repetitive sublime hyperbole in which every other phrase is an exclamation. There are moments of intriguing philosophical insight and visionary intensity, but in the mass his writing is stultifying.

In terms of the representation of the wilderness of the Sierras, Muir wrote the book but Ansel Adams (1902–84) took the pictures. He returned to Yosemite at least once a year from his childhood on, learning to take and process photographs at the Sierra Club lodge there, and publishing them in the Club's *Bulletin*. After his death, the State of California designated over 100,000 acres of the Sierra the 'Ansel Adams Wilderness Area'. Although Adams took around 40,000 photographs, of still-life and documentary subjects as well as caves and canyons, his best known images are his black and white shots of mountains and valleys, in which wilderness attains an iconic status. His images epitomise the purity of the wild in their reduction of landscape to starkly defined regions of sky, rock, water and forest, while their epic scale and eerie stillness conjoin to suggest stoic self-reliance. Adams was a technical perfectionist and developed a sustained mature style that emphasised depth of field and a wide tonal range. He typically took photographs in winter or early spring in only the clearest weather conditions, and used red or green filters for enhanced contrast of rock and snow, sky and cloud. The overall effect is to give the mountains a stark, monumental quality, allowing them to retain the sublime, immeasurable otherness Muir had praised in the Sierra Range: 'In general views no mark of man is visible upon it; nor anything to suggest the wonderful depth and grandeur of its sculpture' (Muir 1992: 614).

Yet William Cronon has identified this 'otherness' as part of 'the trouble with wilderness'. Promoting a more sceptical, less pious ecocritical perspective, Cronon argues that wilderness 'quietly expresses and reproduces the very values its devotees seek to reject' (1996: 80). This construction of alienated urbanites, who buy the works of Muir and his followers but seldom attempt to emulate him, sets up a sacred ideal:

> Wilderness is the natural, unfallen antithesis of an unnatural civilization that has lost its soul. It is a place of freedom in which we can recover

our true selves we have lost to the corrupting influences of our artificial lives. Most of all, it is the ultimate landscape of authenticity.

(Cronon 1996: 80)

This vision has pernicious consequences for our conceptions of nature and ourselves since it suggests that nature is only authentic if we are entirely absent from it. Such 'purity' is often achieved at the cost of an elimination of human history every bit as thorough as that undertaken by pastoral literature. In the case of Yosemite, this myth of an 'uninhabited wilderness' meant that both the Ahwahneechee Indians and the white miners who had lived and worked there were expelled.

Bill McKibben's *The End of Nature* (1990) exemplifies Cronon's myth of wilderness purity. In the past, he argues, pollution and devastation were localised phenomena and even widespread contamination by DDT or fallout from atmospheric nuclear weapons tests would eventually disappear. But the advent of anthropogenic climate change, or 'global warming', has changed the situation, fundamentally contaminating the whole planet:

We have changed the atmosphere, and thus we are changing the weather. By changing the weather, we make every spot on earth man-made and artificial. We have deprived nature of its independence, and that is fatal to its meaning. Nature's independence *is* its meaning; without it there is nothing but us.

(McKibben 1990: 54)

From now on, there will be nothing truly wild and 'a child born now will never know a natural summer, a natural autumn, winter, or spring' (1990: 55). McKibben's horror is justified by the scientific evidence thus far, but it is shaped by an inflection of 'nature' that is by no means universal or inevitable. It might be pointed out, for example, that the methane emitted by termite mounds is substantial enough to make a calculable contribution to global concentrations of greenhouse gases, but these insects have not 'ended nature'. However, McKibben's construction of nature reinforces an idea of wilderness, in which any modification of the environment is a form of contamination.

A further problem is apparent: the ideal wilderness space is wholly pure by virtue of its independence from humans, but the ideal wilderness narrative posits a human subject whose most authentic existence is located precisely there. This model not only misrepresents the wild, but also exonerates us from taking a responsible approach to our everyday lives: our working and domestic lives are effectively irredeemable alongside this ideal, so the activities we carry out there escape scrutiny (see Cronon 1996: 81). Wilderness, then, is ideological in the sense that it erases the social and political history that gives rise to it, extending into reactionary politics as well as Thoreau's occasional misanthropy. At best, the wilderness experience and its deep ecological philosophy risks identification with privileged leisure pursuits that sell authenticity while mystifying the industrialised consumerism that makes them possible. If we correlate the wilderness consciousness with the social forms of life, or social classes, in which it has taken hold, we have the grounds for some of Timothy Luke's cynicism:

> It makes sense for deep ecologists to condemn human overpopulation or resacralize the bioregion they wish to enjoy. Unfortunately, nomadic grub eaters cannot produce high-tech composite surfboards, eighteen-speed bicycles, or sophisticated hang gliders. Who will make such goods or produce food while others seek self-realization and biocentric equality? The antimodern, future primitive condemnation of industrial human civilization by many deep ecologists is not really total, but its contradictory partialities are mystified in the social forms of life that generate this consciousness.
>
> (Luke 1997: 21)

To the extent that it extols the idea of wilderness and the writers who explore it, ecocriticism risks complicity with this ideology. Deep ecology, it might be argued, has conspired with some American ecocriticism to promote a poetics of *authenticity* for which wilderness is the touchstone. To critique this is not to argue for the abandonment of wilderness to the tender mercies of ranchers and developers, but to promote instead the poetics of *responsibility* that takes ecological science rather than pantheism as its guide. The choice between monolithic, ecocidal Modernism and reverential awe is a false dichotomy that ecocriticism can circumvent with a pragmatic and political orientation. The fundamental problem of responsibility is not what we humans *are*, nor how we can 'be' better, more natural, primal or authentic, but what we *do*. Ecocriticism would not then be seeking a more truthful or enlightening discourse of nature, but a more effective rhetoric of transformation and assuagement.

AUSTIN, LEOPOLD AND ABBEY: TWENTIETH-CENTURY NATURE WRITING

The modern canon of American wilderness writing is quite extensive, but the key figures are Thoreau and Muir in the nineteenth century, Mary Austin (1868–1934), Aldo Leopold (1887–1948) and Edward Abbey (1927–89) mainly or wholly in the twentieth. Of these, Leopold is perhaps the least vulnerable to Cronon's argument because he is wary of religious language and imagery, preferring to communicate his natural history observations and philosophical arguments in a relatively self-effacing, low-key idiom. His major achievement for philosophers and historians is his formulation of a biocentric 'land ethic' at the end of *A Sand County Almanac* (1949), where having examined recreational, economic, scientific and other human-centred reasons for preserving wilderness, he concludes that, important as these are, an ethical defence is needed that is not hampered by human chauvinism: '[A] land ethic changes the role of *Homo sapiens* from conqueror of the land-community to plain member and citizen of it. It implies respect for his fellow-members, and also respect for the community as such' (Leopold 1968: 204). His formulation of the land ethic is elegant and apparently simple, bringing together normative criteria that are both aesthetic and scientific: 'A thing is right when it tends to preserve the integrity, stability, and beauty of the biotic community. It is wrong when it tends otherwise' (pp. 224–5). It is not the individual organism that attracts moral consideration, but the 'community' as a whole, a community in which human beings are neither more nor less than 'citizens'.

Beguiling as it may seem, Leopold's dictum raises substantial philosophical and ecological problems. The metaphor of 'citizenship' is appealing, but human societies attach reciprocal rights and duties to citizenship and our duties are exclusively *to* the wilderness; we do not derive any in return. Also, the formula only asserts the moral value of, rather than arguing for, say, a stable biotic community. While it may seem obvious that we should prefer a healthy environment, the non-chauvinistic grounds for wanting one are not supplied. Perhaps more problematic still, the very idea of a 'biotic community' as an identifiable, stable locus of value is extremely problematic from the perspective of modern theoretical ecology. The language of Leopold's ecology is nowadays treated with some caution since it suggests a degree of predictability that is seldom found in natural systems. The idea of a 'community' suggests the ecological whole is greater than the sum of its parts, but, as Brennan argues, 'The possibility remains that when we encounter an apparently stable ecosystem manifesting diversity of species and apparent self-regulation, we . . . may be confronted with an item that just happens to be the way it is' (1995: 211). Many species transgress ecosystem boundaries, and some species benefit from change while others are harmed or eliminated: an entire ecosystem does not stand or fall together. Not only is it very difficult to establish the boundaries of ecosystems, the word itself misleadingly suggests 'the physical concept of the stability of a mechanical system' (Botkin 1992: 42). If the community cannot be properly delineated, and if the ideal stable condition for it cannot be established, then neither 'integrity' nor 'stability' are the objective criteria we need for moral action. It would seem that only beauty remains, which is scarcely easier to define, but which Leopold seeks to exemplify in a series of analogies between the arts of humans and nature.

In Parts I and II of the *Almanac*, Leopold, a professional ecologist and professor of game management, exploits his scientific knowledge to construct a wonderful series of narratives of natural artistry: how the river paints its own landscape; how the tree encapsulates its own history; how the hunting dog reads 'the olfactory poems that who-knows-what silent creatures have written in the summer night' (Leopold 1968: 43). The swampy epic of the whooping crane, the tragedy of the passenger pigeon and even the odyssey of atom X through complex, wilderness biota and simplified, agricultural ones are narrated. In some respects Leopold's idea of wilderness as a retreat or proving-ground for male hunters remains close to the dualistic vision that Cronon criticises. But at the same time, Leopold is the only professional scientist amongst the canonical writers, and he writes for a sceptical audience who work in and with the wilds. His radical land ethic admits the benefits of modernity and the inevitability of human intervention:

> By and large, our present problem is one of attitudes and implements. We are remodeling the Alhambra [desert] with a steam-shovel, and we are proud of our yardage. We shall hardly relinquish the shovel, which after all has many good points, but we are in need of gentler and more objective criteria for its successful use.
>
> (1968: 225–6)

Despite sharing with Leopold an ecocentric perspective, and the admiration of many ecocritics and activists, the writings of Edward Abbey perfectly exemplify the trouble with wilderness. His sojourn as a Park Ranger in the Arches National Monument in Utah is justified in *Desert Solitaire* (1968) as follows:

> I am here not only to evade for a while the clamor and filth and confusion of the cultural apparatus but also to confront, immediately and directly if it's possible, the bare bones of existence, the elemental and fundamental, the bedrock which sustains us. . . . To meet God or Medusa face to face, even if it means risking everything human in myself. I dream of a hard and brutal mysticism in which the naked self merges with a non-human world and yet somehow survives still intact, individual, separate. Paradox and bedrock.
>
> (Abbey 1992: 6)

Thoreau's ascent of Ktaadn embodied a similar paradox. The desire for 'contact', for 'reality', conflicts with the cultural enframing of Thoreau's 'Titan' and Abbey's 'God or Medusa'. Both writers maintain a rigorous individualism at both a political and stylistic level, although Abbey veers at times into vicious paranoia. Nevertheless, Abbey's work is littered with learned literary and philosophical allusions, and, as Daniel Payne comments: 'Although Abbey presented himself as a blunt, straightforward speaker, much of his writing is in fact a complex mixture of personal narrative, journalism, philosophy, natural history, political commentary, and story-telling . . . full of paradox, irony, and humor' (Payne 1996: 153).

Don Scheese, who credits *Desert Solitaire* with changing his life, states approvingly that Abbey is the 'most radical, iconoclastic figure' in the wilderness canon, enjoining us to 'Afford the time to allow for prolonged engagement with and meditation on nature. Enter the wilderness and

experience freedom. Be alive to the redemptive possibilities of the wild'
(1996: 315). Abbey induces us to delight in the apparently unpromising
landscapes of the sandstone deserts he inhabits, and brings justified rage
to his polemics against 'Industrial Tourism' and the damming of Glen
Canyon on the Colorado River. His later novel *The Monkey-Wrench Gang*
(1982) inspired the formation of Earth First! and other direct-action
groups. At the same time, his enthusiasm for guns, paranoia about federal
government and 'big business', and support for violent resistance to
authority risks appearing to ally environmentalists with survivalist
militias. SueEllen Campbell alerts us to some disturbing absences from
Abbey's wilderness; the local Indians, for example, are only briefly and
disparagingly noticed. More strikingly, Abbey does not mention the
atmospheric nuclear tests going on in Nevada at this time, although
Arches was affected by fallout. Campbell's questions reflect Cronon's
concerns: 'What notion of the elemental ignores nuclear fallout? Why
think it's necessary to leave society to find reality? What's *lost* by opposing
wilderness and culture?' (Campbell 1998: 24).

Abbey not only opposes wilderness and culture, he plainly genders
the distinction and eroticises the landscape, wanting to 'embrace the scene
intimately, deeply, totally, as a man desires a beautiful woman' (1992: 5).
But actual women are almost entirely absent from this wilderness, except
as the other end of the 'bloody cord' of civilisation that wilderness helps
a man to cut: '(My *God!* I'm thinking, what incredible *shit* we put up with
most of our lives – the domestic routine (same old wife *every* night),
the stupid and useless and degrading *jobs*, the *insufferable* arrogance of
elected officials, [etc.]) (1992: 155). This despite the fact Abbey married
five times. Nevertheless, it cannot be assumed that the idea of wilderness
intrinsically excludes women, any more than the sublime was reserved
for male Romantic poets: Mary Austin, in particular, provides a useful
counterpoint to Abbey, and even the prospect for a reconfiguration of
'wilderness'.

Austin's landscape is Southwestern, arid and thinly populated like
Abbey's, and she shares his facility for vivid, descriptive prose. In her best-
known work, *Land of Little Rain* (1903), she seems highly attuned to the
presence of birds:

About the time the burrowers and all that feed upon them are addressing themselves to sleep, great flocks pour down the trails with that peculiar melting motion of moving quail, twittering, shoving, and shouldering. They splatter into the shallows, drink daintily, shake out small showers over their perfect coats, and melt away again into the scrub, preening and pranking, with soft contented noises.

(Austin 1996: 13)

According to Buell, 'her protagonist is the land, more particularly the geography of its watercourses and the patterns of life created by water scarcity' (Buell 1995: 80). The extraordinary challenges of the environment lead its inhabitants into strange exigencies: 'There was a fence in that country shutting in a cattle range, and along its fifteen miles of posts one could be sure of finding a bird or two in every strip of shadow; sometimes the sparrow and the hawk, with wings trailed and beaks parted, drooping in the white truce of noon' (Austin 1996: 7).

Yet this is a wilderness for inhabiting, not, like Thoreau, Muir and Abbey, for sojourning, and 'The manner of the country makes the usage of life there, and the land will not be lived except in its own fashion' (Austin 1996: 26). For ecofeminist critic Vera Norwood, this shows that 'Nature and culture are interactive processes: human culture is affected by the landscape as well as effecting change on it' (Norwood 1996: 334). She argues that women write wilderness differently, experiencing immersion rather than confrontation, 'recognition' rather than 'challenge'. Part of the justification for this lies in Austin's self-effacing idiom and narrative structure, which, as Buell observes, 'allows the book to be taken over by other people's stories and her speaker to imagine the desert as it might look through the eyes of birds and animals' (Buell 1995: 176). Whilst Austin's style might be a function of an androcentric prejudice that simply expected reticence of women writers, it might also be seen as a device that decentres the human subject not, as in Muir, by mere assertion, but by subtle insinuation at the level of narrative.

One of the most intriguing, though flawed, works in recent eco-criticism claims that Austin deconstructs the concept of wilderness itself. Combining autobiographical sketches, literary criticism, philosophical reflection and a discussion of desert land management, Barney Nelson's *The Wild and the Domestic* (2000) shows how Austin challenges the myth that wilderness is 'no place for a woman', rewriting the gendered dichotomy of masculine wilderness and feminine domesticity. For example, she notes that the vaunted 'self-reliance' of the heroic Western male consists mainly in the ability to undertake 'feminine' domestic tasks such as cooking and mending clothes themselves, that Western states granted women suffrage long before the East, and that Austin found freedom and self-confidence at home in the rural Southwest.

The centrepiece of Nelson's argument is a contrastive study of Austin and Muir in which she argues that his construction of Yosemite as a pristine wilderness paradise was not only a falsification of history, but also led to the exclusion of working people, white, Hispanic and Indian, from upland pastures that had been in use for as long as 400 years. Whereas Muir betrays contempt for both shepherds and sheep, Austin respects the practical knowledge and philosophy of the people, and the intelligence and hardiness of their animals. Since Muir lost large numbers of sheep during his brief tenure as shepherd in the Sierras (200 ewes and 100 lambs on one occasion) he may have been making a virtue of adversity in constructing Yosemite as a sublime landscape of 'leisure and study, not work', while Austin 'believed land should be valued as home' and fought to protect residents' rights against urban demands for land, water and leisure space (Nelson 1996: 75). Nelson argues that Muir promulgated a 'myth' that ranched sheep and cows were environmentally damaging, calling them 'hoofed locusts' and adversely affecting federal and state policies until the present day.

Nelson's case is far from watertight, since Austin too wonders 'how much the devastating sheep have had to do with driving the tender plants to the shelter of the prickle-bushes' (p. 40). Nevertheless, connecting Austin's literary creations to the specific environmental question of arid land ranching, rather than to very general ecophilosophical issues, makes for refreshing reading, and it emphasises the need for ecocriticism to question even the tropes deployed by environmental organisations. When the Sierra Club argues for more 'wilderness', they are in practice representing the interests of wealthy suburbanites rather than rural working people, and leisure industries rather than extractive or agricultural ones. This attention to the politics of wilderness is especially important in American ecocriticism, which has until recently tended to stress the spiritual and moral, while neglecting the ways in which wilderness is a site of class and gender struggle.

BEYOND WILDERNESS?

An updated wilderness canon would include the work of Annie Dillard, Terry Tempest Williams, Barry Lopez, Peter Matthiessen and Gary Snyder, which has been the subject of much American ecocriticism, particularly in the journal *Interdisciplinary Studies in Literature and Environment* (*ISLE*). It would also address other New World literatures that arguably inflect wilderness in culturally and geographically specific ways: Australia's 'outback' as an interior wilderness space, for example, and Canada's 'North' as both a powerful signifier of an irreducibly 'wild' geography and climate, and a site of contested high-technology industrial and military activities.

In the early 1970s, Canadian cultural nationalism deployed wilderness as a mark of difference as well as an article of ecological faith. Bruce Littlejohn and Jon Pearce claimed in the Introduction to an anthology that 'If there is one distinguishing element that sets Canadian literature apart from most other national literatures, it is the influence of the wild' (1973: 11). Margaret Atwood's early work both reflected this preoccupation with wilderness and, thanks to her talent and success, strongly reinforced it. The unnamed protagonist of *Surfacing* (1979) returns to the landscape of her childhood in Northern Quebec, ostensibly to find out what has happened to her father. The threats to this wilderness from logging, hydroelectric projects and commercial tourism are coded as 'American', driving the protagonist into an increasingly alienated and paranoid state. She sees this 'border country' (p. 20) later as 'occupied territory' (p. 115): 'In the bay the felled trees and numbered posts showed where the surveyors had been, power company. My country, sold or drowned, a reservoir; the people were sold along with the land and the animals, a bargain, sale, *solde*' (p. 126).

Her unresolved grief over an enforced abortion 'surfaces', colliding with her discovery of her father's drowned body in a lake. She eventually leaves the cabin and her friends, denying that she has a name and 'through pretending' to 'be civilized' (p. 162). Ultimately, however, the protagonist feels the need to return, hoping that 'the Americans' can be 'watched and predicted and stopped without being copied' (p. 183).

In the 1970s the paintings of the Group of Seven and Thom Thomson, made in many cases in the first half of the century, had gained fresh appreciation, not only for their striking painterly techniques, but as powerful appeals to emergent Anglophone Canadian nationalism. For example, Thomson's 'Pine Island' (1914) represented the forests and lakes of Ontario as beautifully pure and defiantly hardy, clinging to the rock of the Canadian Shield. In 'Death by Landscape', a short story from *Wilderness Tips* (1991), Atwood layers memories of a childhood wilderness camp with adult meditations upon Group of Seven paintings: 'They are pictures of convoluted tree trunks on an island of pink, wave-smoothed stone, with more islands behind; of a lake with rough, bright, sparsely wooded cliffs; of a vivid river shore with a tangle of bush and two beached canoes, one red, one grey' (p. 110). The attraction the adult protagonist Lois feels for these paintings derives from her uncanny sense that 'there is something, or someone, looking back out'. It emerges that her friend Lucy inexplicably vanished in her company at Camp Manitou, and that she was blamed. The adult Lois has refused to return to the North, but regards her paintings with a fond obsession:

> these paintings are not landscape paintings. Because there aren't any landscapes up there, not in the old, tidy European sense. . . . Instead there's a tangle, a receding maze, in which you can become lost almost as soon as you step off the path. There are no backgrounds in any of these paintings, no vistas; only a great deal of foreground that goes back and back, endlessly . . .
>
> (pp. 128–9)

The twist is that 'Every one of them is a picture of Lucy'; she lives in them, glimpsed only at the edge of vision. Equivocating between the artistic and environmental meanings of 'landscape', and exploring a morbid fascination with the way both paintings and forests recede endlessly, Atwood shows an ironic awareness of the construction of wilderness that was absent from the earlier novel.

Atwood's fiction demonstrates that wilderness can be productively explored in relation to genres other than nature writing. Recently ecocritics have sought to expand the field, as in Adam Sweeting and Thomas Cochunis's analogical study of 'realist' theatrical and wilderness spaces. For example, they observe that the traditional theatre space is sharply demarcated from the audience space by the proscenium arch, just as 'wilderness zones . . . are bureaucratically distinguished from the land from which they have been carved' (p. 326). Both realist theatre and wilderness experience disingenuously 'efface the cultural assumptions and structures that shape our performances, encouraging audiences or wilderness visitors to observe events as though they simply unfold on their own'. This shared 'representational aesthetic' reduces theatre and wilderness to emotive spectacle, preventing recognition of their wider social and ecological context. The authors argue that modern drama theory, which challenges the notion of a fixed, pre-given theatrical space, might help address some of the problems with wilderness spaces that likewise deny their own history and deflect the active agency of their 'audience'. Critics including Andrew Light, David Teague and Michael Bennett have contributed equally innovative essays on the construction of urban 'wilderness' in film and urban planning to the anthology *The Nature of Cities* (1999).

Within nature writing, considerable controversy has been stirred by the work of Rick Bass, especially his discomforting book *Fiber* (1998). The narrator leads us through the four stages of his life, which suggestively parallel Bass's own: oil geologist, literary artist, environmental activist, then an eccentric kind of logger. He inhabits the Yaak Valley in Northern Montana, where Bass lives, and which he has fought vigorously and publicly to preserve from clear-cutting forestry. Yet the narrator also opens up spaces between his persona and Bass, claiming to have an arrest warrant out for one of his earlier incarnations. Gradually the fourth persona emerges, the familiar sojourner 'sinking deeper and deeper into the old rot of the forest' until, he predicts, he becomes one with it. At the same time, unlike most wilderness sojourners, the narrator works in the forest, selectively logging, selling some timber to mills and spooking other local loggers by leaving occasional logs by their trucks. This 'log fairy' persona reflects on the wearying work of the activist, and its corrosive effect on the artist. Then suddenly, in Part IV, this elaborate artifice abruptly disintegrates: 'There is, of course, no story: no broken law back in Louisiana, no warrant, no fairy logs. I am no fugitive, other than from myself. Here, the story falls away' (p. 45). The rest of the narrative seems an enraged rant against the federal government, the Sierra Club and the logging companies, but it still keeps changing tack: 'If you think I'm going to say *please* after what they've already done to this landscape, you can think again' (p. 49). Then, 'I am going to ask for help, after all' (p. 50). Then: 'The valley cannot ask for anything – can only give – and so like a shell or husk of the valley I am doing the asking, and I am saying please, at the same time that I am saying, in my human way, fuck you' (p. 50). The story concludes: 'Somebody please help', with an appendix giving addresses for readers to write letters requesting the protection of the Yaak as a wilderness area.

Scott Slovic has argued that nature writing texts may be characterised as either 'rhapsodic' celebration of natural beauty and wildness, or jeremiad, the 'warning or critique' that challenges the reader to political action and self-reform (1996: 85). Carson's *Silent Spring*, for example, is primarily jeremiadic, while *Land of Little Rain* is mainly rhapsodic. Michael Branch's contribution on Bass to an important ecocritical anthology applies this typology to what he calls Bass's 'Yaak-tivist' writing, showing that it causes 'readers to consider just how much environmental invective they will accept' (2001: 224). The high-powered jeremiad of *Fiber* deliberately unsettles readers who are culturally unused to expressions of open anger, being 'more concerned about good behaviour than about justice' (p. 231). Some readers consider that the literary quality of the work is thereby compromised, but Bass's evocations of rage and grief are artistically sophisticated and sanctioned by a long literary tradition of corrective rhetoric. Branch calls this fusion of fury and almost inconsolable loss 'elegaid'.

Unlike traditional nature writers who assume righteous moral or political positions, Bass is highly self-conscious about his authority as writer. As Karla Armbruster explains, even the title provokes the reader to consider the materiality of the book, and its dependence upon the industry Bass attacks. Bass rigorously interrogates his own rhetorical position, acknowledging his complicity with the activities he castigates and avoiding 'a simplistic, black-and-white version of the situation that would rule out compromise and inevitably end in a stalemate between holier-than-thou environmentalists and the loggers they would see as enemies' (Armbruster 2001: 208).

The 'poet laureate of deep ecology', Gary Snyder, has worked for a long time among such tensions. He achieved fame in the 1950s as one of the Beat Generation, alongside Jack Kerouac and Allen Ginsberg, then took the arduous path of initiation into Zen Buddhism in Japan before moving to Northern California, where he writes, teaches and lectures. Oelschlaeger expresses almost unlimited admiration for his work, arguing that his 'shamanic vision' brings the Great Mother back to life in the postmodern world. Snyder's work is interpreted specifically as a series of injunctions:

> Listen! the poet tells us. This is the Eastern axis of Snyder's spiritual ecology: by listening one quiets the mind, calms the senses, and reestablishes contact with the earth. . . . Go into the wilderness; stand on the rock of granitic truth. Hear the Ur syllables, the seed syllables, of mother earth: *the wind! the moving water! the sighing boughs!* We are her children, she is our mother, we are it, the flowing land . . .
>
> (Oelschlaeger 1991: 274)

In a similar vein, David Robinson applauds Snyder's promotion of a 'new cultural ethic of the wild' made up of four normative claims:

> 1) the necessity of a commitment to the potentialities and limitations of place; 2) the belief in the wild and its processes as the best teacher for humanity; 3) the identification of the wild with the sacred; and 4) the use of the wild as a guide for a diverse, inclusive, participatory democracy.
>
> (1999: 21)

The reader should not, however, be entirely put off by such praise. Much of Snyder's poetry is marred by earnest ecopieties and hectoring propaganda ('For the Children', 'Mother Earth: Her Whales', 'Front Lines', 'Control Burn'), but his adapted translations of Oriental poems are vivid, spare and brilliant, and his own poetry, at best, is rescued by playful eroticism, sharp humour, beautiful language and a degree of self-deprecation. Snyder's youthful experiences of working as a logger, and contact with socialists as well as Buddhists and Native Americans, give his writings a breadth of reference and sensitivity to people's social and material needs that is unusual amongst wilderness writers. His critique of poet Robinson Jeffers in 'Word Basket Woman' might well be extended to many others discussed in this chapter:

Robinson Jeffers, his tall cold view
quite true in a way, but why did he say it
as though he alone
stood above our delusions, he also
feared death, insignificance,
and was not quite up to the inhuman beauty
of parsnips or diapers, the deathless
nobility at the core of all ordinary things

Snyder explicitly and repeatedly rejects the inflection of wilderness as solely a landscape of recreation, recognising the risk and likelihood of commodification, where 'wild and free' as easily evoke 'an ad for a Harley Davidson' as they do 'a long-maned stallion racing across grasslands'. For Snyder, 'Both words, profoundly political and sensitive as they are, have become consumer baubles' (1999: 168). One way of guarding against this risk is to subvert the dualistic construction of wilderness and civilisation that Cronon criticises, and Snyder's most effective technique for accomplishing this is to bring the 'wild' closer to home. For example, he asserts that our bodies are wild, highlighting 'universal responses of this mammal body', such as 'the heart-in-the-throat in a moment of danger, the catch of the breath' (p. 176). In 'Song of the Taste', he restores to us a sense of the wild in our everyday diet:

Eating the living germs of grasses
Eating the ova of large birds

the fleshy sweetness packed
around the sperm of swaying trees

Even human language, the supposedly unassailable marker of culture, is wild in the sense that it 'rises unbidden' and 'eludes our rational intellectual capacities'. It may be domesticated for educational or other purposes, but fundamentally language 'came from someplace else' (p. 177).

Snyder effectively argues that civilisation is the locus of chaos and disorder, while wildness epitomises the free self-organisation of nature. Rather than being simply opposed, the wild ramifies through the civilised and sustains it. The 'etiquette of freedom' this realisation ought to encourage is probably the best we can hope for from wilderness ethics: part deep ecology, part Beat Generation hedonism, and all gentle, humane injunction:

> We can enjoy our humanity with its flashy brains and sexual buzz, its social cravings and stubborn tantrums, and take ourselves as no more and no less than another being in the Big Watershed. We can accept each other all as barefoot equals sleeping on the same ground. We can give up hoping to be eternal and quit fighting dirt. We can chase off mosquitoes and fence out varmints without hating them. . . . The wild requires that we learn the terrain, nod to all the plants and animals and birds, ford the streams and cross the ridges, and tell a good story when we get home.
>
> (p. 182)

5

APOCALYPSE

For at least 3,000 years, a fluctuating proportion of the world's population has believed that the end of the world is imminent. Scholars dispute its origins, but it seems likely that the distinctive construction of apocalyptic narratives that inflects much environmentalism today began around 1200 BCE, in the thought of the Iranian prophet Zoroaster, or Zarathustra. Notions of the world's gradual decline were widespread in ancient civilisations, but Zoroaster bequeathed to Jewish, Christian and later secular models of history a sense of urgency about the demise of the world. From the Zealots of Roman Judaea to the Branch Davidians who perished in Waco, Texas in 1993, Judaeo-Christian believers have fought and died in fear and hope of impending apocalypse, whilst Nazis, communists, Native American Ghost Dance cults, Muslim Mahdists and the Japanese adherents of the Aum Shinrikyo sect have adopted and adapted apocalyptic rhetoric, again with catastrophic results as prophecies of crisis and conflict inexorably fulfil themselves. Yet arguably very similar rhetorical strategies have provided the green movement with some of its most striking successes. With this in mind, it is crucial that we consider the past and future role of the apocalyptic narrative in environmental and radical ecological discourse.

APOCALYPSE AND MILLENNIUM

Eurasians have not always believed that their world will end some day. The prospect of an imminent *eschaton* or End of Time opened up for Judaeo-Christianity in the two centuries on either side of the Christian Year Zero:

> It was mapped out in a new literary genre called apocalypse, from the Greek *Apo-calyptein*, meaning 'to un-veil'. Apocalyptic literature takes the form of a revelation of the end of history. Violent and grotesque images are juxtaposed with glimpses of a world transformed; the underlying theme is usually a titanic struggle between good and evil . . . Apocalypticism has been described as a genre born out of crisis, designed to stiffen the resolve of an embattled community by dangling in front of it the vision of a sudden and permanent release from its captivity. It is underground literature, the consolation of the persecuted.
>
> (Thompson 1997: 13–14)

This definition suggests the following features: the social psychology of apocalypticism that has historically inclined such 'embattled' movements to paranoia and violence; the extreme moral dualism that divides the world sharply into friend and enemy; the emphasis upon the 'unveiling' of trans-historical truth and the corresponding role of believers as the ones to whom, and for whom, the veil of history is rent. But most importantly, for our purposes, apocalypticism is inevitably bound up with imagination, because it has yet to come into being. To use the narratological term, it is always 'proleptic'. And if, sociologically, it is 'a genre born out of crisis', it is also necessarily a rhetoric that must whip up such crises to proportions appropriate to the end of time. This dialectic in which apocalypticism both responds to and produces 'crisis' will be important in our evaluation of it as an ecocritical trope.

To the modern reader, millennial and apocalyptic beliefs may seem bizarre, but even the most lurid anticipations of the fulfilment of scriptural prophecy are based upon interpretations that possess their own argumentative logic. Drawing upon a distinction first suggested by Kenneth Burke, rhetorician Stephen O'Leary has suggested that the drama of apocalypse is shaped by a 'frame of acceptance' that may be either 'comic' or 'tragic'. The choice of frame will determine the way in which issues of time, agency, authority and crisis are dramatised:

> Tragedy conceives of evil in terms of guilt; its mechanism of redemption is victimage, its plot moves inexorably toward sacrifice and the 'cult of the kill'. Comedy conceives of evil not as guilt, but as error; its mechanism of redemption is recognition rather than victimage, and its plot moves not toward sacrifice but to the exposure of fallibility.
>
> (O'Leary 1994: 68)

If time is framed by tragedy as predetermined and epochal, always careering towards some final, catastrophic conclusion, comic time is open-ended and episodic. Human agency is real but flawed within the comic frame, and individual actors are typically morally conflicted and ambiguous. The tragic actor, on the other hand, has little to do but choose a side in a schematically drawn conflict of good versus evil, since action is likely to seem merely gestural in the face of eschatological history.

The contrast between comic and tragic modes may be exemplified by the argument between early Christian millenarians and St Augustine of Hippo. Mathematicians of the End Times such as Hippolytus of Rome often appealed to the notion of a 'Great Week', in which each 'day' lasted 1,000 years. The Second Coming of Christ would occur on the cusp of the Sabbath of the Great Week (6,000 years after Creation, or *Anno Mundi* 6000), ushering in the 1,000 years of his reign on earth announced in the Revelation of St John (Rev. 20:1–6). The mathematicians sought to work back through the genealogies of the Bible to calculate the first year of the world, AM 1, from which the date of the End could be extrapolated. Augustine's solution to the destabilising effects of such calculations was to insist on the figurative nature of the Bible's apocalyptic visions, and to mock those who calculated their literal advent. The End would occur as prophesied, but it was not for humans to second-guess God's timetable. The gradual shift from the *Anno Mundi* calendar to the *Anno Domini* system further dampened Christian apocalypticism, to the point where, according to recent studies, the year 1000 passed off without panic (Thompson 1997: 35–55).

Augustine's eschatology is therefore comic and non-catastrophic, emphasising a drawn-out moral struggle going on not between forces of light and darkness, but within the faithful themselves. This ethical subtlety, along with an emphasis upon free will, supplies a sounder moral ideology for a church wary of millennial enthusiasms: if the End may or may not be nigh, believers must live in the light of its possibility whilst refraining from relinquishing their worldly duties in a fit of utopian hysteria. Tragic narratives of the End, on the other hand, are radically dualistic, deterministic and catastrophic, and have tended historically to issue in the suicidal, homicidal or even genocidal frenzies.

Orthodox, Roman Catholic and, for the most part, Protestant Christianity has promoted comic apocalypticism. The imperatives of scriptural authority, history and popular enthusiasm have rendered the trope indispensable, but a tragic frame tends to produce either schisms or perpetual charismatic revolution, and seems unsustainable in the long term. The implications for attitudes to the natural world, moreover, seem worse in the tragic mode. We may recall Lynn White Jr.'s argument that Christianity is a dangerously anthropocentric religion, and perhaps his parenthetical comment that only Zoroastrianism might be comparable to it. White draws attention to the dualistic conception of humanity and nature that the two religions share, but in addition they are both apocalyptic, which may be the key to the question of Judaeo-Christianity's contribution to environmental problems. Established Christianity balances the long-standing notion of the sanctity of Creation against the dualistic idea of transcendence that White noticed, but millenarian Christianity stresses radical discontinuity: 'And I saw a new heaven and a new earth: for the first heaven and the first earth were passed away' (Rev. 21:1). In its emphasis upon Christians as decisive actors in an imminent epochal conflict, millenarians inevitably brush aside the mild anthropocentrism of the established Christian 'stewardship' tradition, recommended by ecophilosopher John Passmore on account of its long-term, conservationist ethic. Environmental crisis serves modern American conservative evangelists just as natural disasters served mediaeval millenarians: as a sign of the coming End, but not as a warning to avert it. The coincidence of radical anthropocentrism and millennial zeal is epitomised by Ronald Reagan's first Secretary of the Interior, James Watt, who argued against environmental protection on the grounds that

God would soon destroy the old earth. Al Gore criticises Watt in his own apocalypse, *Earth in the Balance*, in the name of mainstream Christianity and a comic eschatology that emphasises human agency. Gore first indulges in tragic apocalyptic rhetoric, evoking Hosea's Biblical prophecy, 'They have sown the wind, and they shall reap the whirlwind', in relation to predictions of terrible hurricanes resulting from the accumulation of greenhouse gases (1992: 263). However, he then attacks the use of such rhetoric by reactionary evangelists as 'an excuse for abdicating their responsibility to be good stewards of God's creation', thereby restating Augustine's case with a 'green' inflection. Despite the temptation to read weather patterns as portents of global warming, Gore acknowledges that sophisticated computer climate models are our prophets now, rather than millennial readings of hurricanes and ice storms.

THE SECULAR APOCALPYSE

Eschatological themes and language in fact escaped the discipline of theology long before the twentieth century. The Romantic poetry of William Wordsworth, Percy Shelley (1792–1822) and William Blake (1757–1827) appropriated apocalyptic rhetoric for secular, often politically revolutionary aims, as did Modernists of the early twentieth century such as T.S. Eliot (1888–1965) and Wyndham Lewis (1882–1957). For the most part, these writers were preoccupied with the fate of human culture, but in the work of D.H. Lawrence (1885–1930) we find a congruence of environmental themes and apocalyptic rhetoric. Hence his writing has exercised a particular fascination over deep ecologists such as Del Ivan Janik, who claims that Lawrence 'saw man as part of an organic universe, living best by acknowledging its wonder and rejecting the temptation to force his will upon it. In this sense he stands at the beginning of the modern posthumanist tradition and of the literature of environmental consciousness' (Janik 1995: 107).

At college, D.H. Lawrence had studied botany and the work of Ernst Haeckel. Friends and enemies alike noted his unusual knowledge of natural history and sensitivity to his environment. Like many other writers of the period, Lawrence was deeply influenced by the writings of Friedrich Nietzsche (1844–1900), who ironically appropriated the arch-dualist Zarathustra as mouthpiece for his call for men to surpass mere human being and become *Übermenschen* ('Over-men'). Unlike the Zoroaster of ancient history who called for transcendence of the earth, Nietzsche's prophet calls for a return to it: 'Let your gift-giving love and your knowledge serve the meaning of the earth. . . . Do not let them fly away from earthly things and beat their wings against eternal walls' (Nietzsche 1982: 188). The Earth that these post-human over-men inhabit, however, will not be that of Romantic poetry, nor even the popularised 'Darwinist' earth of bloody struggle. Indeed, in striving to avoid anthropomorphism, it seems difficult to say anything about it whatsoever, as Nietzsche argues in *The Gay Science* (1882): 'Let us beware of attributing to it heartlessness and unreason or their opposites: it is neither perfect nor beautiful, nor noble, nor does it wish to become any of these things . . . None of our aesthetic and moral judgments apply to it' (1974: 168). Nietzsche, like deep ecologists, seeks a biocentric perspective, but unlike them finds only nihilism in the process.

Lawrence was a major influence upon Rolf Gardiner (1902–72), who founded the Soil Association in 1945 to promote and monitor organic farming. Historian Anna Bramwell claims that Lawrence 'was not a programmatic ecologist . . . but his intellectual background was saturated with a mixture of nature-worship and anti-anthropomorphism', and credits the imaginative power of his 'intuitive but detailed perceptions of landscape, and the people embedded in that landscape' (1989: 112, 113). His unique position is evident from the first chapter of *The Rainbow* (1915), which provides a pastoral depiction of the generations of Brangwen farmers in the valley of the river Erewash. The reciprocity of man and nature is evoked in vivid, rhythmic prose:

> They felt the rush of the sap in spring, they knew the wave which cannot halt, but every year throws forward the seed to begetting, and, falling back, leaves the young-born on the earth. They knew the intercourse between heaven and earth, sunshine drawn into the breast and bowels, the rain sucked up in the daytime, nakedness that comes under the wind in autumn, showing the birds' nests no longer worth hiding. Their life and interrelations were such; feeling the pulse and body of the soil, that opened to their furrow for the grain, and became smooth and supple after their ploughing, and clung to their feet with a weight that pulled like desire . . . They took the udder of the cows, the cows

yielded milk and pulse against the hands of the men, the pulse of the blood of the teats of the cows beat into the pulse of the hands of the men.

(Lawrence 1988: 42)

In this, Lawrence's Genesis, the exile from the original Eden recurs through the generations at and around Marsh Farm; in the first generation, true to the Biblical tradition, the men are awakened by the search of the women for broader knowledge and life. From a world of seasonal, cyclical time the Brangwens fall into linear history, depicted as a disillusioning as well as a liberating process. In the second generation, the despair engendered by modernity seems to demand an apocalyptic resolution, and Will Brangwen welcomes a vision of 'cities and industries and civilisation' swept away, 'leaving only the bare earth with plants growing and waters running' (p. 235). Yet Lawrence is concerned to locate his millennium beyond both this nihilism and the 'blood-drowse' of the first chapter. Ursula Brangwen, the third generation in the novel, experiences an epiphany in a cellular biology class that draws upon Haeckel's idea of an organic 'life force':

Suddenly in her mind the world gleamed strangely, with an intense light, like the nucleus of the creature under the microscope. Suddenly she passed away into an intensely-gleaming light of knowledge. She could not understand what it all was. She only knew it was not limited mechanical energy, nor mere purpose of self-preservation, and self-assertion. It was a consummation, a being infinite. Self was oneness with the infinite.

(pp. 491–2)

Ursula's reservations about scientific method are identical to those expressed by deep ecologists:

firstly, that modern science works with an analytical method which is reductionist and thereby reduces the natural world in various ways which undermines its integrity, wholeness and interconnectedness; secondly, that its metaphysics is dualist, so that whereas humans are seen as not just physical but also mental and spiritual beings, the rest of nature is seen in purely mechanical terms; and finally, that this justifies a disregard for nature.

(Hayward 1995: 16)

Her acceptance of a holistic perspective is linked to the Revelation that ends the novel:

And the rainbow stood upon the earth. She knew that the sordid people who crept hard-scaled and separate on the face of the world's corruption were living still, that the rainbow was arched in their blood and would quiver to life in their spirit, that they would cast off their horny covering of disintegration, that new, clean, naked bodies would issue to a new germination, to a new growth, rising to the light and the wind and the clean rain of heaven.

(Lawrence 1988: 548)

The Rainbow follows the development of three generations, focused largely upon the women, in an extraordinary path which brings Ursula back to the organic awareness of the first generation of men, only at a higher level of consciousness that links it to a more general redemptive vision. It self-consciously appropriates Biblical narrative structures, and something of the poetry of the Authorised Version, whilst thematising the critique of Christian anthropocentrism. Dolores LaChapelle's ecocritical study *Future Primitive* (1996) links Lawrence's ecological vision to his hope for reconfigured and revitalised sexual relation, arguing that ties between Ursula's new 'awareness of the greater whole of nature' and her discovery of her 'deepest sexual nature' show us how 'a fulfilling human society could be built in harmony with the greater cosmos' (1996: 48). LaChapelle's book is an excellent example of the pious strand of eco-criticism: her detailed research has yielded intriguing results and her enthusiasm and hope are appealing and infectious, but she takes her deep ecological standpoint entirely for granted and seems inclined to minimise, rationalise or ignore the less palatable aspects of Lawrence's work. Her faith in the power of Lawrentian sexual awakening to inaugurate a new world of authentic human relations with nature is correspondingly excessive.

Much of the remainder of Lawrence's œuvre after *The Rainbow* substitutes for its utopian promise an obsession with masculine power correlated to a blankly nihilistic apocalypticism. Thus Birkin, in the pseudo-sequel *Women in Love*, envisages a millennium entirely without humans, arguing 'Man is a mistake, he must go' (Lawrence 1989: 128). It is this biocentric inhumanism that seems to appeal to deep ecologists, although the character of Ursula Brangwen remains as a slight counter-balance: 'She herself knew too well the actuality of humanity, its hideous actuality. She knew it could not disappear so cleanly and conveniently. It had a long way to go yet, a long and hideous way' (ibid.). The contrast between a tragic and a comic apocalypticism is pointed, but there is also a more subtle exposure of the inconsistency of Birkin's view, who is like a man imagining his own funeral, unable to comprehend his own absence. Ursula's perspective suggests that Birkin's inhumanism is self-contradictory, his brand of apocalypticism nihilistic. These limi-tations afflict other forms of anti-anthropocentrism too, at least insofar as they imagine a blank apocalypse: an *eschaton* without a utopia to follow.

ENVIRONMENTAL APOCALYPTICISM

Buell has argued that 'Apocalypse is the single most powerful master metaphor that the contemporary environmental imagination has at its disposal' (1995: 285). Several of the most influential books in the environmentalist canon make extensive use of the trope, from Carson's *Silent Spring* through Paul Ehrlich's *The Population Bomb* (1972) to Al Gore's *Earth in the Balance*. Apocalyptic rhetoric is deployed in the activist literature of Earth First!, the philosophical reflections of Bill McKibben and the poetry of Robinson Jeffers. Even the commonplace notion of 'environmental crisis' is inflected by it.

The most influential forerunner to the modern environmental apocalypse is the *Essay on the Principle of Population* (1798) by Thomas Malthus, which set out to contradict the utopian predictions of endless material and moral progress made by political philosopher William Godwin (1756–1836). Malthus was the first thinker to insist that social policy be guided by ecological necessity, and his theories of population founded the science of demographics, providing the basis for the theories of natural selection of Charles Darwin (1809–82) and Alfred Russel

Wallace (1823–1913) and, later, the emergence of ecology. Malthus acknowledges the attraction of Godwin's optimism, but points out that 'the power of population is indefinitely greater than the power in the earth to produce subsistence for man' (1982: 71). This is because each generation of humans can beget a still larger next generation, whereas increases in agricultural production by cultivation of new ground can be achieved only incrementally: a contrast between a geometric, or exponential progression, and an arithmetic one. Unchecked population growth, in other words, would always outrun subsistence, as Malthus demonstrates:

> Taking the population of the world at any number, a thousand millions, for instance, the human species would increase in the ratio of – 1, 2, 4, 8, 16, 32, 64, 128, 256, 512, etc. and subsistence as – 1, 2, 3, 4, 5, 6, 7, 8, 9, 10, etc. In two centuries and a quarter, the population would be to the means of subsistence as 512 to 10: in three centuries as 4096 to 13, and two thousand years the difference would be almost incalculable, though the produce in that time would have increased to an immense extent.
>
> (pp. 75–6)

Population will always increase to the point where 'misery and vice' halt it, Malthus claimed, so even the most egalitarian utopia must eventually revert to conflict and competition for scarce resources. Malthus's *Essay* is basically anti-apocalyptic in that population and food are supposed to remain in permanent competition, rather than building to a dramatic crisis. Nevertheless, its gloomy prognostications have since provided the scientific basis for much more lurid eschatologies.

The apocalypticism of Carson's *Silent Spring* goes beyond the 'strange blight' that falls upon the pastoral scene in 'A Fable for Tomorrow'. The association of radioactive fallout and pesticide pollution mentioned in the Introduction is exceptionally potent because the imagery of nuclear detonation redefined popular conceptions of the end of the world, both religious and secular, whilst the fear of lethal fission products such as Strontium-90 undetectable to the senses provided a perfect model for the all-pervasive insinuation of pollutants such as DDT, lindane and dieldrin:

> The most alarming of all man's assaults upon the environment is the contamination of air, earth, rivers, and sea with dangerous and even lethal materials. This pollution is for the most part irrecoverable; the chain of evil it initiates not only in the world that must support life but in living tissues is for the most part irreversible. In this now universal contamination of the environment, chemicals are the sinister and little-recognized partners of radiation in changing the very nature of the world – the very nature of its life.
>
> (Carson 1999: 23)

Here we can see characteristic features of tragic apocalyptic rhetoric. The warning is presented in terms of absolute authority; the material threat is 'evil', and so, by association, are the authors of it; the consequences of failure to heed the warning are catastrophic, and the danger is not only imminent, but already well under way. Another of Carson's rhetorical strategies is to radically dissociate key agents in the drama. As Randy Harris has shown, the environmentally sensitive 'Good Guys' are named, admired and cited without demurral, whilst the 'Bad Guys' who promote pesticides are 'faceless bureaucrats and salesmen' whose claims are cited sardonically, with frequent reference to their commercial sources of research funding (Harris 2000: 138). Moreover, popular environmentalism has adopted her use of 'scare quotes' whenever industry safety claims are made: 'What then can be a "safe dose" of DDT?' (2000: 209). This powerful citational strategy casts doubt on the very idea of a 'safe dose' and dissociates the author, her favoured experts and the implied reader from compromised, unreliable industry scientists.

The precise function of Carson's apocalyptic rhetoric is a matter of debate. For Buell, she offers little hope that catastrophe may be averted because the threat she outlines is so pervasive and irreversible. Jimmie Killingsworth and Jacqueline Palmer, on the other hand, argue that 'the conflicting narratives of apocalyptic doom and millennial hope strive for dominance in *Silent Spring*' (2000: 190). They point out that the book immerses the reader in the impending blighted world where 'no birds sing', whilst holding out the possibility of 'the other road'. Carson's alternative is not an ecocentric or anti-interventionist vision, but rather a pragmatic environmentalism in which limited, targeted chemical pesticides combine with biological controls in an integrated pest-management approach. Consequently her enlightened anthropocentrism has been criticised by deep ecologists for whom the crisis is vaster and more intransigent. Like Birkin in *Women in Love*, such critics do not necessarily even hope for the survival of the human species.

After *Silent Spring*, the most important environmentalist book was Paul Ehrlich's *The Population Bomb*, a neo-Malthusian classic that relied on horrifying apocalyptic projections for its persuasive force: 'The battle to feed all of humanity is over. In the 1970s and 1980s hundreds of millions of people will starve to death in spite of any crash programmes embarked upon now. At this late date nothing can prevent a substantial increase in the world death rate' (1972: xi). In the first of two 'scenarios', Ehrlich imagined that overpopulation would bring about environmental collapse, international instability and nuclear war in the mid-1980s. In the second, overpopulation would facilitate an epidemic of Lassa fever. Failure to regulate birth rates would result, according to Ehrlich's remorseless Malthusian logic, in rocketing death rates as population pressure loosed 'three of the four apocalyptic horsemen – war, pestilence, and famine' (1972: 48). What radically distinguishes Ehrlich from Carson is that for the former it is the human species itself that represents the teeming, burgeoning, eco-pathological threat, which he compares to a cancer, with its 'uncontrolled multiplication of cells'. 'Treatment of symptoms' might offer temporary comfort, but 'radical surgery' is the only real hope for the patient. Food aid and medical assistance, then, would be replaced by compulsory sterilisation and a 'triage principle' in famine relief, whereby countries deemed incapable of self-sufficiency would not receive food, but 'nature' would be allowed to take its course (1972: 156). The moral responsibility for such a tragic outcome would rest, according to Ehrlich, with whoever had failed to prevent overpopulation.

The neo-Malthusian approach to demography as a 'numbers game' is actually deeply misleading. For example, bioregionalist Kirkpatrick Sale presents the following Malthusian scenario:

> For well over a century, year after steady year, the British encouraged and the Irish developed a near-total dependency upon a single dietary mainstay, the potato, and the population of the island grew from 2 million people to more than 8 million. Then suddenly in 1845 a natural

competitor for the potato came along in the form of a parasitic fungus that got to the tubers somewhat before the people did and turned the potatoes into sticky inedible, mucous globs. Crash: within a generation the country was devastated . . .

(Sale 1985: 27)

Sale's facts are, in outline, correct. Over a million Irish people starved to death or died of diseases of malnutrition during the famine of 1845. What he fails to mention is that Ireland continued to export food throughout the famine, but control of this surplus lay with British and Anglo-Irish landlords. Irish peasants were not simply short of food, but short of money, land and power. Scotland was similarly dependent upon potatoes and was badly hit by blight, but there was no starvation. In fact all modern famines might be seen as political and economic crises rather than mere collisions of population increase and food production collapse. The supposedly objective limit on population represented by the ecological 'carrying capacity' of a region is meaningless when applied to human societies that always mediate food supply with political, military and economic power. On this point, cornucopians and social ecologists agree, albeit from very different political perspectives (see North 1995: 11–94 and Ross 1994: 237–73). Neo-Malthusianism has been used to justify stronger immigration controls in rich countries to protect their threatened carrying capacity, as well as ending food aid to famine-struck countries that have allegedly overshot their ecological limits. In both cases biological models are applied to human situations with results that directly corroborate an extreme right-wing politics even when they do not derive from them.

Demographers agree that Malthus got his sums right as regards the exponential growth possibilities of any population, from bacteria to humans, but that his projections of possible increases in food production were little more than speculations. He also failed to predict the phenomenon known as 'demographic transition', whereby scientific advances reduce death rates, populations soar and agricultural production struggles to keep up. But then the process of modernisation gradually produces economic and cultural incentives to reduce family sizes, and so birth rates fall. Most developed countries now have stable or falling populations, but they have paid for the transition in economic growth fuelled by non-renewable energy sources, first coal and then oil. Neo-Malthusians argue that our finite planet cannot support such transitions for all developing countries.

However, it may be that transition does not require economic growth of the rate or extent experienced by developed countries. The 1994 UN Conference on Population and Development exhibited remarkable agreement that non-coercive population control is a priority both for economic development and environmental sustainability, proposing that education and primary healthcare, especially for women, were the most effective means available. These would certainly seem to be the sort of 'sugarcoated solutions' that Ehrlich rejected in *The Population Bomb* (1972) on the grounds that apocalyptic famine was imminent, although he recently supported such measures in *The Population Explosion* (1990). Perhaps this is because the most recent projections of global population suggest that transition may occur earlier, and at a lower level, than previously feared.

The problems with *The Population Bomb* are in fact representative of the more general difficulty surrounding dire predictions in environmental literature. In October 1999, the estimated world population passed 6 billion, six times the world population in 1850. As Gore observes, most of this increase has occurred recently:

> from the beginning of humanity's appearance on earth to 1945, it took more than ten thousand generations to reach a world population of 2 billion people. Now, in the course of one human lifetime – mine – the world population will increase from 2 to more than 9 billion, and it is already more than halfway there.
>
> (1992: 31)

Just as Lawrence's horrified rhetoric was influenced by the catastrophe of the First World War (1914–18), so Ehrlich's is explained by the rapidity of the increase in world population, and the undeniable environmental costs associated with it. At the same time, his projections of global anarchy failed to be realised, and the famines that did occur in such countries as Ethiopia and Somalia were a consequence of ethnic, political and economic conflicts, not simply population pressure. Widespread and worsening chronic malnutrition in some regions during this period, particularly in sub-Saharan Africa, did not prevent cornucopian critics of Ehrlich such as Julian Simon from declaring victory.

Killingsworth and Palmer note that *The Population Bomb* is the most popular environmental book ever published, which they attribute partly to its shocking apocalypticism. However, they defend Ehrlich against critics who point out the failure of his 'scenarios' to materialise, arguing that 'these writings are not to be taken literally. Their aim is not to predict the future but to change it' (1996: 40–1). This claim is bolstered by Ehrlich's own cautionary comment prefacing his scenarios: 'Remember, these are just possibilities, not predictions' (1996: 52). Environmental apocalypticism, on this view, is not about anticipating the end of the world, but about attempting to avert it by persuasive means. Yet this categorical distinction between prophecy and exhortation is one that neither the history of apocalypticism nor rhetorical theory will sustain. The classical distinction between *ethos*, *logos* and *pathos* sets out the three contributory elements in a rhetorical stance, which might be crudely rendered as moral authority, facts and arguments and the emotional inflection an utterance is given. Ehrlich's *ethos* derives directly from his status as a scientist capable of extrapolating tested hypotheses into just the sort of predictions, or *logos*, he undertakes so strikingly in the opening pages of *The Population Bomb*. The affective power or *pathos* of the book will not rely entirely upon falsifiable claims, of course, but nor can it be completely severed from them.

Ehrlich's strategic hyperbole might be justified in the interests of successful persuasion, but the long-term dangers this approach poses for environmentalist causes may outweigh its rhetorical usefulness. It is clear that later eco-apocalypses have learned circumspection from the Ehrlich example. Gore, as we have seen, flirts with tragic apocalypse only to retreat to the more cautious claims that fit both scientific uncertainty and mainstream green Christian thought, and *Betrayal of Science and Reason* (1998), in which Anne and Paul Ehrlich set out to demolish cornucopian claims, is a paragon of comic apocalyptic rhetoric. The book mounts a rearguard defence of some of the claims of *The Population Bomb* whilst acknowledging some of its failings, but the most striking change is that while the facts or *logos* presented are little changed, both the *ethos* and *pathos* of the book are dramatically altered. Whereas the implicit locus and authority of the rhetor in the first book was that of a lone Jeremiah sending back an incontestable warning from the wilderness, *Betrayal* repeatedly calls upon the scientific truth claims of almost the entire scientific community. Indeed, the Ehrlichs even append a list of scientists and scientific associations that make up the consensus on environmental crisis. The cornucopians, whose claims are cited in bold throughout, are positioned as the crazy Polyannas and industry apologists. Furthermore, the emotional tone is far less confrontational and dramatic, reaching out to 'loggers, miners, farmers and fishers' and urging international action to alleviate poverty, illiteracy and oppression of women in order to slow population growth. The Ehrlichs claim that it was Paul's decision to include 'scenarios' in *The Population Bomb* that made it vulnerable to criticism, but the rhetorical shift identified here suggests that it was the tragic apocalyptic inflection of the population issue that produced both its phenomenal success and enduring scandal.

Just like Christian millennialism, environmental apocalypticism has had to face the embarrassment of failed prophecy even as it has been unable to relinquish the trope altogether. Clearly there is much greater latitude for reasonable disagreement in environmental science than there is with divine intervention. However, religious and secular narratives of the End in the tragic mode seem to share a propensity to lapse into either unintentional comedy or self-fulfilling horror. As Buell points out, 'in the era of *Cat's Cradle*, *Doctor Strangelove* and *Star Wars* it is hard for apocalypticism to keep a straight face' (1995: 300). And, conversely, the author of *The Population Bomb*, proponent of the 'triage test' and 'radical surgery', ought to admit indirect responsibility for coercive population control strategies implemented in China and India in the wake of his revelation.

Environmental apocalypticism is not limited to popular scientific publications. The American poet Robinson Jeffers (1887–1962) espoused a philosophy of 'inhumanism' that was decidedly at odds with the anthropocentric assumptions ingrained in literary critics and academics, but clearly indebted to Nietzsche and Lawrence. The exact tenets of inhumanism are debatable, but it seems to epitomise apocalyptic ecocentrism as a poetic creed. Oelschlaeger appropriates it as an affirmation of wilderness pantheism that 'turn[s] love outward from humankind to the transhuman magnificence of the beauty of things, the cosmic whole that enframes the human odyssey and, indeed, is itself divine' (1991: 252). Certainly the beauty of nature is frequently asserted, but less often shown than might be expected of an 'ecocentric' poet. Jeffers's 'The Purse-Seine' admits as much, as the poet struggles to describe the terrible beauty of the night-fishing of a phosphorescent shoal: 'I cannot tell you / How beautiful the scene is'. But then the trapped fish

> . . . wildly beat from one wall to the other of their closing destiny the phosphorescent
> Water to a pool of flame, each beautiful slender body sheeted with flame, like a live rocket

(Jeffers 1987: 55)

The inevitability of the analogy between trapped fish and human b/ is also acknowledged, as the poet looks over the lights of 'a wide cir d cannot 'help but recall the seine-net / Gathering the luminous fis he 'inevitable mass disasters' as the net of Progress tightens around v not the occasion for warning or mourning, but rather a grim s/ ction at the working-out of an inexorable natural law. Jeffers' poer in fact full of apocalyptic imagery: 'the dance of the / Dream-led / :s down the dark mountain' ('Rearmament'), 'man . . . blotted ('To the Stone-Cutters'), and the meteoric 'mortal splendor' of a d/ d America ('Shine, Perishing Republic'). At times it is associated a qualified compassion for humanity, as when the earth itself d/ of a heavily symbolic cleansing storm in 'November Surf' and ,ines how 'the two-footed / Mammal' might regain 'The dignity of room, the value of rareness' (1987: 39). In 'The Inquisitors', a horrified human is depicted observing as three mountain-like giants 'inspect' a handful of people. Splitting open the skull of a young 'female' to reach the origin of the problem, the giants debate the thermonuclear progeny of this brain:

> 'A drop of marrow. How could that spoil the earth?' 'Nevertheless,' he answered,
> 'They have that bomb. The blasts and the fires are nothing: freckles on the earth: the emanations
> Might set the whole planet into a tricky fever
> And destroy much.' 'Themselves,' he answered. 'Let them.
> Why not?' 'No,' he answered, 'life.'

(Jeffers 1987: 73)

The unimaginable threat of nuclear weapons, like a rocketing population, is an ample stimulus to apocalyptic thinking. Lawrence was writing in the midst of the most horrific war ever seen, and Jeffers' republic had just deployed the most devastating weapon ever devised. Nevertheless, the misanthropic ecocentrism of Lawrence's Birkin, Jeffers's giants or even Nietzsche's over-men is ethically troublesome, as a truly ecocentric perspective would arguably be morally *neutral* regarding human impacts on the environment.

As a comparison, we might look at James Lovelock's *Gaia: a New Look at Life on Earth*, which argues that the Earth may be thought of as a kind of super-organism thanks to its biochemical and climatic 'homoeostatic' self-regulation. The Gaia hypothesis seems to support an ecocentric perspective, because it enjoins us to consider policies in terms of their effects on the biosphere as a whole. However, Lovelock's conclusions are not necessarily amenable to radical ecologism; he argues that 'large plants and animals are relatively unimportant. They are comparable rather to those elegant salesmen and glamorous models used to display a firm's products, desirable perhaps, but not essential' (1982: 40). Lovelock concludes:

> It may be that the white-hot rash of our technology will in the end prove destructive and painful for our own species, but the evidence for accepting that industrial activities either at their present level or in the immediate future may endanger the life of Gaia as a whole, is very weak indeed.
>
> (1982: 107–8)

Jeffers's giants reach the same conclusion:

> 'It is not likely they can destroy all life: the planet is capacious.
>   Life would surely grow up again
> From grubs in the soil, or the newt and toad level, and be beautiful again. . . . '
>
> (1987: 73)

The paradox, then, is this: the long view enjoined by radical ecologists in fact favours fatalism as regards individual species, including our own.

From the giants' perspective, humans, dinosaurs and dodos are equally dispensable. Only the 'drop of marrow' inside the human skull is capable of caring about the fate of rhinos or redwoods, only we construct apocalyptic narratives and therefore even a biocentric ethic must remain anthropogenic. At this extreme, the sort of in- or post-humanism preached by Nietzsche, Lawrence and Jeffers is simply self-contradictory, because achieving it would at the same time render it pointless. Such implications are discussed further in the final chapter.

Earth First!, which established itself during the 1980s as one of North America's most radical environmental organisations, combined revolutionary inhumanism, apocalyptic beliefs and direct action to protect wilderness areas. It was made up initially of activists from existing mainstream groups such as the Sierra Club and the Wilderness Society who were fed up with the compromises demanded of them as Washington lobbyists, and who decided that only resolute confrontation with the forces of modernity could prevent 'biological meltdown'. According to M.F. Lee, Earth First! combined tragic apocalypticism and deep ecological beliefs:

> They . . . advocated biocentric equality, the belief that all species are intrinsically equal and therefore have an equal right to life. Earth First! transplanted these ideas from the realm of philosophical spec-ulation to the realm of political action, adding to them the urgency of a belief in an imminent apocalypse. It is this millenarian transformation that directly motivated Earth First!'s actions and determined its development.
>
> (1997: 124)

These beliefs gave Earth First! an extraordinary zeal and courage in its defence of wilderness areas. Its proponents also developed a millennial vision of a future primitive world, where postmodern hunter-gatherer 'tribes' would subsist in the aftermath of industrial civilisation. Earth First! grew rapidly, attracting ecofeminists and social ecologists as well as wilderness advocates. But then, as Lee shows, the organisation began to encounter tensions inherent in its core beliefs, as the original activists' millenarian beliefs gave way to blank apocalypticism and Malthusian nightmares of overpopulation gave rise to grotesque inhumanity, as evidenced by the figure of Christopher Manes. Writing under the pseudonym 'Miss Ann Thropy', Manes argued that AIDS should be welcomed by radical ecologists for its contribution to population reduction. Earth First! was riven by such disputes, with many of the newer, socially orientated members and some deep ecologists attacking the apocalypticism of the wilderness advocates. Eventually many founder members such as Dave Foreman left Earth First!, claiming that it had betrayed its early uncompromising stance. Lee argues on the basis of her study that

> the most radical of environmental doctrines may initially support, but cannot sustain, a millenarian faith. The biocentric beliefs of Earth First!'s apocalyptic faction deny the human species a pivotal role in history. When it is pushed to its limits, this belief system provides a justification for any action undertaken in defence of the wilderness, regardless of whether or not human beings are harmed. Individuals who hold such beliefs are capable of wreaking significant havoc on the human civilization in which they live.
>
> (1997: 133)

In the terms used earlier, the inhumanist faction of Earth First! were distinguished from the social ecologists by their espousal of tragic, rather than comic, apocalypticism. Their fears of imminent ecological catastrophe were articulated in terms of a dualistic moral schema that crudely opposed humanity and the wild. Their opponents saw people as differentiated in their responsibility for environmental problems according to gender, class and ethnicity, and envisaged radical political change through negotiation as well as direct action. The inhumanist faction were also accused of fostering androcentric, paranoid and potentially violent attitudes in the organisation.

THE TROUBLE WITH APOCALYPSE

Apocalyptic rhetoric seems a necessary component of environmental discourse. It is capable of galvanising activists, converting the undecided and ultimately, perhaps, of influencing government and commercial policy. In the United States, in particular, it can draw upon deep wellsprings of popular and literary apocalyptic sentiment. The news media often report environmental issues as catastrophes not only because this generates drama and the possibility of a human interest, but also because news more easily reports events than processes. Apocalypse provides an emotionally charged frame of reference within which complex, long-term issues are reduced to monocausal crises involving conflicts between recognisably opposed groups, such as Greenpeace versus whalers. John Hannigan's study of the sociology of environmental conflict specifies the most common inflection: 'Employing a series of medical metaphors, our planet is depicted as facing a debilitating, perhaps terminal, illness' (1995: 72). Ehrlich's *Population Bomb* is an early example of the rhetorical link that is now commonly made between the ancient apocalyptic trope and the inflection of ecology as a science of *planetary health*, as discussed further in Chapter 8.

Eschatological narrative, then, brings with it philosophical and political problems that seriously compromise its usefulness, especially in its radical, tragic form. It tends to polarise responses, prodding sceptics towards scoffing dismissal and potentially inciting believers to confrontation and even violence, a pattern familiar from conflicts between liberal society and apocalyptic cults. On the other hand, while radical ecological groups are rhetorically akin to traditional millenarians, they are sociologically very different, stressing openness to diverse beliefs and maintaining a solid resistance to charismatic leadership. Even if this is allowed, however, the propensity of apocalypticism to turn ugly in relation to population growth must be confronted.

A more general problem is that the rhetoric of catastrophe tends to 'produce' the crisis it describes, as in the Malthusian depiction of extreme poverty as 'famine'. Moreover, as Richard North shows in two detailed case studies, the political objectives of campaigning organisations may dovetail too neatly with journalistic desire for scientific integrity to be sustained in the reporting of ecological 'disaster'. North analyses media responses to the 1993 sinking of the oil tanker *Braer*, and claims that they show a marked preference for apocalyptic comments from campaign organisations over less dramatic assessments from government or oil industry scientists:

A Greenpeace comment seems to have several prime journalistic merits. It stresses the possibility of ecological disaster. It comes from the heart. It is short and understandable. It comes from people who are not part of 'the establishment'. The media and Greenpeace share an understanding of the world. Things go wrong because vested interests are careless, and they stay wrong because of the cover-ups which vested interests go in for. Neither the media nor Greenpeace ever admit that they too are vested interests, with readers and supporters to keep amused and excited.

(1995: 99)

North argues that environmental 'doom merchants' may literally be selling bad news. Another example is the journalistic propensity to interpret every drought or ice storm as a 'sign' of catastrophic global warming, while climatologists consistently adopt a comic apocalyptic rhetoric that denies the possibility of linking specific weather events to global climate change. Such caution is compromised by the need for authoritative pronouncements in the interests of policy, but also by the danger that projections are often popularly interpreted as predictions.

Bill McKibben's *The End of Nature*, already discussed as a 'Wilderness' narrative, is haunted by both the ubiquity and unreliability of the 'signs' of climatic change. McKibben's 'nature' is not merely threatened by the possibility of apocalypse, but in some sense already beyond it, for if nature is inflected as wilderness, the very thought of human interference is enough decisively to contaminate its purity. In an inversion of blank apocalypse, a world purified by human absence is replaced by one irretrievably altered by human emissions, where we can no longer know what a season or temperature is 'supposed' to be. For McKibben, the end of nature is not the end of the world itself, but an apocalypse of the imagination. This End is already behind us, leaving nothing more than various options for managing a nature rendered thoroughly and permanently domestic. However, not only is McKibben's inflection of nature as wilderness rather specific to the USA, but human activities such as deforestation, hunting and farming have been crucial ecological agents since the evolution of the species. McKibben's apocalyptic rhetoric effectively produces the irreparable crisis it claims only to identify.

Apocalyptic rhetoric furthermore fosters a delusive search for culprits and causes that may be reductively conceived by conflating very varied environmental problems within the concept of a singular, imminent 'environmental crisis'. Deep ecologists, for example, attack 'humanity' or 'civilisation', or, at the conceptual level, 'anthropocentrism'. Ecofeminists criticise androcentrism or the dualistic logic of domination. Environmental problems, whilst they should not be seen in isolation, might seem more amenable to solution if they are disaggregated and framed by comic apocalyptic narratives that emphasise the provisionality of knowledge, free will, ongoing struggle and a plurality of social groups with differing responsibilities. In this way, problems are not minimised, but those who describe them become less vulnerable to the embarrassments of failed prophecy and to the threat of millennial enthusiasms.

If radical ecologists and some environmentalists are apocalyptic, then, is environmental 'crisis' unreal, a discursive construct worthy of deconstruction but not millennial panic? Whilst the strategic dangers of such rhetoric may be identified along with its somewhat disreputable genealogy, its validity must ultimately be judged by a careful consideration of the evidence, derived from historical trends and from the variety of projections of, say, global population or climate change that legitimate scientific dissension will produce. Ecocritics must assess the scale and import of scientific consensus, and in the final analysis defer to it, even as they analyse the ways such results are shaped by ideology and rhetoric. At present, the consensus accurately set out in the Ehrlichs' *Betrayal of Science and Reason* does not sustain a traditional tragic conception of a singular, catastrophic 'end of time', or even the immediate doom of Western civilisation, although their assessment is far from optimistic. Nevertheless, it could be argued that the real moral and political challenge of ecology may lie in accepting that the world is *not* about to end, that human beings are likely to survive even if Western-style civilisation does not. Only if we imagine that the planet *has* a future, after all, are we likely to take responsibility for it.

6

DWELLING

The tropes that have been examined so far contribute to the ways in which we understand nature, but from an ecocritical perspective they are all faulty in one respect: none suggests a mode of practical existence as an immediate reality. Pastoral and wilderness tropes typically imply the perspective of the aesthetic tourist, while the apocalypse encodes the vision of a prophetic imagination. However, other literatures explore the possibility of coming to dwell on the earth in a relation of duty and responsibility. 'Dwelling' is not a transient state; rather, it implies the long-term imbrication of humans in a landscape of memory, ancestry and death, of ritual, life and work. This chapter will consider models of dwelling in the literature of farming known as 'georgic', before turning to the 'primitive' models supposed by some critics to be exemplary of an authentic dwelling on earth.

GEORGIC

We have considered the claim that Judaeo-Christian monotheism has provided modern European civilisation with ecologically damaging attitudes. Lynn White Jr. argues that Genesis 1:26, 'And God said, Let us make man in our image, after our likeness: and let them have dominion over the fish of the sea, and over the fowl of the air, and over the cattle, and over all the earth', constitutes a scriptural licence for whatever exploitation we think fit within the framework of moral laws set out elsewhere. Clearly much depends upon the force and meaning of the word 'dominion', however, and philosophers who argue against White's thesis claim that stewardship or 'usufruct', rather than despotism, is enjoined (Attfield 1983; Passmore 1974). Jeanne Kay has argued that both positions misread nature's role in the Bible: 'Nature is God's tool of reward and punishment, and its beneficence depends on human morality' (Kay 1998: 214). Ecological catastrophe in the Old Testament descends for a whole range of transgressions, on innocent and guilty, humanity and nature alike. Kay proposes that the Bible is neither anthropocentric nor ecocentric, but theocentric in a way and to a degree difficult for the modern reader to fully accept: 'A society which explains destruction of pasturage as the result of God's anger over idolatry or insincerity in Temple sacrifices rather than as the direct outcome of climatic fluctuations or overgrazing may have little to offer modern resource management' (Kay 1998: 219). It is certainly difficult to sustain a direct link between contemporary environmental problems and Judaeo-Christianity as such, be it archaic or modern. As theologian Stephen Clark sardonically observes, 'Maybe "the West" has been more successfully rapacious for the last few centuries, but not because we have been more careful Christians!' (Clark 1998: 46).

Virgil's *Georgics* shares with the Bible an emphasis on the relationship of agricultural productivity and ritual observance, although the Roman obsession with astrology and augury differentiates it from the practices represented in the Old Testament. All non-secular agricultural societies ascribe religious significance to key agricultural practices, but Virgil foregrounds the practical aspects of farming, such as the planting of fertility-enhancing legumes before hungry cereals. His aim is not the dispensation of sacred law to a chosen people, but the promotion of good husbandry and the restoration of Roman social virtues in the countryside. The Virgilian emphasis on agriculture is not depicted as a curse for disobedience, as in the Bible, but rather as the god Jupiter's challenge to human ingenuity. Whereas the Old Testament gives advice of a highly localised nature for inhabitants of a Promised Land, Virgil reflects the scope and variety of the Roman Empire in his careful survey of soil types, climates and crops. It is clearly advice for neither the unlettered peasant nor the absentee landowner, but for the citizen-farmer whom Virgil sets up as the ideal Roman:

> O farmers, more than happy if they've realised their blessings,
> for whom earth unprompted, supreme in justice, pours out
> a rich livelihood from her soil, far from the clash of armies!
>   . . . he neither
> grieves in pity for the poor, nor envies the rich.
>
> (2002: 52–4)

Such overt politicisation of the georgic finds clear echoes in the conservative agrarianism of Thomas Jefferson (1743–1826), which idealises a free, land- and slave-owning and farming citizenry as the foundation of the American republic and extols the georgic virtues of industry, thrift and measured self-interest.

The British radical William Cobbett (1763–1835) understood the politics of farming very differently, taking the part of the agricultural labourer and, with reservations, the English farmer against the depredations of rural capitalism. Presumably it is also against such political appeals that Thoreau inveighs in 'The Bean-Field' experiment in *Walden*, during which he works his small plot with only meagre results as measured in beans. He contemptuously dismisses helpful suggestions from his hard-working neighbours since the true harvest is measured in wild animals and birdsong, meditation and instruction, as well as in dollars and cents:

> By avarice and selfishness, and a grovelling habit, from which none of us is free, of regarding the soil as property . . . the landscape is deformed, husbandry is degraded with us, and the farmer leads the meanest of lives. He knows Nature but as a robber.
>
> (Thoreau 1992: 131)

The farmer, as Cobbett shows and Thoreau reminds us, is often an enthusiastic agent of rural capitalism rather than a centre of resistance to it, and is, therefore, ill-suited to the stabilising role suggested by Virgil and assigned by Jefferson.

The political consequences of idealising the rootedness of rural folk in place and ancestral time are illustrated most starkly by Martin Heidegger.

In his 1935 lecture 'On the Origin of the Work of Art', Heidegger criticises various philosophical interpretations of 'things' for their abstraction of objects from a context of life and work. Meditating on the shoes depicted in Van Gogh's painting *A Pair of Shoes* (1886), he finds that they reveal the true 'thingness' of things at the heart of a way of life:

> From the dark opening of the worn insides of the shoes the toilsome tread of the worker stares forth. In the stiffly rugged heaviness of the shoes there is the accumulated tenacity of her slow trudge through the far-spreading and ever-uniform furrows of the field swept by a raw wind. . . . In the shoes vibrates the silent call of the earth, its quiet gift of the ripening grain and its unexplained self-refusal in the fallow desolation of the wintry field. . . . This equipment belongs to the *earth*, and it is protected in the *world* of the peasant woman.
>
> (Heidegger 1995: 159–60)

The shoes provide the gathering nexus of the inhuman and the human, the earth from which they are made and to which they hark, and the world in which they have meaning and use. A temporal landscape of long inhabitation and ancestry coincides here with a known physical landscape, its soil and climate, placing the rural dweller in profound opposition to the mobile, deracinated urbanite. If the shoes themselves disclose both 'earth' and 'world', Van Gogh's painting reveals this revelation, opening up for the viewer a silent attentiveness to Being that they, presumably, lack. Nor is it insignificant that the peasant woman herself is inarticulate, since words might reveal her as one of Thoreau's grasping, chattering neighbours. As Kate Soper points out, 'Heidegger's presentation of a mute and earthy peasantry, as embodying the "pre-understanding" that is lost to technological wisdom, has proved inspirational as a rallying cry to the establishment of "authentic" relations with nature, but it functions only by denying to this "peasantry" a Heideggerian consciousness of its own participation in Being' (1998: 237). The shoes, it turns out, were Van Gogh's own, which indicates the way in which Heidegger is able to extrapolate a lengthy meditation from a basis that is, in this case, simply false.

The timing of Heidegger's lecture is significant, since the philosopher was an enthusiastic Nazi. His georgic philosophy was all too congruent with the strand in Nazi ideology that stressed the relationship of German blood and soil, or '*Blud und Boden*'. Anna Bramwell, the foremost historian of the links between Nazism and ecology, explains 'blood and soil'as 'the link between those who held and farmed the land and whose generations of blood, sweat and tears had made the soil part of their being, and their being integral to the soil' (1985: 54). The Nazis not only appealed to small farmers and georgic philosophers, but also to conservationists, enacting the world's first comprehensive nature conservation and animal welfare laws. An enthusiastic proponent of organic farming, Richard Walter Darré, was appointed Reich Peasant Leader, and the town of Goslar was made into a national neopagan shrine to and for the peasantry. The Nazis even tried to limit the environmental cost of their massive autobahn-building project, establishing 'strict criteria for respecting wetlands, forests and ecologically-sensitive areas' (Biehl and Staudenmeier 1995: 15). The pursuit of harmonious dwelling for the German people was ultimately extended, in an obscene paradox, into industrial total war and genocide, as the invasion of the East secured *Lebensraum* or 'living space' for the implementation of a brutal imperial georgic. Even the extermination of the Jews could be justified in part by their internationalism and urbanism; not only by their 'blood' but by their supposed lack of allegiance to German soil. The outcome was a hideous hybrid of modern and antimodern elements; as Timothy Luke puts it:

A reenchantment of Nature in Nordic myth and new Aryan ritual produced V-2s, Auschwitz, ME-262s, and nuclear fission, while covering itself in fables of Teutonic warriors true to tribal *Blut und Boden*. Industrial fascism in Germany openly proclaimed itself to be *antimodern* and *future primitive*.

(1997: 13)

Both Nazi ecology and Heidegger's Nazism are highly controversial (see Ferry 1995). Clearly, the virtues of nature conservation and organic farming are in no way compromised by their promotion by Nazis, and there is no sign in any major part of the modern environmental movement of fascist authoritarianism. Nevertheless, it is significant that environmentally orientated georgic ideology should have been so easily appropriated. Bate's *The Song of the Earth* gives careful consideration to 'the question concerning Martin Heidegger: is the relationship between the Nazism which he never renounced and the theory of dwelling which he developed in his late essays contingent or necessary?' (2000: 268). Was it merely a personal mistake or, as Heidegger thought, a deep congruence that might bear upon contemporary thinking? Whilst the virulent racism of Nazi georgic is wholly contingent, and its nationalism easily substituted with a regional or individualistic focus, the social conservatism of an appeal to ancestry, family and tradition rooted in place seems intrinsic to georgic in its familiar and traditional forms. Heidegger is important to ecocritics because he set out to 'think dwelling', but in doing so became a nexus of georgic philosophy and the vast destruction wrought by German National Socialism.

MODERN GEORGIC: BERRY, BERGER AND SALE

The foremost proponent of georgic today is the Kentuckian Wendell Berry, whose defiantly homespun, plain prose contrasts as much with Heidegger's violent portentousness as his eclecticism and humane values show up the philosopher's political myopia. His work is also distinct from that of the American nature writers alongside whom he is usually considered, since his landscape is not wilderness but farmland, and his characteristic technique not the shock tactics of nature writers like Edward Abbey but 'repetition and reassurance, always intensifying descriptive detail or adding layer upon layer of perception' (Slovic 1992: 118). Berry has explicitly situated himself within a Christian georgic tradition, seeking a 'practical harmony' inspired by both the long-term demands of a 'beloved country' and a sense of sacred duty called 'stewardship' in the abstract, but repeatedly promoted figuratively as a 'marriage' of man and place, culture and nature. In the first place, Berry rejects the primacy of science, even ecological science, in favour of a resolute emphasis on the affections, since 'To be well used, creatures and places must be used sympathetically, just as they must be known sympathetically to be well known' (1990: 116). This love, founded on daily working knowledge, corresponds to a Christian adherence to 'the idea of stewardship as conditioned by the idea of usufruct' (pp. 98–9). The 'justice' and 'charity' demanded of Christians are practical rather than merely abstract virtues, and cannot be restricted only to man on scriptural grounds. Man's divinely ordained dominion is not simply a dispensation of power, but a demand from God that we take responsibility for the natural world. Berry argues that the Christian denominations have failed adequately to acknowledge this burden, let alone to exhort their followers to assume it. At the same time, this duty carries with it the right of just and charitable use of God's 'properties', the usufruct ideally practised by a loving and sustainable agriculture.

The slaughter of a hog, for example, that to modern industrial agriculture represents merely an economic and logistical problem within the limitations set by welfare legislation, is, for Berry, a sacramental act. 'For the Hog Killing' adopts the antiphonal structure found, for example, in Psalm 95, beginning with injunction:

> Let them stand still for the bullet, and stare the
> shooter in the eye,
> let them die while the sound of the shot is in the
> air, let them die as they fall . . .
>
> (Berry 1980: 5)

The preoccupation here is not the welfare of the animal in itself, but rather the authenticity of the encounter and the gratitude and respect evinced by the killer. Properly carried out, the slaughter does not erode but enhances his humanity:

> for today we celebrate again our lives' wedding with
> the world,
> for by our hunger, by this provisioning, we renew
> the bond.
>
> (ibid.)

The injunction finds vindication in Berry's master metaphor of marriage, that unifies his social and ecological concerns under the banner of his key virtue: fidelity. Berry's poetry, fiction and essays continually ask us, not to stand apart from the earth and one another, but to become part of a biotic and human community.

Berry's frank piety is apt to disarm cynics, and his practical vision can probably be shared by non-Christians, although they would have to look elsewhere for philosophical justifications. However, Buell is generous when he argues that '[Berry's] favorite analogy of man:woman = culture: nature is more problematic than he realizes, but he seeks to rehabilitate and purify it with an idealistic passion that can only be called patriarchal in the heroic sense' (Buell 1995: 161). As if in recognition of this, Buell's later treatment of Berry's communitarianism attempts to counterbalance the implication that his is a 'white backcountry enclave' ruled by wise and loving male farmers, with dialectical consideration of Gwendolyn Brook's black, urban, woman-centred equivalent (Buell 2001: 157–67).

Alongside marriage, Berry's locus of literal and figural value is land, and more specifically soil. In 'The Work of Local Culture', Berry recalls the story of a bucket left hanging from a tree by his father's black labourers. Over a span of some fifty years, it has accumulated falling leaves, insects and bird droppings, beginning gradually to make soil. Its literal significance for Berry is that production and maintenance of soil fertility is the most basic duty of a human community. Metaphorically 'It collects stories, too, as they fall through time' (1980: 154). These two fields of meaning do not just coincide in the bucket accidentally, however:

> A human community, too, must collect leaves and stories, and turn them to account. It must build soil, and build that memory of itself . . . that will be its culture. These two kinds of accumulation, of local soil and local culture, are intimately related.
>
> (Berry 1980: 154)

To be fully human, then, is to be a part of such a community. More ominously, the reverse is logically true too: not to belong to such a community is to be less than human, although one might say so either as a lament or an indictment. While it is not impossible to imagine an urban equivalent of Berry's neo-Jeffersonian utopia, it is somewhat easier to imagine escapees from oppressive rural communities, be they female, black, gay, Jewish, short on piety or keen on anonymity, wanting none of it.

An instructive contrast with Wendell Berry is provided by the British novelist and art critic John Berger, whose long residence in the French Alps has resulted in the trilogy *Into Their Labours*. The first novel *Pig Earth* (1979) exemplifies georgic dwelling as shaped by socialism, rather than Christianity and American agrarianism. It begins, strikingly, with a frank, detailed and dispassionate account of the slaughter of a cow. Once the animal has been shot:

> The son pushes a spring through the hole in the skull into the cow's brain. It goes in nearly twenty centimetres. He agitates it to be sure that all the animal's muscles will relax, and pulls it out. . . . [He] cuts by the throat and the blood floods out onto the floor. For a moment it takes the form of an enormous velvet skirt, whose tiny waist band is the lip of the wound. Then it flows on and resembles nothing.
>
> (Berger 1979: 4)

The narrator's blunt prose, offering a metaphor and then retracting it, reflects the eminent pragmatism of farmer and butcher, an orientation repeated in other stories involving animals. The relationships of humans and domestic animals in *Pig Earth* are funny, compassionate and humane without sentimentality or anthropomorphism. Furthermore, although the work of both Berry and Berger implies criticism of factory farming, the latter situates it within a political rather than a theological context. Thus, whereas farming ideally offers Berry a blessed refuge from capitalism, for Berger the peasant way of life is precariously balanced on its jagged edge: 'The peasant checks the meter. He has agreed to nine francs a kilo. He gets nothing for the tongue, the liver, the hooves, the head, the offal. The parts which are sold to the urban poor, the rural poor receive no payment for' (1979: 6).

Berger does not simply oppose town and country, field and factory, honest farmer and corrupt capitalist, but carefully traces their inter-relations, transactions and transformations. In 'The Value of Money', apple farmer Marcel, whose sons have left the land, explains why he keeps planting trees that will outlive him in the classic georgic terms of responsibility to the past as well as the future:

> I dig the holes, wait for the tender moon and plant out these saplings to give an example to my sons if they are interested, and, if not, to show my father and his father that the knowledge they handed down has not yet been abandoned. Without that knowledge, I am nothing.
>
> (Berger 1979: 67)

Resisting his sons' attempts to replace the mare with a tractor, he concedes that 'Men have dreamed of machines like these for centuries' (p. 69), but goes on to enumerate the process by which capitalisation of agriculture divides generations and neighbours, destroys communities and concentrates power and wealth in the hands of fewer and fewer agricultural businessmen.

Marcel's resistance is crystallised when the State tries to tax his home-brewed cider brandy. This '*gnôle*' has both practical benefits and deep symbolic meaning, as has the distillation engine that produces it: 'Its secret is to transform work into spirit. What is emptied into the vases is work; what comes out of the beak is imagination' (Berger 1979: 80). But when Marcel is caught in the act by the inspectors, he is driven to kidnap them and lock them in a stable to teach them a lesson, informing them of taxes to pay on 'worry', 'pain' and 'shivering' and asking 'Have you filled in the form for your pain?' (p. 90). Ultimately, however, he releases them and is imprisoned, realising that the inspectors could only see his act as a bid to make money, and 'would never know what [he was] avenging'. Marcel's defiance is not simply a gesture against a modern bureaucracy, but an example of the long peasant resistance to the expropriation of his 'surplus' production. The methods change with transformations in the general political and economic system – from feudal tithes through capitalist taxes and socialist production norms – but the demand is the same.

Berger is far from idealising the peasant way of life. He vividly depicts the oppressive narrow-mindedness of the Alpine community, and its incessant labour on the boundary of a voracious, changing economy and a harsh, unpredictable ecology. Moreover, he states plainly that, since the peasantry is always a class produced by oppressive socio-economic relations, 'In a just world [it] would no longer exist' (Berger 1979: xxv). Yet he argues that the georgic inflection of nature can function as a critique of both capitalism and modernising, industrial versions of socialism:

> Productivity is not reducing scarcity. The dissemination of knowledge is not leading unequivocally to greater democracy. . . . The peasant suspicion of 'progress,' as it has finally been imposed by the global history of corporate capitalism and by the power of this history even

LIVERPOOL JOHN MOORES UNIVERSITY
LEARNING SERVICES

over those seeking an alternative to it, is not altogether misplaced or groundless.

(p. xxvi)

Here Berger's fiction might suggest an avenue as yet inadequately explored in ecocriticism, in which environmental critique meets the post-colonial politics of resistance to economic globalisation (see Chapter 8). Nevertheless it remains essential to maintain a discrimination between such democratic socialist ambitions and the genocidal 'back to the land' movements in China and Cambodia. Berger does not acknowledge it, but Maoists have experimented with the centrally planned implementation of georgic, with catastrophic results.

Berger exemplifies socialist georgic, but in the western USA a movement has emerged that seeks to combine traditional agrarianism with more radical social ecological or anarchistic leanings. The term used to describe this movement is 'bioregionalism'. Kirkpatrick Sale's seminal work *Dwellers in the Land* (1985) explains the idea of a bioregion as an eco-political unit that respects the boundaries of pre-existing indigenous societies as well as the natural boundaries and constituencies of mountain range and watershed, ecosystem and biome. Opposing what they call 'giantism' at every level, bioregionalists promote decentralisation of the economy, in the form of regional diversification and self-sufficiency, as well as the anarchistic dismantling of the centralised nation-state in favour of confederated self-governing communities of 1,000 to 10,000 people. Sale asserts that 'Here, where people know each other and the essentials of the environment they share, where at least the most basic information for problem-solving is known and readily available, here is where governance should begin' (1985: 94–5). Bioregionalism is therefore a politics of 'reinhabitation' that encourages people to explore more deeply the natural and cultural landscape in which they already live.

Bioregionalism has a number of attractive features as a version of georgic. First, it can act as a political nexus, bringing together indigenous, vernacular and regional movements struggling against homogenising global culture, with anarchistic and social democratic political movements and transregional environmental organisations working at a local level. Conflicts between such groups would certainly continue, but the bioregion might form a geopolitical context within which they might be addressed more meaningfully than at a state or national level. Second, bioregionalism can counteract the cultural and economic concentricity of urban cultures, emphasising the ecological dependence of cities on countryside and wilderness and undermining the false oppositions inherent in pastoral and wilderness myths. Third, it is demandingly pragmatic. In an attempt to move away from an exclusive focus on Sale's influential book, Doug Aberley argues that: 'Bioregionalism is best understood from the "inside," not from reading one or several texts. Gatherings should be attended, ephemeral periodicals reviewed, restoration projects participated in, and place-based rituals and ceremonies shared' (Aberley 1999: 31). He goes on to identify a wide range of, mainly grass-roots American, bioregional initiatives. The creation of the ethnic bioregion of Nunavut Territory in Canada in 1999 and 'the restructuring of regional governance units in New Zealand to match major watershed boundaries' (p. 34) are larger-scale examples.

However, bioregionalism is vulnerable to some important objections. The problem of defining boundaries in ecological terms is usually countered by an appeal to the scientifically informed intuition of reinhabitants. It is likely to be less problematic where, as in North America and Australia, the sovereign state is larger than the bioregions that will compose it, since this will ensure there are fewer collisions with pre-existing jurisdictions. Bioregions based on, say, the River Jordan watershed or the Congo, would have to incorporate hostile ethnic groups who are deeply rooted in their geographical locations as presently defined. At the same time, emerging conflicts over water extraction and pollution would seem to necessitate some sort of bioregional consciousness even in these places if water wars are to be averted. A further challenge is that many of the indigenous societies whose knowledge and lococentric values bioregionalists admire are already thoroughly deracinated. Forced and voluntary ethnic migration has changed the world's cultural landscape just as the deliberate and accidental movement of plant and animal species has transformed the world's biogeographical landscape. As Mitchell Thomashow explains, it will paradoxically be necessary to develop a 'cosmopolitan bioregionalism':

> In the twenty-first century we face the prospect of multiple ecological and cultural diasporas, millions of migrants attempting to salvage their

> ecological and cultural integrity. . . . In the twenty-first century, having
> a homeland will represent a profound privilege. Living-in-place may
> become a quaint anachronism, reinhabitation a yuppie utopian vision.
>
> (1999: 123)

Bioregionalism may well represent a positive influence in the ecocritical search for a culture of dwelling, or a viable modern georgic, but it is not a panacea. In addition, its tendency to idealise indigenous cultures links it to the other major ecocritical inflection of dwelling, the notion of the Ecological Indian.

THE 'ECOLOGICAL INDIAN'

The Georgic model of dwelling is of diminishing relevance for most North Americans and Europeans. 'We' apparently cannot dwell in working harmony with nature, but perhaps other cultures are able to do so. Since the sixteenth century at least, 'primitive' people have been represented as dwelling in harmony with nature, sustaining one of the most widespread and seductive myths of the non-European 'other'. The assumption of indigenous environmental virtue is a foundational belief for deep ecologists and many ecocritics. Native Americans, or American Indians, are the *locus classicus* for this assumption, although South American Amazonian Indians have more recently come to the fore as exemplary dwellers in the rainforest (see Slater 1996). Most particularly, the Plains Indian societies of the Lakota/Sioux, Blackfoot, Crow, Cheyenne and others have been transformed from Western film villains into noble-but-doomed heroes of a supposedly primal culture attuned to the Earth and its creatures. When the environmental organisation Keep America Beautiful, Inc. wanted to capitalise on the mass environmentalist sentiment of the early 1970s, they produced an advertising campaign in which a tear rolled down the furrowed cheek of an Indian called Iron Eyes Cody, with the slogan 'Pollution: it's a crying shame'. It implied that white people, not Indians, make pollution, and that Indian ethics of respect for nature were needed to counteract white greed and destructiveness. As historian Shepard Krech III has argued, this advert helped to crystallise a cultural stereotype of 'Ecological Indians' that had deep roots in Euro-American culture. From book covers to movie screens to gallery exhibitions, 'the dominant image is of the Indian in nature who understands the systemic consequences of his actions, feels deep sympathy with all living forms, and takes steps to conserve so that earth's harmonies are never imbalanced and resources never in doubt' (Krech 1999: 21) The minimal ecological impact claimed for Indians is not supposed to be based only on low population densities or pre-Columbian material cultures lacking metal weapons, guns and horses, but upon animistic belief systems that constrained their actions. Environmental philosopher J. Baird Callicott claims that:

> the typical traditional American Indian attitude was to regard all features of the environment as enspirited. These entities possessed a consciousness, reason, and volition, no less intense and complete than a human being's. The Earth itself, the sky, the winds, rocks, streams, trees, insects, birds and all other animals therefore had personalities and were thus as fully persons as other human beings.
>
> (1983: 243)

Callicott's contrast between these ecocentric beliefs and practices and destructively anthropocentric Euro-American beliefs and practices is exemplified in the film *Dances with Wolves* (1990), in which cavalry officer John Dunbar (Kevin Costner) joins a Sioux band and learns a deep admiration for them. In a pivotal scene, they come across a field of buffalo (more properly called 'bison') carcasses with only the hides and tongues missing, leading Dunbar to muse that the white hunters who presumably killed them were 'without value and without soul, with no regard for Sioux rights'. Later, when the Sioux hunt the buffalo, it is an heroic, albeit brutal, struggle showing, as Ingram argues, 'the Sioux hunting buffalo for sustenance rather than for financial profit, within a ritual context, and in an environmentally harmonious way' (2000: 78). In accordance with the Sioux's seemingly timeless traditions, all the body parts of the animals are utilised to make a vast range of artefacts. The film ends with the cavalry closing in on the Sioux, their way of life in danger of vanishing forever.

A more detailed and subtle depiction of Plains Indian life in the late nineteenth century is found in James Welch's novel *Fools Crow* (1986), about a Pikuni (Blackfoot) leader struggling to keep peace with the Napikwans (whites) as the massacre of buffalo and invasion of Indian lands gathers pace. The fate of animals and people is intertwined, since 'Without the blackhorn [buffalo], the Pikunis would be as sad as the little bigmouths [coyotes] who howled all night' (1986: 47). This profound interdependence is reflected in the magic realist conventions of the narrative: it is written conventionally, told by an omniscient, third-person narrator with a linear timescale and believable, rounded characters, yet animal helpers and other spirit beings such as So-at-sa-ki (Feather Woman) mingle with them as part of everyday reality. In the middle of the novel, Fools Crow takes his wife Red Paint to the mountains for a holiday, but then hears from Raven about a white hunter who kills indiscriminately and does not butcher the animals:

> For three more sleeps I followed this strange Napikwan that leaves his meat. He killed a long-tail, a bighead, three real-dogs and five wags-his-tails. He even tried to kill your brother, Skunk Bear [wolverine], but I flew ahead and warned him. In anger, the Napikwan took a shot at me, scared the shit out of me, so I left. But for many moons now the hunter kills animals until they become scarce. I fear he will kill us all off if something isn't done.
>
> (p. 164)

When Fools Crow hesitates over killing a white man, Raven taunts him, claiming that '"he would see his brothers, the four-leggeds and the flyers, perish and not put up a fight"' (p. 165). Shooting the stinking, rapacious Napikwan in a gripping struggle, the Indian is depicted as a fighter for both ecological survival and the survival of his human kin. At the end of the novel, Feather Woman grants to Fools Crow an appalling vision of the decimation of his people by disease and war, their containment on bleak reservations and betrayal by the US government, and the annihilation of the buffalo, the key herbivore of the Plain.

Welch's elegiac lament is justified. The absence of epidemic diseases in the pre-Columbian Americas meant that Indians were appallingly vulnerable to familiar Old World illnesses from the common cold to measles. This, combined with the superiority of European military technology and the aggressiveness of the imperialist ideology that drove it, led to a catastrophe of inconceivable proportions. James Wilson's history of

Native America, *The Earth Shall Weep* (1998), says of the survivors at the end of the nineteenth century:

> The emotions of Native Americans themselves are hard to imagine. In under four centuries, disease, warfare, hunger, massacre and despair had reduced their population from an estimated 7–10 million to less than 250,000. As well as costing them their independence and more than ninety per cent of their land, the long struggle against Europeans and Euro-Americans had ruptured their sense of reality.
>
> (1998: 283)

The onslaught on America's wildlife was similarly awesome in scale: 40 to 60 million bison were reduced to fewer than 1,000 animals by the end of the century, while the vast flocks of passenger pigeons, totalling an estimated 5 *billion* birds, were wiped out completely (Ponting 1992: 168–9). America's rapidly growing wealth in the nineteenth century was based on destruction and consumption of forests and wildlife so astonishingly voracious that, in places, it amounted to an 'ecocidal' campaign to exhaust and refashion whole habitats. Invariably Indians had previously dwelt in the habitats under threat, transforming and managing them in their own ways.

Therefore the history of the colonisation of America has to be seen, at least in large part, in ecological terms. According to Alfred Crosby (1995), European imperialism is not solely an ideological or even just a human phenomenon; on every continent, environments with similar climates to Europe were invaded by a 'portmanteau biota' including domestic, feral and wild animals and plants as well as epidemic and epizootic pathogens. On the Plains, a whole European biota ultimately supplanted a native American one in a well-documented campaign of what Crosby calls 'ecological imperialism': whites brought ploughs, cattle, pigs, tough short-stemmed grasses, European weeds, smallpox, measles and whooping cough and drove out, in a combined ecological assault, Indians, tall grasses and bison. Wherever the climate was less temperate or the native flora and fauna more resilient, as in most parts of Africa, biological colonisation was less complete and slower. In North America, New Zealand and Australia, it was extremely rapid, near-total and incredibly destructive.

The image of the Ecological Indian is certainly potent, but it does not accurately represent the environmental record of historical Native Americans. There seems little reason to question the destructiveness and, at times, genocidal racism of the Euro-American culture that opposed it. Yet the idealisation that would make Indians and other indigenous people models of ecological dwelling arguably derives primarily from the latter, not the former, culture. Wilson points out that Indians are subjected even by sympathisers to a derogatory colonial vocabulary that substitutes 'tribe' for 'nation', 'medicine man' for 'doctor' or 'priest'. He goes on to observe that the romantic elegy for the 'vanishing' Indian assumes the colonist's viewpoint since '*vanishing* is a kind of innate quality, as in *vanishing cream*, something you do rather than something that is done to you' (Wilson 1992: xxii). One of the most famous texts in the history of the Ecological Indian is the alleged speech of Chief Seattle, or Seathl (Suquamish), that was widely promoted during the 1960s and after as a testament to Indian ecological values. In 1854, Seathl accepted a demand from the US Government that he concede more land. However, in the version of the speech that became famous over a century later, Seathl also said that 'Every part of this earth is sacred to my people . . . We are part of the earth and it is part of us' (1994: np). He went on to castigate the white man for his indifference to the land: 'One portion of land is the same to him as the next. For he is a stranger who comes in the night and takes from the land whatever he needs.' The contrast neatly epitomises the putative difference between Native and Euro-American inflections of dwelling.

It now seems, however, that the speech was first given during treaty negotiations, translated into the trading jargon Chinook, then into English, then reconstructed from notes over 30 years later by white physician Henry Smith. Seathl's original words cannot be determined with certainty, but it is likely that a negotiation demand for access to ancestral burial grounds and secure reservation boundaries was transformed by a white sympathiser into a combination of ecological testament and elegy for the vanishing 'Red Man'. The enthusiastic appropriation of this apocryphal speech by environmentalists in the twentieth century demonstrates the sway of the Ecological Indian.

The idea of the 'primitive' from which the Ecological Indian descends is an ideologically charged piece of rhetoric, although unlike the other tropes we have examined it seems not to have such important Judaeo-Christian or Graeco-Roman antecedents. It is a construction of intra-human difference, introduced by humanistic philosophers such as Michel de Montaigne (1533–92) and Jean-Jacques Rousseau (1712–78), that responded to, and in turn influenced, European encounters with indigenous Americans. In their attempts to understand human nature without the burden of irrational religious prejudices, philosophers such as Rousseau tried to articulate a vision of man before the advent of civil society. They took indigenous peoples as possible representatives of such a state. Their desire to distinguish between 'us' and 'them' by means of ethnic or racial constructions of difference is not unique to Euro-American culture. Often such distinctions are drawn geographically, reflecting the territorial claims of the different groups. The metaphor of 'the primitive' is unique, however, because it transforms a geographical differentiation into an historical or evolutionary one, so that Indians or aborigines can be seen as being *behind* Europeans in an inevitable progression from a natural to a civilised state. Since all contemporary human societies are, in a sense, as modern as each other, this metaphor of the primitive can be seen as an ideological mystification. It was shared, from the seventeenth century until well into the twentieth century, both by those who viewed Native Americans as noble savages and as irredeemable heathens and cannibals. Rousseau and Montaigne to some extent lamented progress rather than celebrating it, but they left the basic polarity of civilised and savage man in place. In the nineteenth century, romantic social commentary in the tradition of Rousseau found a practical outlet in woodcraft and Scout movements that praised Native skills and virility, and in the twentieth century the Ecological Indian resulted from an alliance between this frontier primitivism and anti-modernist environmentalism.

The Ecological Indian is clearly a stereotype of European origin, although it provides some Indians with a source of pride and aspiration for themselves and their societies. Many contemporary Native writers also evince annoyance at the indiscriminate appropriation of Native cultures, under the banner of ecology, by the New Age industry and its Euro-American customers, and more generally the failure to recognise the differences between tribes and bands. Critics try to avoid stereotyping by identifying a writer's origin by tribe and even village, as I do here, but the distinctive cultures of the Plains Indians are often assumed to be representative of all Native Americans. 'Adventures of an Indian Princess', an angry tale by Patricia Riley (Cherokee), sees an Indian girl fostered by a white family dressed up in faux-Indian gear and made to pose with a 'cut-and-paste "Indian"' at a tacky 'Indian trading post': 'This man had his tribes all mixed up. He wore a fringed buckskin outfit, with Plains-style geometric beaded designs, a Maidu abalone shell choker, and moccasins with Chippewa floral designs beaded on the toes' (Trafzer 1993: 137). At its crudest, the Ecological Indian represents a homogenisation of the 600 or so distinct and culturally diverse societies in pre-Columbian North America, or even the 314 federally recognised tribes in the USA today.

For similar reasons, writing about pre-twentieth century Indians presents problems. Native writers assume a certain responsibility to bear witness to their history in their writing, countering the distortions and suppressions of the dominant culture. Yet to write about, especially, nineteenth-century Plains culture is to risk collusion with it, as Native Canadian Thomas King observes:

> Feathered warriors on Pinto ponies, laconic chiefs in full regalia, dusky, raven-haired maidens, demonic shamans with eagle-claw rattles and scalping knives are all picturesque and exciting images, but they are, more properly, servants of a non-Native imagination.
>
> (King 1990: xiii)

At the same time, just as Indians are culturally and genetically mixed up in Euro-American society, so Indian writing in English is inevitably a 'hybrid' form. Neither the novel nor lyric poetry were part of traditional Native cultures, meaning that writers have had to graft oral traditions onto them. This often implies a sense of community response and responsibility, where 'Much oral storytelling conveys a religious sensibility that stresses ideals of reciprocity, wholeness and beauty and so expresses a deep sense of attachment between a people and the land they inhabit' (Padgett 2001: 18). While some people might be especially talented story-tellers, everyone contributed to and benefited from the formation of a communal narrative memory. The 'community' implied, moreover, goes beyond the tribe, even beyond the human; as King explains, Native Americans and

Canadians express a widely shared perspective in the common phrase 'all my relations':

> [It] is at first a reminder of who we are and of our relationship with both our family and our relatives. It also reminds us of the extended relationship we share with all human beings. But the relationships that Native people see go further, the web of kinship extending to the animals . . . to all the animate and inanimate forms that can be seen or imagined. More than that, 'all my relations' is an encouragement for us to . . . [live] our lives in a harmonious and moral manner (a common admonishment is to say of someone that they act as if they had no relations).
>
> (King 1989: ix)

WRITING 'RELATIONS': SILKO AND ERDRICH

Leslie Marmon Silko's novel *Ceremony* (1977) exemplifies many of these characteristics. This novel is about the ritual realignment of damaged mixed-race war veteran Tayo with 'all his relations'. It tries to enact such an alignment by incorporating parallel stories from the oral Pueblo tradition about culture heroes and spirits, such as Ts'its'tsi'nako, Thought Woman, who thought the world into existence. Tayo's recuperation from the horror of the war in the Pacific against the Japanese involves trying to escape the shadow of his lost, drunk Indian buddies from the army, and returning to the ways of the Laguna people. The medicine man Ku'oosh tries to help him by explaining the people's relationship to a world that is, in English, 'fragile': 'The word he chose to express "fragile" was filled with the intricacies of a continuing process, and with a strength inherent in spider webs woven across paths through sand hills where early in the morning the sun becomes entangled in each filament of web' (Silko 1986: 35). As Tayo starts to engage with his people, he comes to perceive connections between, to Euro-American eyes, disparate events, such as the drought on the reservation, his buddies' alcoholism and violence and the day in the Philippines he cursed the jungle rain. He sees the war as having alienated the young men both from their own people and, when they returned home to find racism just as prevalent as when they left, from America beyond the reservation. Eventually he comes to see a great spiritual conspiracy or 'witchery' at work, using white people in particular as tools in an apocalyptic ceremony that links the uranium-bearing rocks of the reservation to the nearby Trinity nuclear test site and thence to the atomic bombs dropped on Japan, and also linking the war to global environmental crisis, the crisis in the Pueblo and to Tayo's own struggle:

> the lines of cultures and worlds were drawn in flat dark lines on fine light sand, converging in the middle of witchery's final ceremonial sand painting. From that time on, human beings were one clan again, united by the fate the destroyers had planned for all of them, for all living things; united by a circle of death that devoured people in cities thousands of miles away, victims who had never known these mesas, who had never seen the delicate colors of the rocks which boiled up their slaughter.
>
> (Silko 1986: 246)

Against this, Silko sets the possibility of hybrid ceremonies combining old and new, Pueblo and Euro-American elements designed to confront the 'witchery' and save Tayo, the people and the world.

Ceremony powerfully represents the environmental racism directed at Pueblo and other 'borderland' peoples since, as Killingsworth and Palmer observe, Tayo overcomes his alienation in part by identifying with a larger community of relations damaged by the war machine (1998: 203). Joni Adamson's *American Indian Literature, Environmental Justice and Ecocriticism* quotes a 1987 report that claimed that '60 per cent of African Americans and Latinos, and more than 50 per cent of Asian/Pacific Islanders and Native Americans were living in areas with one or more uncontrolled toxic waste sites' (2001: xvi). This book is part of a movement in ecocriticism from a preoccupation with pastoral and wilderness towards a social ecological perspective. Adamson points out that:

> novels such as [Silko's] *Ceremony* . . . are not set in the 'pristine wilderness areas' celebrated by many mainstream American environmentalists and nature writers. They are set on reservations, in open-pit uranium mines, and in national and international borderlands. These novels question and confront our most popular assumptions about

'nature' and 'nature writing' by inviting us to take a hard look at the
contested terrains where increasing numbers of poor and marginalized
people are organizing around interrelated social and environmental
problems.

(2001: xvii)

As Adamson acknowledges, Native Americans are often both victims
and employees of polluting industries. Her critique therefore represents a
shift away from the notion of the Ecological Indian towards a nuanced
appreciation of the complex ecopolitical issues that permeate contemporary Native American culture and literature; from a poetics of
authenticity towards a poetics of responsibility.

Lawrence Buell praises the 'fusion of regionalism and globalism'
in *Ceremony* and its brilliant hybridisation of oral tradition, realist novel
and apocalyptic fable (1995: 286), but then criticises it for an almost
utopian ending. Whilst he is right to point this out, it is probably the
only workable ending to a novel that has so thoroughly imbibed Judaeo-
Christian apocalyptic motifs. A similar problem afflicts Silko's story 'The
Return of the Buffalo', where the orator Weasel Tail interprets the ills
of modern society as a spiritual affliction caused by white guilt, and
predicts the vanquishing of Euro-American society: 'You think there is
no hope for indigenous tribal people here to prevail against the violence
and greed of the destroyers? . . . You forget the earth's outrage and the
trembling that will not stop. Overnight the wealth of nations will be
reclaimed by the Earth' (Trafzer 1993: 492). By reducing social, national
and ecological conflicts to a dualistic spiritual confrontation of 'witchery'
and 'ceremony', or 'natives' and 'destroyers', Silko forfeits the subtle
discrimination needed to respond to environmental justice issues in
favour of a one-off drama that can only issue in disaster or utopia.

Louise Erdrich's novels present a far more complex picture of the
social and ecological interrelations of Indian and Euro-American societies.
She often uses two or more narrators, sometimes in disrupted historical
sequences, to explore the complex interrelationships of generations
of North Dakota Chippewa, dwelling with each other and their landscape
and, as Padgett comments, 'She conjures an environment in which
an animistic world view prevails even as a growing proportion of the
reservation's population distances itself from traditional Chippewa

culture' (2001: 38). But unlike the third-person narration of Silko's novel, Erdrich's multiple perspectives include sceptical as well as credulous ones, inviting the reader to position themselves self-critically in relation to them. When in *Love Medicine* (1984, 2nd edn 1993) the glamorous Lulu Lamartine adopts the attitudes and jargon of the American Indian Movement, a radical civil rights group, and helps to bring buffalo back to the reservation, her son Lyman mocks her well-fed primitivism. Looking out at the animals, Lulu reflects on:

> 'The four-legged people. Once they helped us two-leggeds.'
> This was the way her AIM bunch talked, as though they were translating their ideas from the original earth-based language. Of course, I knew very well they grew up speaking English. It drove me nuts.
> She went on, musing, and I tried to listen. 'Creation was all connected in the olden times.'
> 'It's pretty much connected now,' I said. 'As soon as my plumbing's hooked in I'll be part of the great circle of life.'
>
> (Erdrich 1994a: 307–8)

The prequel *Tracks* (1988) reaches back to the end of the nineteenth century through the conflicting narratives of neurotic, mixed-blood Pauline Puyat, who is determined to deny her Indian heritage and conquer paganism with a horrific brand of Catholicism, and of Nanapush, 'a turn-of-the-century embodiment of the archetypal Chippewa trickster Nanabozo' (Westling 1996: 158). The lives of both narrators span a period of intense change. Despite ending up as a tribal politician, Nanapush was once a great hunter: 'I think like animals, have perfect understanding for where they hide, and in my time I have tracked a deer back through time and brush and cleared field, to the place it was born' (Erdrich 1994b: 40). In an extraordinary scene, he helps Eli, Fleur's lover, to track and kill a moose in midwinter by means of a ritual song. Eli then ties the butchered flesh onto his own body in order to carry the meat and protect himself from the cold. Pauline still believes in the power of such old ways, but they are anathema to her. This hatred binds her to her enemies, so that when Fleur, a character who sustains a close relationship with the spirits, suffers a miscarriage, Pauline not only fails to help effectively, but also accompanies her on a strange journey to a frozen limbo full of buffalo and dead Indians to try to win back the infant's life.

At the end of the novel, Fleur is betrayed and her allotment sold to a white timber company. Outright warfare against people, animals and landscape has been replaced by a more insidious, though no less effective, kind of invasion led by federal Indian agents and extractive industries (see Wilson 1998: 289–329). Nevertheless, when the lumber men come to her property, Old Woman Pillager has the last word:

> Around me, a forest was suspended, lightly held. The fingered lobes of leaves floated on nothing. The powerful throats, the columns of trunks and splayed twigs, all substance was illusion. Nothing was solid. Each green crown was held in the air by no more than splinters of bark.
>
> Each tree was sawed through at the base.
>
> . . . With one thunderstroke the trees surrounding Fleur's cabin cracked off and fell away from us in a circle, pinning beneath their branches the roaring men, the horses.
>
> (Erdrich 1994b 223)

As Westling asserts, it is a 'Pyrrhic victory' but one that exposes what Euro-American writers effaced in their pastoral visions of the closing of the frontier: 'Colonization, genocide, legal chicanery, and corporate pillage' (Westling 1996: 164). Adamson argues that Erdrich identifies electoral and cultural politics, as well as animist spirituality, as the proper weapons of Native Americans against environmental racism, and that '*Tracks* . . . is cultural critique that calls for change and participation in altering the power relations at the root of social and ecological problems' (Adamson 2001: 112). Moreover, Erdrich's novels portray not simply an inevitable annihilation of Indian ways of life, as in the myth of the 'vanishing Indian', but ongoing struggles against improbable odds in which no conclusions can be taken for granted.

THE TROUBLE WITH ANIMISM

It is one of the most widespread, and least carefully examined, assumptions in American ecocriticism that the affirmation of community and spiritual tradition represents a quest for ecological dwelling that is relevant today. Ecofeminist critics, in particular, have correlated Native animism with both ecology and feminism, drawing in part upon matrifocal and matriarchal traditions in some Indian tribes. For example, Westling suggests that Erdrich's novels solve the problem of gendered landscapes that Euro-American pastoral had posed, and Greta Gaard's account of ecofeminist pedagogy 'Hiking Without A Map' (1998) traces the responses of a seminar class to *Ceremony*, reflecting the importance of Indian literature to the ecocritical canon, but making no mention of critical questions about either its apocalypticism or the problematic relationships of spirit, science and politics that it raises. Indeed, in contemporary ecofeminist readings, spiritual 'ecology', or animism, not only complements scientific ecology, but is at times posited as a superior wisdom. Paula Gunn Allen suggests that Einsteinian physics approximates to the Indian understanding of the identity of spirit and matter, but that it 'falls short' of the latter because it fails to see energy as 'intelligence manifested in yet another way' (1996: 246–7). In the assessment of J. Donald Hughes, Indian traditions deserve to be seen as 'an ethnic science':

> Indians were keenly observant and rational, but would make expla-
> nations that would be excluded even as hypotheses by modern Western
> science, because they were often subjective and mystical. But they were
> always based upon empirical observation and experience.
>
> (Hughes 1996b: 79)

The relationship between animistic beliefs and environmentally sustainable dwelling is rarely questioned in historical, literary or ecocritical contexts, despite very mixed historical and anthropological evidence. There is no doubt that, until decimation, displacement and colonisation supervened, Indians thoroughly knew and cherished the places they inhabited, but this does not necessarily correspond to ecological under-standing and responsibility in a modern sense. The famous example of the buffalo hunt and its historical transformations exemplifies the distinction.

Hughes, who explicitly prefers the accounts of contemporary Indians to archaeological and other sources of evidence in his book *North American Indian Ecology*, speaks for both white and Indian traditions when he says that 'Indians were living in ecological balance with the herds of buffalo' (1996b: 42) before mass hunting by whites began. He also tries to show that Native beliefs, rather than low population density or lack of technological means, prevented them from overexploiting the herds. However, the Plains Indian way of life that Euro-Americans both feared and admired was only around a century old by 1850, a testament to the adaptability of Indian societies rather than to their 'timeless' harmony with nature. Martin Lewis's survey of the mixed environmental record of 'primal people' argues that 'No harmonious relationship between prey and predator could have been established in this short, demographically unstable period', especially given the alacrity with which some tribes catered to the Euro-American demand for buffalo products (Lewis 1992: 65).

Shepard Krech III's detailed account shows that Indians did indeed view and treat buffaloes as 'other-than-human persons', surrounding their hunts with elaborate rituals suggesting great respect for them, but also that, in the case of Piegan and Cree, their beliefs included the fear that buffaloes who escaped the hunt could warn the others. Before the arrival of the horse transformed Plains societies, buffalo were often driven into rivers or over bluffs to kill them, or forced into pounds to be slaughtered, and the Indians' belief therefore entailed killing all the animals they could in order to prevent escapees foiling future drives. Remains from bluffs used over hundreds or thousands of years suggest that some drives produced far more carcasses than could be completely butchered.

A more widespread and well-attested belief, held by Arapahoe and Cheyenne, was that buffalo wintered in underground caves or pastures underneath lakes, a factor that may have militated against conservation. After all, 'If buffaloes returned each year from the earth because they were of the earth, how could they possibly go extinct?' (Krech 1999: 149). Respect was due primarily to the animals' spirit master, ensuring that rigorous regard for proper treatment of the creatures would never system- atically align with modern notions of animal welfare or conservation. Among some Cree in Canada, belief in animal reincarnation meant that the more animals they killed, the more there would be, provided that the correct ritual preparation of the hunter and treatment of the carcass were observed (pp. 205–6).

If animism is not necessarily ecological, neither is ecology the science of harmony and balance that certain critics have assumed. The most recent ecological theory is markedly wary of the rhetoric of classical ecology since it too often fails to accord with observed reality. For example, Michael Pollan discusses the destruction by a tornado of an old-growth forest called Cathedral Pines. Classical theories of forest succession would predict that, undisturbed, it would go through a predictable series of intermediate states, eventually reverting to its 'balanced' condition before the storm: the 'climax' forest. The reality is far more complex and unpredictable, as 'Nature may possess certain inherent tendencies, ones that theories such as forest succession can describe, but chance events can divert her course into an almost infinite number of channels' (Pollan 2002: 198–9). Pollan's claim is based in part on the work of ecologist Daniel Botkin, who, in his controversial book *Discordant Harmonies: A New Ecology for the Twenty-First Century* (1990), sets out a series of scientific case studies that demand a fundamental philosophical reassessment of ecology, arguing that the prevalent view of 'a very strict concept of a highly structured, ordered, and regulated, steady-state ecological system' is now known to be 'wrong' (Botkin 1992: 9).

The rhetoric of balance and harmony that sustained the Ecological Indian is at least as problematic as, historically and politically, the stereotype is itself: 'In a balanced, harmonious, steady-state nature, indigenous people reproduced balance and harmony. In an open nature in which balance and climax are questionable, they become, like all people, dynamic forces whose impact, subtle or not, cannot be assumed' (Krech 1999: 23). Such sceptical views of the overarching master narrative offered by classical ecology, in which undisturbed nature inevitably sustains a balanced ecology, are sometimes called 'postmodern ecology'. This perspective will be discussed further in the final chapter.

The analysis presented here should not undermine a proper respect for the ways of life of Native peoples, although it does enjoin suspicion of any attempts to make them figures of ecological piety and authenticity. The figure of dwelling is crucial, as it inflects nature as the troubled ground of work, knowledge, economy and responsibility, whereas the Ecological Indian inhabits an improbable Eden untouched by ignorance, stupidity or greed. Indians, we should assume, radically transformed landscapes long before Europeans, as far as possible in their own interests, with considerable knowledge and skill but always within the terms of their own cultural cosmos. Neither contemporary Indians nor other Americans can readily understand that world, let alone inhabit it, as much of the best Native writing affirms. Andrew Ross argues that overemphasis on spiritual ideas obscures 'the fact that a society bound together by a nature philosophy holds no guarantee of ecological well-being if it is governed by a pyramidal social hierarchy that depends upon selective access to natural resources to maintain its power' (Ross 1994: 71). Supposedly 'primitive' peoples may internalise the myths propagated about them, but they may also manipulate and deploy them in their own economic and political interests. According to this social ecological analysis, circumventing primitivism may lead us to a new perspective altogether, perhaps even to a society 'in which conscious organization of political, economic and cultural life is directed towards maximizing the diversity of natural life by minimizing social inequality' (1994: 72).

Interpretation and critique of the various inflections of dwelling is a major task for ecocritics interested in a predominantly political, rather than moral or spiritual, project of cultural critique that can take us beyond pastoral and nature writing, from the landscapes of leisure to the uneven terrain of real work.

7

ANIMALS

The study of the relations between animals and humans in the Humanities is split between philosophical consideration of animal rights and cultural analysis of the representation of animals. A remarkably recent phenomenon, it derived impetus primarily from Peter Singer's revolutionary *Animal Liberation* (1975), which examined an issue until then discussed in passing by moral philosophers but seldom fully explored.

Singer drew upon arguments first put forward by Utilitarian philosopher Jeremy Bentham (1748–1832), who suggested that cruelty to animals was analogous to slavery and claimed that the capacity to feel pain, not the power of reason, entitled a being to moral consideration. Singer gives the label 'speciesism' to the irrational prejudice that Bentham identifies as the basis of our different treatment of animals and humans. Just as, say, women or Africans have been mistreated on the grounds of morally irrelevant physiological differences, so animals suffer because they fall on the wrong side of a supposedly 'insuperable line' (cited in Singer 1983: 8) dividing beings that count from those that do not. Yet it turns out to be impossible to draw that line in such a way that all animals are excluded and all humans are included, even if we turn, as many have done, to the faculties of 'reason' or 'discourse': for Bentham 'a full-grown horse or dog is beyond comparison a more rational, as well as a more conversable animal, than an infant of a day or a week or even a month old' (1983: 8). The boundary between human and animal is arbitrary and, moreover, irrelevant, since we share with animals a capacity for suffering that only 'the hand of tyranny' (ibid.) could ignore.

The Utilitarian 'principle of equality' states that everyone is entitled to equal moral consideration, irrespective of family, race, nation or species, and for Singer 'If a being suffers there can be no moral justification for refusing to take that suffering into consideration' (1983: 9). Differences between the objects of our concern will make a difference to what, exactly, we do, so it would be senseless to campaign for votes for animals, but Singer contends that the suffering of a human should not automatically count for more than the suffering of an animal. This argument derives from the Utilitarian tradition in ethics, which holds that actions are not right or wrong in themselves, but only insofar as they bring happiness or cause pain. Singer's inclusive version of it is presented in the first chapter of his book, while the remainder is devoted to the promotion of vegetarianism and the exposure of horrifying vivisection and factory farming practices, arguing throughout for the liberation of animals.

A less radical position than Singer's 'liberationist' stance is espoused by Mary Midgley, whose book *Animals and Why They Matter* (1983) remains an excellent introduction to animal 'welfarism'. She qualifies the principle of equality, arguing that we are sometimes right to prefer the interests of our human kin, and criticises Singer's analogy of racism and speciesism:

> Overlooking somebody's race is entirely sensible. Overlooking their species is a supercilious insult. It is no privilege, but a misfortune, for a gorilla or a chimpanzee to be removed from its forest and its relatives and brought up alone among humans to be given what those humans regard as an education.
>
> (Midgley 1983: 99)

At the same time, she explores the concept of anthropomorphism. It is worth noting here that the few who oppose the liberationist stance on factory farming on philosophical, not economic, grounds (e.g. Leahy 1994) have criticised anthropomorphism, arguing that we mistakenly ascribe human attributes, such as our own desire for freedom, to the animals involved. Midgley looks back to the origins of the term, which was first applied to the false attribution of human shape and qualities to

God. The problem for theologians who attacked anthropomorphism was that their scepticism seemed to deny God any qualities whatsoever. Similarly, the sceptical attack on sentimental views of animals risks making it impossible to describe animal behaviour at all. The problem therefore is to distinguish between kinds of anthropomorphism, which is often a very practical matter. An example is the 'mahout' or elephant handler:

> Obviously the mahouts may have many beliefs about the elephants which are false because they are 'anthropomorphic' – that is, they misinterpret some outlying aspects of elephant behaviour by relying on a human pattern which is inappropriate. But if they were doing this about the basic everyday feelings – about whether the elephant is pleased, annoyed, frightened, excited, tired, sore, suspicious or angry – they would not only be out of business, they would often simply be dead.
>
> (Midgley 1983: 115)

Jeffrey Masson and Susan McCarthy's survey of evidence for animal emotions suggests that scientific researchers insulate themselves from moral qualms by rejecting as 'inappropriate' the descriptive language more usually used for human behaviour, so that 'A monkey is not angry, it exhibits aggression. A crane does not feel affection; it displays courtship or parental behaviour' (Masson and McCarthy 1996: 45). This can extend to a reluctance to give observed animals ordinary names: 'Granted that a number is more dehumanised than a name, does that make it more scientific? Assigning names to them . . . can be called anthropomorphic, but so is assigning numbers. Chimpanzees are no more likely to think of themselves as F2 or JF3 than as Flo or Figan' (1996: 47). Their study gives remarkable examples of a variety of emotions in animals, including hope, grief, happiness and rage, although their examples of very complex emotions such as compassion and shame are less convincing. Liberationist criticism seeks to enhance the status of animals by undermining the 'insuperable line' between humans and animals criticised by Bentham. The ultimate implication is that even the opposition between technology and nature is unsustainable, as electro-mechanical and biological processes become ever more closely interfused. Contemporary 'cyborg' criticism takes Bentham's argument to the extreme, claiming that postmodern technologies such as artificial body organs are challenging the traditional distinction between machine and organism, thereby threatening the notion of the 'human' itself.

The activist orientation of liberationist criticism is formulated in ethical debates, but the distinctive inflection of modern Cultural Studies comes from John Berger's essay 'Why Look at Animals?' (1980), which examines the animal question as a social and aesthetic issue. When we look at animals, they return our gaze, and in that moment we are aware of both likeness and difference. Hence the peasant 'becomes fond of his pig and is glad to salt away his pork' (Berger 1980: 5). For the integrated, pre-modern sensibility, the fondness and the slaughter are not contradictory. It is only through industrialisation that most animals are removed from everyday life, and the meat production process hidden away. Once marginalised in this way, the few animals still visible to us can be only 'human puppets' as family pets or Disney characters, or else the objects of spectacle, most often wildlife books and films, where

> . . . animals are always the observed. The fact that they can observe us has lost all significance. They are the objects of our ever-extending knowledge. What we know about them is an index of our power, and thus an index of what separates us from them. The more we know, the further away they are.
>
> (Berger 1980: 14)

If the pet is just a mirror, reflecting back our gaze with no autonomy, TV wildlife is powerless to make its gaze register at all against our imperial eye. To the morality of liberation, which he might regard as a further symptom of our alienated distance from animals, Berger adds the rather different politics of representation.

Neither of these is directly related to ecology, not least because environmentalism and animal liberation conflict in both theory and practice. Animal liberationists generally draw the line of moral consideration at the boundary of sentience or feeling. For Singer, this is somewhere between crustaceans and molluscs, leaving mussels on the menu but taking crab and lobster off. Environmental ethics, on the other hand, places far less emphasis on the individual organism, but demands moral consideration for inanimate things such as rivers and mountains, assuming pain and suffering to be a necessary part of nature. These ethical conflicts have practical consequences, in that liberationists are generally opposed to hunting, whereas ecophilosophers argue that in some cases exploding populations of a certain species must be culled if they threaten a local environment as whole (see Callicott 1995: 39). Such conflicts have become especially pressing in cases where non-native predators or destructive herbivores threaten fragile ecologies. However, since much livestock farming is objectionable on both environmental and welfare grounds, liberationist cultural studies may be seen as an important ally of ecocriticism if not strictly a branch of it.

We have seen how 'pastoral' and 'wilderness' function as tropes, but 'animal' too has a range of important functions as a trope. At the simplest level, we are familiar with animal similes of the form 'as stubborn as a mule'. The play of likeness and difference in the relationship of humans and animals in general may be analysed in terms of the distinction of metonymy and metaphor:

> The distinctive peculiarity of animals is that, being at once close to man and strange to him, both akin to him and unalterably not-man, they are able to alternate, as objects of human thought, between the contiguity of the metonymic mode and the distanced, analogical mode of the metaphor.
>
> (Willis 1974: 128)

Humans can both be, and be compared to, animals. There is, therefore, an extensive 'rhetoric of animality', as Steve Baker calls it, that is as functional in descriptions of human social and political relations as it is in describing actual animals. Liberationist cultural critics typically focus on the place of domestic animals within this rhetoric, whereas ecocritics study the representation of wild animals, a difference in emphasis that roughly corresponds to Berger's family/spectacle dichotomy, and the animal rights/environmental ethics contrast. These provisional distinctions will form the basis for a separate consideration of the two strands in the remainder of this chapter.

DOMESTIC ANIMALS AND CYBORGS

An excellent example of liberationist criticism is Steve Baker's *Picturing the Beast* (1993), which analyses the use of animal stereotypes in political contests and animal cartoon strips. Baker insists that the common-sense distinction between actual animals and images of them, represented earlier in terms of the different interests of Singer and Berger, ought not to lead us to trivialise the image in favour of the actual, to prioritise ethics over aesthetics, since:

> much of our understanding of human identity and our thinking about the living animal reflects – and may even be the rather direct result of – the diverse uses to which the concept of the animal is put in popular culture, regardless of how bizarre or banal some of those uses may seem. . . . Culture shapes our reading of animals just as much as animals shape our reading of culture.
>
> (Baker 1993: 4)

One case is the use of animals in a 'rhetoric of moral and social regulation' (1993: 89); for example, violent or sexually immoral behaviour is routinely condemned as 'bestial' or 'animal'. Baker wonders whether this usage reflects, or sustains, the contempt for animals some modern practices imply, and he shows how British Labour politicians were discredited in the early 1980s by newspaper cartoons that metaphorically *likened them* to animals. By contrast, Second World War cartoons deployed metonymic images in which 'the lion *stands for* Britain . . . the bald eagle *stands for* the United States' (Baker 1993: 108). The Labour politicians were represented 'therianthropically', combining human and animal characteristics for purposes of mockery, whereas the lion and the eagle were 'theriomorphic' images of Britain and America. Theriomorphism is the reverse of anthropomorphism, and is often used in contexts of national or racial stereotyping, such as when Nazis depicted Jews as rats.

One of Baker's major contributions to liberationist criticism is his elaboration of 'disnification' as a critical term: 'With regard to the animal, the basic procedure of disnification is to render it stupid by rendering it visual' (Baker 1993: 174). Anthropomorphic animal narratives are generally denigrated as 'childish', thereby associating a dispassionate, even alienated perspective with maturity. Disnification exacerbates this existing association, as reflected in the colloquial use of 'Mickey Mouse' to describe something as trivial or worthless. The visual cue of disnification is 'neoteny', or the set of characteristics we instinctively associate with infant humans and animals: large eyes, a big head relative to the body, short limbs and a generally rounded configuration. Both the real panda and the WWF logo in which it appears exemplify neoteny, and also the disnified 'cutesy' relation to nature that it implies. Baker claims that 'there is little point in complaining about this: it is simply how disnification seems currently to operate' (1993: 182), although his final chapter suggests how non-disnified images of animals might be promoted.

Looking further back, Erica Fudge's *Perceiving Animals* (2000) traces in the early modern period, specifically 1558–1649, an overlapping series of attempts, in theology, law and other disciplines, to define the 'insuperable line' between humans and animals. Fudge starts with an anecdote: the visit of the Italian Alessandro Magno to the Bear Garden on the South Bank in London in 1562. Her stated aim thereafter is to account for the evidently considerable pleasure that he, and many others, derived from watching animals being torn to pieces. Her explanation is that people felt the need perpetually to reassert human dominance over, and separation from, the animal kingdom by baiting horses, bears, monkeys and bulls, but that this attempt was doomed to fail in a vicious circle of anxiety and sadism: 'To watch a baiting, to enact anthropocentrism, is to reveal, not the stability of species status, but the animal that lurks beneath the surface. In proving their humanity humans achieve the opposite. The Bear Garden makes humans into animals' (Fudge 2000: 15) Fudge supports her argument by citing sixteenth-century critics of baiting, who derided the people who enjoyed it as being 'bestial', thereby rhetorically undermining the very 'humanity' it was supposed to reinforce. Apologists for blood sports then and now assert that the suffering of the animal is not their object, but Fudge points out that their activities would be entirely meaningless were there no emotional reaction from the animal at all. There could be no 'sport' in bear-baiting or fox-hunting if the participants were insentient. However, it might be argued that her attempt to deconstruct the boundary between human and animal fails, as it wrongly assumes that when opponents of bear-baiting castigated those who enjoyed it as being 'bestial', their rhetoric of animality may be taken to subvert a putatively superior 'humanity'. Kate Soper argues, on the contrary, that such abuse actually reinforces the notion of human difference because it sustains what she calls 'negative anthropomorphism', or in Baker's terminology, theriomorphism:

> The animal is here used to police rather than confuse the human–nature divide; by associating all our 'lowlier' characteristics and bodily functions with animality, we assert the importance of sustaining those higher or more spiritual attributes that grant us human sovereignty over the beast.
>
> (Soper 1998: 86)

So while Fudge's historical detail testifies to considerable debate about the proper treatment and theological status of animals, it does not sustain the more dramatic claim that 'in each exercise of dominion the antithetical position emerges: humans become the animals they attempt to dominate' (1998: 143).

There are many, varied ways of tracing the 'insuperable line', from the possession of an immortal soul through existential freedom, neurological differentiation and symbolic language use to the anatomy of the human hand that enables sophisticated tool-making. Fudge shares with a number of other liberationist critics the assumption that this plethora of claims and arguments does *not* prove the unassailable security of our position as top species. On the contrary, it betrays an anxious, self-defeating need to construct and continually reinforce a difference that nature has not supplied, so that our dominionist beliefs and practices may continue unmolested. Singer's notion of a moral overlap of 'higher' mammals and 'lower' humans translates in liberationist criticism into attacks on the paranoid frontier mentality of successive generations of self-deluding humanists. These derive much of their force from their subversion of the boundaries of the human.

One of the most intriguing post-human critiques is Michael Shapiro's analysis of Philip K. Dick's *Do Androids Dream of Electric Sheep?* (1968) and the popular film adaptation *Blade Runner* (1982). In Dick's novel, bounty hunter Rick Deckard pursues escaped androids or 'replicants' in a post-apocalyptic future where the few animal species that remain command exorbitant prices. With each replicant he 'retires', Deckard gets closer to the day that he can replace his robot sheep with a real goat, but as he tracks down and kills six of the advanced bio-electronic Nexus-6 type androids, his sense of human superiority is challenged and finally shattered. As Shapiro observes, Dick's novel explores the challenge posed to human identity not only by animals but also by cyborgs. In the novel, the standard Voigt-Kampff test used to expose replicants relies on measuring empathetic responses, often to imaginary scenarios involving injury to animals. The androids' failure to respond to the pain of animals both identifies them and legitimates their retirement, but precisely because they are so realistic, they also threaten the bounty hunter's own sense of his animal-loving, empathetic humanity:

> To dissociate themselves from androids, humans must associate themselves with animals (which are in turn disassociated from androids if they are 'real'). Accordingly, Deckard attempts to retire rogue androids in order to be able to afford a live pet, which he wants in order to distinguish himself from androids.
>
> (Shapiro 1993: 68)

In this world teetering on the edge of final collapse, the insuperable line between human and animal is undermined in order to bolster the boundary between human and android. Deckard is exposed to the inconsistencies involved in his profession in the following conversation with an opera-singing replicant called Luba Luft:

> 'Do you have information that there's an android in the cast? I'd be glad to help you, and if I were an android would I be glad to help you?'
>
> 'An android,' he said, 'doesn't care what happens to another android. That's one of the indications we look for.'
>
> 'Then,' Miss Luft said, 'you must be an android.'
>
> That stopped him; he stared at her.
>
> (Dick 1997: 79)

Deckard's position is fatally compromised by a sexual relationship with Rachael Rosen, a Nexus-6 sent by the manufacturers. She shows a painful degree of self-consciousness about her being: '" . . . We're not born; we don't grow up; instead of dying from illness or old age we wear out like ants. . . . *I'm not alive!* You're not going to bed with a woman. Don't be disappointed; okay?"' (p. 146). Her words are somewhat self-contradictory given that these androids combine biological and electro-mechanical elements. Repeatedly in the novel, the boundaries break down, and many humanity-confirming animals turn out, like Deckard's sheep, to be machines. Moreover, Deckard's injured human colleague Dave Holden receives a prosthetic implant to save him, making him part cyborg, while another bounty hunter Phil Resch evinces a callousness towards replicants that seems psychopathic in its own right.

Animals play a far less prominent role in Ridley Scott's film than in Dick's novel, with a greater emphasis falling on the pathos of the replicants' struggle for life and identity. Shapiro argues that this is thematised from the opening moments of the film through the motif of the eye, 'representing both vision as the "eye" and identity as the "I"' (Shapiro 1993: 75). The Voigt-Kampff test closely monitors involuntary eye movements in order to gauge empathy, and therefore identity. When the replicant leader Roy Baty confronts his maker, he kills him by gouging out his eyes, and when he meets the subcontractor who manufactured the Nexus-6 eyeballs, he comments, with superb ambiguity, 'If only you could see what I have seen with your eyes.' As in the novel, Deckard's role as bounty hunter, or 'blade runner', ultimately clashes with precisely those human sentiments that he is supposed to defend: 'Replicants weren't supposed to have feelings, but neither are blade runners. What was happening to me?' In a climactic fight scene, Roy Baty injures and mutilates, then rescues and redeems Deckard. Reflecting upon his all-too-brief existence, Baty says, 'I've seen things you people wouldn't believe.' Yet even as the witness of his eyes confirms an identity beyond the narrow configurations of the human, he recognises his own mortality: 'And now, it's time to die.' This more than anything renders the human/cyborg boundary impossible to sustain.

The implications of this second frontier for ecocriticism have not been widely explored, despite the emergence of a vibrant field of 'cyborg studies' founded principally on the work of Donna Haraway (see Gray 1995). In her seminal 'Cyborg Manifesto', she points out the ubiquity of the cyborg in science fiction, modern medicine and high-technology warfare. The cardiac patient with a pacemaker and the attack heli-copter pilot with a gunsight that tracks eyeball movement are becoming monsters almost as familiar as the Terminators (1985, 1991, 2003). The cyborg is quickly becoming autonomous, subverting an apparently limitless number of dualistic schema, according to Haraway: animal/human, organism/machine, male/female, physical/non-physical. It is located at the nexus of change in both microelectronics and biology, as computers begin to mimic and to incorporate biological processes, thus transforming the science of living organisms into 'a powerful engineering science for redesigning materials and processes' (Haraway 1991: 165). The Internet emerges as the natural home of the cyborg, even as nature loses its capacity to offer 'a source of insight and promise of innocence' (p. 153). This seems to leave us adrift in a compromised society bereft of metaphysical consolation or despair, yet although Haraway demonstrates the '*pleasure* in the confusion of boundaries', she nevertheless insists upon the need for '*responsibility* in their construction' (p. 150). In Haraway's case, the cyborg is a thoroughly political animal, committed to socialism and feminism.

The cyborg will be a key figure in a poetics of responsibility because its irreverence and keen sense of irony are quite incompatible with traditional pastoral, wilderness and apocalyptic tropes: 'The cyborg would not recognize the Garden of Eden; it is not made of mud and cannot dream of returning to dust' (Haraway 1991: 151). Not having 'fallen', the cyborg does not need to be redeemed, only to survive; it remains outside the 'salvation history' that underlies some ecophilosophical and ecocritical positions. Haraway argues that cyborgs need to develop political strategies of resistance that do not depend upon the kind of dualistic model of technology versus nature found in Carolyn Merchant, Heidegger and many deep ecologists. Her position acknowledges 'that science and technology are possible means of great human satisfaction, as well as a matrix of complex dominations' (p. 181). She even goes so far as to claim it is necessary to 'advocate pollution' to the extent that such a tactic undermines the principle of moral and material purity that was outlined in the Introduction. Some of the most enthusiastic cyborgs are to be found in youth cultures centred on music, dance and 'neurotechnologies' (formerly known as 'drugs') ancient and modern, 'natural' or not. Andrew Ross claims that:

From the electric boogie style of early breakdancing to the braindraining energy worship of hardcore techno, hybrid species of high technology have been a material presence in recent popular music, comfortably coexisting with ancient oral traditions in rap, and with neopagan forms of tribal communing among ravers.

(Ross 1994: 235)

For Haraway and Ross, the cyborg represents an opportunity to flout the boundaries of gender and species, although as Ross points out, Arnold Schwarzenegger's cyborg incarnation in the first *Terminator* film offers scant grounds for optimism given his violent, exaggerated masculinity.

The example of the 'Oncomouse', a patented species of mouse that spontaneously grows tumours and is therefore invaluable in cancer research, clearly shows that cyborg biotechnologies transgress the animal/technology boundary as well as the human/technology boundary, yet *Blade Runner* reduces Philip Dick's triangle to only the latter two terms. Shapiro's focus on the cyborg rather than the animal frontier seems to reinforce the film's exclusion of the animal, a move that Jhan Hochman claims also occurs in *The Silence of the Lambs* (1991). In a series of more or less tenuous associative links, Hochman describes the characters in the film in terms of a 'theriomorphic bestiary'; Hannibal Lecter is not only a cannibal, but associated by name with control of animals, while the killer Buffalo Bill is obviously associated with ruthless hunting and skinning. Several female characters are associated with birds, as in the surnames of the detective Clarice Starling and the victim Catherine Martin. Although his prose is overheated and the argument sometimes strained, Hochman offers a brilliant and surprising analysis of the role of lambs in the film. In a pivotal scene, Hannibal Lecter extracts from detective Clarice Starling the story of a childhood trauma in which she tried to save a lamb from slaughter on her uncle's farm. Hochman contends:

Clarice grows up and accepts the killing of lambs . . . but not the screaming that some associate with the mushy, childish, and effeminate side of her constitution. The screaming *inside her head* must be stopped. She attempts this through metaphor – Christian lambs and women in need – for screaming lambs. If she rescues Catherine Martin, Clarice might also save herself.

(Hochman 1998: 39)

Leaving the house of killer 'Buffalo Bill' near the end of the film, Clarice carries Martin's lamb-like poodle in her arms, and later confirms to Hannibal that the lambs have stopped screaming. But as Hochman reminds us, these are lambs of the mind whose fate displaces that of real lambs, an erasure that eliminates the topic of animal cruelty that is unwittingly revealed by the title of the film.

Ecocriticism therefore shares with liberationist and cyborg criticism a sustained and sustaining interest in the subjectivity of the non-human, and in the problem of the troubled boundaries between the human and other creatures. All three critical discourses invite an encounter with the pleasures and anxieties of a possible post-human condition. However, animals and animal products have recently become the site of a new range of concerns. As a result of the advent of BSE ('mad cow disease') and the huge outbreak of foot and mouth disease in the UK in 2001, traditional significations and narratives involving animals have come under threat. Most obviously, the mass burning and burial of slaughtered livestock severely damaged the pastoral image of modern farming. Moreover, as Richard Kerridge argues, the BSE crisis seemed to elude traditional narratives of catastrophe thanks to the scientific uncertainties involved, since there could be no dramatic climax contained within a reassuring narrative of resolution. Neither the warning given by the jeremiad nor the confrontational excitement of the apocalyptic thriller were appropriate since consumers were faced with a threat that might have existed long before anyone had the power or knowledge to prevent it. The health risk might either affect a very small number of people or virtually an entire nation, so as Kerridge puts it, 'The thriller works us up and then withholds its climax' (1999: 118).

If the supposed infectious agent was a model of indeterminacy, its probable origin in the practice of feeding sheep-based products contaminated with scrapie, a natural disease of sheep, to cattle in the form of anonymous, manufactured feed pellets epitomises the sinister side of cyborg boundary-crossing. Furthermore the beef products in which the pathogen might lie unseen turned out to be terrifyingly ubiquitous.

Kerridge's prose itself seems infected by breathless panic in the face of one of the postmodern megahazards discussed in my Introduction:

> In its imagery, BSE confronted the public with spectacles of bodies – animal bodies – being rendered, bursting out of their limits and being boiled down to an essence which would then disperse uncontainably. The dissolution of bodies appeared first as a ruthlessly managed process, but then, revealing the hubris of this notion of control, as an unmanageable process, uncontainable. That which is dispersed ceases to be containable and seems to be present everywhere: beef derivatives were revealed to be ingredients of biscuits, yogurt, medicines, ice cream. Semen, tallow and gelatin, the three beef derivatives whose export was banned by the European Community in addition to the ban on meat itself, seemed to stand for the uncontainable afterlife of the body, after the extinction of the self. Against such dispersal, acts of volition by the good old humanist unified self – mere resolutions not to eat the stuff – were powerless. As were narratives giving primacy to that self.
>
> (Kerridge 1999: 120)

The sublime threat to received notions of the self, nature and culture 'BSE stories' inadvertently narrate might force us to develop alternatives, Kerridge suggests, to established ways of presenting and containing environmental crisis. These would have to cope with indeterminacy, long timescales, complex problems of agency and responsibility and the postmodern problem of the unseen, unquantifiable cyborg risk.

WILD ANIMALS AND BIODIVERSITY

Liberationist criticism typically attempts to undermine the moral and legal distinctions between humans and animals, but it takes for granted the difference between wild and domestic animals. We are rarely enjoined to prevent the suffering of wild animals because our moral responsibility principally applies to the animals we use for food, transport and companionship. Ecocritics also rely on the distinction, but tend to venerate wild animals while treating cattle, sheep and cats as the destructive accomplices of human culture.

Earlier we argued that wilderness narratives deploy a gendered hierarchical distinction between wild and domestic animals in which the former are linked with masculine freedom, and often predation, while the latter are denigrated as feminine servants of human depredation. Barney Nelson shows that Mary Austin challenged this entire system of associations and distinctions: 'She finds wildness in both genders and domesticity in both, just as she finds wild animals very domestic and domestic animals very wild' (Nelson 2000: 132). She argues convincingly that the urban notion of 'domestication' barely describes many livestock, with its connotations of docility, stupidity and lack of autonomy, while protected bears and mountain lions habituated to humans are now a serious problem in many 'wild' areas of North America. In many parts of the world, dogs and cats move freely back and forward across the conceptual divide, suggesting that a detailed analysis of *ferality* as both theoretical construct and historical practice may be opportune in ecocriticism. Nelson cites archaeological evidence that some animals, such as gazelle and Barbary sheep, have been domesticated and then returned to the wild again.

Zoo animals cross the same boundary as feral animals. As Berger shows, they are the objects of the imperial gaze we turn on wild animals, in which our alienated distance is proportionate to our power. Liberationists claim that zoo confinement is cruel, which may be true in some cases, but an ecocritical perspective is more concerned with the politics of representation implied by the zoo experience. Randy Malamud's *Reading Zoos* (1998) is an exhaustive analysis of zoo stories, mainly from English literature, that seeks to demonstrate that zoos distort our perception of animals as well as being a spectacle of imperial or neocolonial power:

> In the same way that the nineteenth-century London Zoo was designed to make visitors proud of vicarious engagement in their culture's imperial prowess, today's zoos are marketed to flatter spectators' roles as active members of a gloriously affluent consumeristic society.
>
> (Malamud 1998: 91–2)

This continuous role has been only slightly affected by recent attempts by zoos to market what Malamud calls the 'feel-good ecoactivism' of captive breeding programmes to protect endangered species. He finds that many writers have intuited and exposed the dominionist assumptions behind zoos, and his survey is valuable for depicting a widespread sense of unease surrounding the welfare and politics of wild animals in captivity. However, Malamud becomes less convincing when his liberationist convictions lead him into a general dismissal of the educational, scientific and preservationist possibilities of zoos.

For most modern readers, it is not the zoo but the wildlife documentary or movie that predominantly shapes their perceptions of wild animals. Informed critique of the way these productions shape our ideas is perhaps the most important way that we can enhance our ecocritical awareness beyond the realms of literature. There is no question that wildlife films and documentaries have made important contributions to environmental campaigns: *Flipper* (1963) is credited with creating a constituency of young dolphin admirers who, as adults, joined the tuna boycott that transformed fishing practices that are lethal to marine mammals. At the same time, critics claim that nature programming may misrepresent its objects in various ways, substituting error for ignorance. In particular, the way the relationship of the viewer to the wildlife is constructed may be highly problematic, narrowing our experience of nature from full sensory, intellectual and political engagement to a purely visual relation that is further distorted by overemphasis on violence and sex. Nature programming, in other words, may be little better than 'eco-porn'.

No book-length treatment of the subject has yet been written, but Alexander Wilson and David Ingram have provided outline histories of documentaries and films respectively. The early Disney documentaries are a source of appalling misrepresentation, sentimental anthropomorphism and outright fakery, as was the case when brown lemmings were captured in large numbers, then driven over the edge of a cliff to illustrate their 'suicidal' mass migrations. In fact, it is Norway lemmings who occasionally migrate in this way, and it is inconceivable that they would jump off cliffs unless forced over by a film crew. The examples Wilson critiques often involve the use of wildlife to enforce social norms such as monogamy and hard work, as in the 1950s films *Bear Country* and *Beaver Valley*. They are deeply indebted to pastoral traditions, but also draw on the stylistic devices of Disney cartoons, such as, in Wilson's analysis, the 'orchestrated vignettes of organic rhythms' for instance: 'Mud gurgles, frogs croak, blooms bloom. Grebes stage pageants, pelicans perform classical ballet. It's enthralling; the world hums and cooks to a human choreography and middle-brow orchestral music' (Wilson 1992: 129) Wilson charts a shift 'from pastoralism to scientism' from these early efforts to the 1980s, as environmentalist values came to challenge anthropomorphism. Audiences demanded more accurate information, combined with a degree of conservationist advocacy. Nevertheless, the demand for spectacle tends to lead to an obsessive interest in predation, usually enhanced by the exciting music and slow-motion, fast-edited sequences that audiences might expect of a thriller. The desire to inform as well as entertain has created the sort of conflicts that Wilson finds in the National Geographic production *White Wolf* (1989). He points out that the overt, verbal message and the implicit meaning of the action sequences are far from complementary, where 'the biologists speculate about wolf language and child rearing, play, security and feeding', but 'the tension of the show is a *dramatic* tension, organized around an edited hunting episode rather than the ideas set out by the biologists'. For Wilson, 'The structure of the movie undercuts the script' (Wilson 1992: 141). Likewise, documentaries often carry the conservationist message that an animal is rare, but then depict large numbers of them. Absent animals do not make for exciting viewing.

The favourite location for wildlife documentaries is the African savannah with 'charismatic megafauna' such as elephants and giraffes, where the camera sometimes seems to stand in for the colonial figure of the white game hunter. Despite the fact that Africans have coexisted with these species since ours evolved there, humans are either totally excluded from the scene, or introduced in one of two roles: destroyers or saviours. All too often, black hunters are simply the demonised 'poachers' while white conservationists are valorised, and the complex economic and political factors involved in poaching and game management are ignored. Wilson praises some productions, such as the Canadian Broadcasting Corporation's long-running *The Nature of Things*, that attempt to incorporate conservationist advocacy, social commentary, natural history and science, and anthropological programmes such as *Millennium: Tribal Wisdom and the Modern World* (1992) that explore the creative and destructive interrelations of human cultures and nature.

In the 1980s, as documentaries were attempting to change perceptions with more responsible and accurate reporting, Hollywood, however, was producing films that exploited and reinforced theriophobia, or fear of animals. Ingram argues that the *Jaws* series, for example, represents a backlash against conservationist ideas in which an 'evil, threatening nature is eventually mastered through male heroism, technology and the blood sacrifice of the wild animal' (2000: 90). In the fourth film, *Jaws: the Revenge* (1987), the marine biologist Mike Brody's environmentalist concerns are effectively ridiculed as his colleague is eaten by the enraged fish; he joins the hunt for it and the shark in turn hunts him down.

The most useful discussion of wildlife programming thus far is Karla Armbruster's 1998 essay 'Creating the world we must save', which draws on the work of both Berger and Wilson, in order to survey a range of criticisms of TV nature documentaries. For example, Armbruster points out that an hour-long documentary represents an extraordinary compression of time and space, in which weeks of waiting and hours of filming is edited down to a brief, enthralling spectacle. Far from connecting us with nature, this is likely to contrast strikingly with direct experience, as 'a fulfilling experience with the natural world involves more than passively sitting back to be informed and entertained' (Armbruster 1998: 224). This rather fundamental objection aside, Armbruster's essay also criticises specific techniques and practices. Even the fantastic photography of the recent BBC series *The Blue Planet* (2001), which captures myriad species in numerous locations over eight programmes, may come to represent a distinctly narrowed vision if we interpret it with her strictures in mind. Some of the most extraordinary scenes are indeed of mass predation, as in the 'Open Ocean' programme where a school of sardines is set upon simultaneously by striped marlin, yellowfin tuna and frigate birds, with a sei whale rushing up from the deep to engulf the survivors.

Armbruster criticises the phenomenon of the absent narrator, claiming that it encourages a sense of innocent unobtrusiveness in the viewer, and argues that 'By identifying with the narrator, and with the perspective of the camera that so often appears to be the narrator's eye, the viewer is constructed as omniscient and capable of penetrating the most inaccessible reaches of the natural world' (Armbruster 1998: 232). As the metaphor of penetration might indicate, the illusion of unrestricted access into a mysterious or forbidden space produces a relation of subject to object that is structurally similar to that involved in pornography in which the eye/I derives pleasure from an obtrusive gaze that its object cannot challenge or return. *The Blue Planet* articulates an underlying contradiction at its outset, first admitting that the vast oceans remain barely explored and mysterious, but then promising us a privileged, deeper, closer, 'never before seen' perspective. The narrator in this case is Sir David Attenborough, a virtual culture hero in the United Kingdom, whose familiar voice lends the programme the sense of omniscient authority that Armbruster identifies. Nonetheless, he could hardly appear on this programme, as he has on many land-based ones, and he has himself voiced some of the criticisms that Armbruster makes of irresponsible documentaries.

In most respects, *The Blue Planet* is exemplary, starting off the series with a contextualising overview of oceanic ecology that interrelates wind, tides and currents, and stresses movements of nutrients as well as massive migrations of species. This contrasts with documentaries that isolate events or individual species, reducing the significance of ecological connections and processes. The narrative wrestles with anthropomorphism when a pod of killer whales capture a seal pup and torment it for a prolonged period before leaving it to die, and Attenborough openly struggles to account for their behaviour without condemning it. For the most part, though, the documentary does tend to 'naturalise' its perspective. The people and sophisticated technology needed to obtain the pictures remain unseen, thereby, Armbruster claims, undermining environmental advocacy. She lauds documentaries that admit that they are particular, and partial, constructions of nature rather than posing as unmediated truth, and criticises 'the seamless insertion of "technical events"' such as 'passages of slow motion, changes in viewpoint such as the shift from a close-up of a coyote hunting a weasel to a wider perspective that includes them both, and shots into hard-to-access locations such as a nest of termites' (Armbruster 1998: 231). In the case of *The Blue Planet*, some of these events, such as the use of image intensifiers at night, are obvious enough, and the programme on 'The Deep' could not help but show the submersible, but most were seamless. Slow motion is perhaps more misleading than its opposite effect, time-lapse photography. Slow motion is generally used to enhance tension in dramatic scenes, adds little extra insight and may not be detectable as such by the viewer, whereas time-lapse photography shows gradual processes under way to great effect and is invariably obvious. 'Tidal Seas' made good use of the latter to show changes at the ocean's edge.

One of the key concerns of wildlife documentaries is that some species may become extinct. Many wildlife biologists believe that we are in the early stages of a mass extinction episode not seen since the annihilation of the dinosaurs at the end of the Cretaceous Period 65 million years ago. Humans have been held responsible for many local extinction episodes; for example, the arrival of human settlers in both Madagascar and New Zealand was followed by the extinction of numerous species of flightless birds. More controversially, Native Americans have been blamed for Palaeolithic extinctions of American camels, elephants, giant armadillos, ground sloths and many other species. Such anthropogenic extinctions are thought to have risen rapidly in the last 200 years from an estimated loss rate of one species per year (already 100 times the natural background rate) at the turn of the nineteenth century, largely as a result of extensive destruction of biologically rich tropical rainforests and coral reefs. Norman Myers, in his *Scarcity or Abundance?* debate with cornucopian Julian Simon estimates that we might be losing 27,000 species a year, but suspects that with a more accurate reckoning the annual total might well become 'a good deal larger' (Myers and Simon 1994: 76).

The most accessible examination of the science of extinction is David Quammen's *The Song of the Dodo* (1996), which shows how and why island ecologies are especially vulnerable to anthropogenic impacts. As Alfred Wallace and Charles Darwin found in their crucial field trips, to the Malay Archipelago and the Galapagos Islands respectively, evolution operates most obviously in the biological isolation afforded by islands. They came independently to the conclusion that a single ancestor species, arriving or becoming isolated on the island in the past, could evolve by natural selection into a variety of different species, a process known to modern ecologists as 'adaptive radiation'. As Quammen shows, island ecologies have given rise to an enormous range of odd species such as the tree-climbing kangaroos of New Guinea and the giant lizard or 'dragon' of Komodo (1996: 137–8). Birds typify the combination of variety of species and scarcity of individuals found on islands such as New

Zealand, home to the kiwi, a flightless parrot called the kakapo, the large, flightless takahe and the kea, a carnivorous parrot. The dodo (*Raphus cucullatus*) of Mauritius is the most famous flightless island bird because it is also the first species known to have been driven to extinction by human activity in modern times. Quammen explains that the rarity of such a species is exacerbated by hunting, habitat destruction, competition from introduced species such as goats and pigs, and predation from aliens such as rats, mongooses and cats. These 'deterministic' factors reduce the population to the point where it is exceptionally vulnerable to random or 'stochastic' factors such as catastrophic weather events, normal variations in birth and death rates, and inbreeding. In a series of detailed case studies, Quammen shows how extensive island extinctions have been, and argues that habitat destruction is now also forcing mainland species into ever-diminishing ecosystems that are effectively 'islands'. Of the 171 extinct species and sub-species of bird counted since 1600, 90 per cent were from islands, even though such species make up just 20 per cent of the total number of bird species (Quammen 1996: 264). Quammen imagines the death of the last dodo with moving immediacy:

> *Raphus cucullatus* had become rare unto death. But this one flesh-and-blood individual still lived. Imagine that she was thirty years old, or thirty-five, an ancient age for most sorts of bird but not impossible for a member of such a large-bodied species. She no longer ran, she waddled. Lately she was going blind. Her digestive system was balky. In the dark of an early morning in 1667, say, during a rainstorm, she took cover beneath a cold stone ledge at the base of one of the Black River cliffs. She drew her head down against her body, fluffed her feathers for warmth, squinted in patient misery. She waited. She didn't know it, nor did anyone else, but she was the only dodo on Earth. When the storm passed, she never opened her eyes. This is extinction.
>
> (1996: 275)

The death of an individual is also the death of its kind. Quammen's elegy therefore shuttles uneasily between imaginative lament and eco-logical explanations with lists of species lost, exemplifying the problem of representing absence on such a scale. The narrative incorporates scientific analysis and anecdotes from the history of ecology within a travelogue, in which Quammen functions as itinerant witness to the extinction, past or imminent, of species, as well as heroic efforts to conserve a few.

Julia Leigh's novel *The Hunter* (2000) represents extinction very differently. The anonymous protagonist travels to Tasmania posing as a conservationist in order to track down the last thylacine, a marsupial wolf believed to be extinct but still occasionally reported (see also Quammen 1996: 279–306). His task is to kill the animal in secret and collect samples for a biotechnology company that intends to capitalise upon its unique DNA in the development of biological weapons. One of Leigh's major achievements is to associate believably the rhetoric of closeness to nature with such a morally bankrupt individual. Out in the bush, the protagonist seeks to identify totally with the creature as well as to understand its environment fully, as in this scene in which a kind of shamanistic transformation takes place:

> Lying there on the hard ground inside his tent he performs his favourite trick: he changes shape, swallows the beast. The eyes in his head are no longer his own, short thick fur runs along the back of his neck, and his spine grows thick and strong, right out of his back, out into a long still tail. He hangs his body off this strong spine, hollows out his belly, shrinks his gangly limbs. His arm is bent at the elbow, and a paw, not a hand, rests against his bony convex chest. He sleeps and hopes to dream.
>
> (Leigh 2000: 91)

Ultimately the hunter's quest is successful, and his dissection of the last thylacine is thorough and efficient, though not without a hint of tenderness. Richard Kerridge compares this powerfully depressing scene with Quammen's depiction of extinction, showing that while regret is only implied by its distressing absence in Leigh's novel, the inevitability of the outcome is no more in question there than in the elegiac narrative of the dodo's demise. He points out that 'conventional plot structures require forms of solution and closure that seem absurdly evasive when applied to ecological questions with their extremes of timescale and complexities of interdependency' (2002: 99). Writing extinction involves not simply the problem of representing absence, but also the difficulty of narrating ongoing systemic crises within intrinsically individualising forms such as the travelogue and the novel.

The representations of animals discussed so far are predominantly concerned with individuals or, at most, species. Likewise, much conservation activism has in the past centred on pandas, say, or whales, with regulatory frameworks ranging from early international measures to conserve fur-bearing seals (1911) to the Convention on International Trade in Endangered Species (CITES, 1973) that maintains a list of banned or controlled species. In the late 1980s, however, a new scientific and political discourse emerged that sought to integrate various levels of environmental concern within an overarching global framework. The Convention on Biological Diversity, agreed at the UN-organised Rio Earth Summit in 1992, codified a new understanding of the threat of extinction that shifted from the conservationist, species-based model to a concept of 'biodiversity'. Stephen Yearley argues that there are three levels of biodiversity: 'diversity between and within ecosystems and habitats; the diversity of species; and genetic variation within species' (1996: 121–2). This increasingly ecological, or systems-orientated, perspective aims to reframe local conservation issues in the language of global biodiversity. Yet, as Leigh's novel shows, genetic diversity is increasingly seen as a resource for biotechnology companies as well as the object of potentially comprehensive protection. The 'global' discourse of biodiversity is highly contested because of its complex and politically explosive relations with economic and cultural globalisation. Many environmentalists from the wealthy industrialised countries seek to protect biodiversity from both local people (poachers, illegal loggers) and transnational corporations. At the same time, commentators from ecologically rich Third World countries, such as Vandana Shiva, see such environmentalism as neo-colonialism, and suspect an unholy alliance between ecology and biotechnology. As Suzanne Biggs observes:

> The articulation of this new language of biodiversity is concomitant with the new biotechnologies which can isolate genes from an organism, manipulate them in the laboratory and insert them stably into another organism. Nature is no longer a process embedded in space and time expressing itself in natural living species through the process of evolution taking place over time, within spatially delineated ecosystems.

The component parts of nature can be disembedded and their relationship to space and time appear likely to be overcome. . . . Biodiversity
and biotechnology are intimately connected.

(1998: 120–1)

Thus the figure of the cyborg is complemented by that of the genetically
engineered organism (GEO) within a new, globalised frame of reference.
Liberationist criticism, which had been concerned with the rights of
individual domestic animals, must cope with the emergence of boundary
figures such as the cyborg and the feral animal. Ecocriticism similarly
must come to terms with GEOs and global biodiversity, as well as individual species. From a global perspective, an enlarged 'common future'
might be envisaged alongside the prospect of worldwide 'biopiracy'. It is
therefore the figure of the Earth itself that demands attention at the close
of this book.

8

FUTURES: THE EARTH

Jonathan Bate concludes *The Song of the Earth* with a Wallace Stevens poem called 'The Planet on the Table' and a request to the reader:

> As you read the poem, hold in your mind's eye a photograph of the earth taken from space: green and blue, smudged with the motion of cloud . . . so small in the surrounding darkness that you could imagine cupping it with your hands. A planet that is fragile, a planet of which we are a part but which we do not possess.
>
> (2000: 282)

As Stephen Yearley points out, 'The photographic portrayal of the globe viewed from an orbiting spacecraft has been used repeatedly to evoke the Earth's isolation in space, its fragility and wonder, and the sense that the beings on it share a restricted living space surrounded by an unwelcoming void' (1996: 65). Media analyst John Hannigan, like Bate, takes the meaning of the image for granted when he cites evidence that 'the single most effective environmental message of the century was totally inadvertent: the 1969 view from the moon of a fragile, finite "Spaceship Earth"' (1995: 62). Somehow this image, without commentary or design, seems unambiguously to communicate a powerful message.

The history of the Earth image, however, does not sustain the notion that it has a single meaning. Repeating Bate's experiment, we must acknowledge that the same act of imagination could grasp the earth as either a fragile totality 'of which we are a part but which we do not possess', or else a biological system for producing unlimited non-monetary wealth given fully rational management, and that both inflections might fairly claim to be ecological. The concept of 'Spaceship Earth' was in fact proposed by architect, inventor and cosmologist R. Buckminster Fuller (1895–1983), who took the Earth image as a figure for the possibility of the total, cornucopian management of the planet in human interests (see Fuller 1969).

Andrew Ross, one of the few ecocritics working on popular rather than literary culture, counts a photograph of the Earth taken by Apollo astronauts, amongst his 'images of ecology':

> In recent years, we have become accustomed to seeing images of a dying planet, variously exhibited in grisly poses of ecological depletion and circulated by all sectors of the image industry, often in spots reserved for the exploitation fare of genocidal atrocities. The clichés of the standard environmental image are known to us all: on the one hand, belching smokestacks, seabirds mired in petrochemical sludge, fish floating belly-up, traffic jams in Los Angeles and Mexico City, and clearcut forests; on the other hand, the redeeming repertoire of pastoral imagery, pristine, green, and unspoiled by human habitation, crowned by the ultimate global spectacle, the fragile, vulnerable ball of spaceship earth.
>
> (Ross 1994: 171)

We seem here to return to pastoral on an almost cosmic scale. Yet as Ross demonstrates, it is also crucial to consider the 'ecology of images': 'the social and industrial organization of images' and the 'ecological arguments to be made about those processes' (p. 172). The astronauts' pictures of the planet were won at considerable cost to it, not only in terms of the $25 billion space programme, or the £5.6 million of fuel on each Saturn 5 rocket, but also the interrelations between the Apollo programme and the Cold War military-industrial complex. As Ross shows, the US military has historically evaded environmental legislation, while preparing for wars that wreak extraordinary ecological damage upon foreign lands.

So the Earth image is contested and, arguably, compromised by the institutions and practices that made it possible. It is, moreover, a false perspective that allows us to see what only a handful of US astronauts have actually seen, a 'god's eye view' that promises a kind of transcendental power that we, as individuals or as a species, do not possess (see Legler 2000: 245). Nevertheless, it is essential for ecocritics to give greater consideration than they have thus far to the transformation in the dominant meaning of the word 'earth': from the most immediate ground of existence, the soil, to life's largest relevant context, the biosphere. The need not only to 'think globally' but to think about the globe demands a politicised reading practice more akin to social ecology and Cultural Studies than to deep ecology and traditional literary studies. Such a practice would consider constructions of the Earth provided by eco-nomics, politics and biology, as well as literature, TV and film. This chapter will examine two key inflections of the Earth, in order then to suggest possible futures for ecocriticism, beyond the problematic tropes of pastoral and wilderness, place and locale. The first inflection stems from the key concern of postmodern social thought, globalisation, and gives us the Earth as a technologically and economically enframed globe. The second is Gaia, which inflects the Earth as a living thing.

GLOBE

The Apollo photographs are just one means by which people all over the world are now able to apprehend its form. This globalisation of the imagination is powerfully reinforced by counterparts that operate, according to Yearley, in finance, communications, culture, business and politics. Transnational financial organisations demonstrated that they could marshal greater resources than national governments on several occasions during the 1990s: 'As capital markets become global, the fate of whole countries' economies can fall prey to the fears and imaginings of investors in the international money markets' (Yearley 1996: 4). These activities are made possible by global satellite-based communications, including the Internet, which eliminate traditional considerations of physical distance from transactions involving the communication of information. The local communities beloved of anti-modern ecocritics are being supplanted by 'virtual' communities brought together by shared interests, including environmental concerns. The globalisation of culture is both a cause and an effect of this process, as transnational cultural icons provide transnational talking points within and across these communities.

Globalisation, for some, represents homogenisation in which diverse local cultures are supplanted by 'monocultures of the mind' promoted and sustained by transnational culture industries based mainly in North America, Japan and Western Europe. The aspect of globalisation most often targeted by environmentalist critics is the growth of companies with turnover exceeding that of many nations and who possess a commensurate political power. While many industries remain necessarily locally or nationally based, the omnipresence of brand-based companies such as Nike or Coca-Cola seems to produce, sustain and rely on a homogenous global market. Cornucopian enthusiasts for globalisation argue that this presents an opportunity for poverty-stricken countries to develop economically, following the example of some Asian and South American nations. They claim that deregulation of markets and the elimination of trade barriers will encourage international investment, give Third World countries access to foreign markets and liberate domestic entrepreneurial capital, leading to a circle of wealth creation and the kind of social and environmental progress seen mainly in rich countries. At the same time, 'structural adjustment' policies imposed on Third World countries by international financial institutions such as the World Bank can have crippling effects on existing social and environmental pro-grammes, forcing governments to end price controls on basic goods, cut public spending and privatise nationalised industries. Even then, the economic benefits of free-market solutions may not accrue because of adverse domestic conditions or because transnational corporations realise most of the profits from liberalised trade. This has led to vigorous anti-globalisation resistance in both First and Third World countries. While the proportion of people in the world enduring absolute poverty is declining, population growth means that total numbers are continuing to increase, and power remains unevenly distributed. The statistics lessen neither the misery of the poor nor the scandal of First World wealth. As ecocritics interpret the meaning of the Earth, they will increasingly have to engage with globalised political conflicts.

The inflection of the globe as market place requires institutions to promote and enforce it. The most powerful of these are the World Bank, the International Monetary Fund (IMF) and the recently formed World Trade Organisation (WTO). All three are explicitly dedicated to the promotion of international capitalism, although the World Bank in particular incorporates questions of social development and environmental protection into negotiations with Third World countries. Some environmental organisations such as the World Wide Fund for Nature, Friends of the Earth and Greenpeace International have become substantial global actors, reflecting the scale and scope of the issues they address. The planet is developing a meaningful, though fragmented, political identity, in which a range of distinctively globalised social and environmental issues are contested.

As discussed earlier, it was a global political meeting, the Rio Earth Summit in 1992, that redefined the local or national problem of nature conservation as the globalised issue of 'biodiversity'. Yet the affirmation of a common interest in the future of the world's herring or rainforests conceals considerable differences of interpretation and conflicts of interest. Not only are there variations between countries in terms of method and extent of data collection, but as J.A. Hannigan's 1995 study shows, the biodiversity agenda had to overcome several major problems before it could become a 'successful' issue: accurate claims about extinctions are difficult to sustain, there are no obvious villains or simple solutions and few First World environmentalists would be affected directly by the losses. Third World countries that are biologically rich but economically impoverished can easily see the costs of preservation but, wildlife tourism aside, may not be able to see substantial benefits (Hannigan 1995: 146–61). Moreover, the universalising scientific and moral discourse of biodiversity is seen by some critics as a cover for First World pharmaceutical and agricultural corporations seeking to expropriate Third World biological wealth.

From the fifteenth century onwards, new territories discovered by European explorers were granted to national governments and their agents by charters, patents and Papal Bulls, with little concern for the rights of indigenous peoples. Vandana Shiva claims in *Biopiracy* (1998) that this colonial appropriation of land by means of legal instruments, which led to the domination, enslavement or extermination of non-Europeans in the populated continents, has a modern counterpart in the patents on genetically engineered organisms granted by courts in the developed world and assiduously protected by the WTO. Trade Related Intellectual Property Rights (TRIPs) are demanded by biotechnology companies to protect their investments in research and development, but Shiva claims that they represent a neo-colonial appropriation of the traditional biological knowledge of indigenous peoples and the 'inner spaces' of DNA, in processes that can be likened to 'the second coming of Columbus' (Shiva 1998: 11). She argues that genetic modification is misrepresented as a predictable, deterministic process of 'engineering' that creates organisms worthy of patent protection. On the contrary, this mere 'tinkering' with DNA, as she calls it, involves both processes and products that rely on nature's own capacity for self-organisation and reproduction, so that a patent effectively appropriates for biotechnology companies the inherent creativity of nature. If, as Shiva believes, the latter deserves reverence in itself, patenting even hybrid seed varieties would be a form of blasphemy. She makes a strong case for the legal protection of indigenous knowledge, albeit without explanation of how it differs from biotechnology as an appropriation of nature. Shiva also shows that the WTO and the Biodiversity Convention, which seem to represent opposite poles of exploitation and protection, may not be quite so antagonistic. The latter may lead to the identification and protection of Third World biological resources in the name of ecology that the former then allows First World companies to appropriate in the name of profit. Thus the comforting Planet Earth of ecologists may collude with the exploitative globe of transnational capital.

We have already observed that globalisation requires sophisticated communications technologies, which in turn require satellites in space. The various space programmes have not only supported commercial and military ends, however: meteorological and hydrological satellites supply vital information to scientists about global and local environmental issues, from ozone thinning to soil erosion. This process arguably represents a fresh inflection of the Earth as the object of new regimes of environmental surveillance and disciplinary design. This rather paranoid-sounding view derives from ecocritic Tim Luke's critique of the influential environmentalist organisation, the Worldwatch Institute, which is loosely based upon the work of philosopher Michel Foucault. Worldwatch collects environmental data from a vast array of sources, produces computer models and develops alternative future scenarios that are extrapolated from various possible starting points. Each year they publish a comprehensive report on the *State of the World*, including 'bioeconomic' information on natural resources, biodiversity, water supplies, population and so on.

Luke does not deny that Worldwatch is an effective environmental organisation. Rather, he criticises the inflection of the planet implied by Worldwatch's quest for sustainable modernisation: no longer a wild, mysterious Earth, but rather 'an ensemble of ecological systems, requiring human managerial oversight, administrative intervention, and organizational containment' (1997: 90). Lukes points out that Worldwatch reports identify bioeconomic inefficiencies that can be rectified, and individual or state policies that might be modified, but do not critique global capitalism as such. In the process, the science of ecology is reduced to a managerial or disciplinary role in the mitigation of environmental problems. Luke argues that the Earth is thereby inflected as an errant subject requiring techno-scientific correction, or 'environmentalization': 'As biological life is refracted through economic, political and technological existence, "the facts of life" pass into fields of control for disciplines of ecoknowledge and spheres of intervention for their management as geopower at various institutional sites' (1997: 91) From the social ecological perspective of Luke's analysis, world-watching leaves in place the 'basic logic of commodification and exchange that causes ecological destruction' (1997: 93). Because it fails to challenge the wealth of the First World, world-watching ensures that the burden of attaining sustainability will fall disproportionately on the Third World.

One of the most striking successes for world-watching was the 1987 Montreal Protocol that introduced global controls on ozone-depleting chloro-fluoro-carbons (CFCs). This agreement is often cited as evidence of the role science can play in addressing an emerging environmental problem decisively and effectively. As one US negotiator put it:

> The Montreal Protocol was the result of research at the frontiers of science combined with a unique collaboration between scientists and policymakers. Unlike any previous diplomatic endeavor, it was based on continually evolving theories, on state-of-the-art computer models, simulating the results of intricate chemical and physical

reactions for decades into the future, and on satellite-, land-, and rocket-
based monitoring of remote gases measured in parts per trillion.

(cited in Yearley 1996: 107)

The protocol and later amendments achieved a complete phased elimination of CFCs and related compounds in response to evidence that they were destroying the ozone layer over Antarctica. Ozone is a relatively rare form of elemental oxygen in which three atoms are present rather than the more usual two. At low altitudes, ozone is a corrosive component of smog and a greenhouse gas, but in the upper atmosphere it forms a 'layer' that filters out ultraviolet radiation that would otherwise be extremely damaging to animals and plants. In the 1970s it was claimed that CFCs, chemicals used in aerosol sprays and refrigeration, were capable of destroying atmospheric ozone. This claim was confirmed when scientists in the Antarctic found that the ozone above them was severely depleted during the spring, as a combination of atmospheric conditions unique to the region led to rapid destruction of stratospheric ozone.

This account makes it clear that the ozone problem is an objective, scientific phenomenon of global import that was successfully addressed by scientifically informed global political action. Kate Soper in *What is Nature?* assumes and propagates this view when she comments that 'it is not language that has a hole in its ozone layer' (151). This neat, memorable phrase has been cited by a number of critics to exemplify the emphasis on literal truth, rather than social construction, that marks ecocriticism out from other literary critical schools (Barry 2002: 252; Rigby 2002: 154). Ironically, Soper may have picked the wrong example to make her point. The 'hole in the ozone layer' is actually a good example of the scientific and cultural construction of global environmental problems, since the terms 'hole' and 'layer' are strictly metaphorical in this context. The latter is an area of increased concentration of ozone, which is actually present throughout the atmosphere. As Hannigan observes, images of the ozone hole are really simulated graphic maps:

> The NASA satellite pictures of the ozone hole . . . transformed con-
> tinuous gradations in real ozone concentration into an ordinal scale that
> is colour-coded, conveying the erroneous impression that a discrete,

identifiable hole could actually be located in the atmosphere over the South Pole.

(1995: 45)

These images raise the question of access to the means of representation and policy formation. It was the rich nations that drove forward the Montreal negotiations, demanding cuts in their own emissions and those of Third World countries, even though the latter were much smaller and had started more recently. Deploying science allowed developed countries to claim to speak for the whole world, a process called 'scientification': '*The conviction that science speaks objectively and disinterestedly means that one need have no qualms about excluding other people from decision-making since they would, in any event, have arrived at the same conclusions as oneself*' (Yearley 1996: 118; italics in original). The image of the ozone hole suggests the possibility of undemocratic and even neo-colonial environmental scientification. Ecocriticism demands attention to literal and irreducibly material problems such as ozone depletion, but it also depends upon the insight that scientific problems are never fully separable from cultural and political ones. The ozone problem is real, but it is mediated by a popularising metaphor, and framed within international political discourses that are not scientific, but ideological. Such an insight is congruent with the *critical realism* elaborated by Soper in her analysis as a whole.

The problem is therefore to establish the role of simulation for an ecocritical perspective on the globe. For the poetics of authenticity, it is the unmediated encounter with the real world that rescues the subject from the corrupt modern world of representation and simulation. In *The Age of Missing Information* (1992) Bill McKibben, one of the most persuasive of the proponents of this view, contrasts the insights provided by 24 hours on top of a mountain in the Adirondacks with the torrent of programming recorded from 100 cable TV channels in the same period. The latter, McKibben concedes, provides occasional doses of knowledge and a fair bit of entertainment, but at the same time fatally narrows our range of perception and response. Far from an Information Age, he claims, we live in a period of 'Unenlightenment', cut off from in the lessons taught by nature: 'Subversive ideas about how much you need, or what comfort is, or beauty, or time, that you can learn from the one great logoless channel and not the hundred noisy ones or even the pay-per-view' (McKibben 1992: 23). McKibben argues that TV promotes a violently compressed sense of time, and that it substitutes a bland, minimal comfort for the strife of exertion, discomfort, relaxation and sensuality that makes real happiness possible. Putting on warm, dry clothes after a hike in the rain is a pleasure fundamentally antithetical to immersion in the flickering glow of the TV set, not least because it involves senses of touch and smell that the latter simply does not address. Nonetheless, for ecocritics alert to the implications of postmodernity, his dualistic view of TV versus nature is unsustainable. The ozone hole is real and simulated, literal and metaphorical; global warming is a phenomenon generated by complex computerised climate models.

However, it is not only because climate change and ozone depletion are simulated crises that the world of simulations cannot simply be counterposed to the real world of nature. As we have seen, our encounters with the natural world are inflected by metaphors and every perception is, to some extent, a simulation. Conversely, as Katherine Hayles shows in 'Simulated Nature and Natural Simulations', the functionality of 'virtual reality' (VR) programmes and other simulations depends on an intimate fit between technology and nature, which implies a critique of the poetics of authenticity:

> If nature can be separated from simulation in a clear-cut way, then we risk believing that nature is natural because it is unmediated, whereas simulation is artificial because it is constructed. But there is an important sense in which nature is constructed . . . and simulation is natural . . . Only because simulation technologies employ precise and detailed knowledge about human perceptual transformations can they create simulations that strike us as compelling and realistic. A VR simulation appears three-dimensional to us because the images are offset, simulating the "natural" spacing of our eyes.
>
> (1996: 418)

Yet even as Hayles argues that the real and the simulated are not simply opposed and incommensurable categories, she takes for granted the validity of the distinction between them. French philosopher Jean Baudrillard claims in his influential 'Simulacra and Simulations' (1981) that communications technologies, capable of infinite replication and wide dissemination of information, have initiated a world of simulation, that now functions to supplant the real world. Modernity was characterised by growth in forms of representation, such as writing or the map, in which the real thing and its representation could always be clearly distinguished. In the postmodern world, however, mass-reproduced representations lose their origins so that now 'it is the map that engenders the territory' (2001: 169), and the real is scarcely discernible. Baudrillard identifies four 'phases of the image':

1   It is the reflection of a basic reality.
2   It masks and perverts a basic reality.
3   It masks the *absence* of a basic reality.
4   It bears no relation to any reality whatever: it is its own pure simulacrum.

(2001: 169)

Disneyland exemplifies all four of these orders; it represents pirates, and Main St USA (1), and also, obviously, misrepresents them (2). But it also embodies a more subtle misrepresentation: 'Disneyland is there to conceal the fact that it is the "real" country, all of "real" America, which *is* Disneyland' (p. 175). In this third phase of the image, the unreality of Disneyland obscures the more ominous unreality of America, although the 'unreality' in both cases is due to a surplus of representations rather than a lack of substance. Both Disneyland and America, then, are not less than real, but 'hyperreal', since the distinction between the real and simulated has collapsed, and what is left is a hall of mirrors of 'simulacra' (4). Michael Branch's essay 'Cosmology in the Casino' (1999) exemplifies this notion by examining the 2-hour cycle of day and night projected inside the dome of the Silver Legacy Resort Casino in Reno, Nevada, and expresses concern that this simulacrum may feed a desire for the hyperreal as a satisfactory substitute for the real. Baudrillard's scepticism towards the 'real' diametrically opposes him, and his theoretical conception of postmodernity, to most ecocritics.

Don DeLillo's novel *White Noise*, discussed earlier, explores the relationship between a postmodern world of simulations and environmental crisis. For example, during the toxic airborne event, officials appear from a state emergency preparedness organisation, SIMUVAC, that simulates catastrophes. For them, this actual emergency is an opportunity to rehearse, although the real can disappoint, as one official remarks: 'There's a probability excess. . . . You have to make allowances for the fact that everything we see tonight is real' (1986: 139). Jack's exposure to the toxic cloud leaves him adrift in uncertainty, as the SIMUVAC computer attempts to calculate a projected risk to his health. The official's reassurance is indistinguishable from threat:

> "It's what we call a massive data-base tally. Gladney, J.A.K. I punch in the name, the substance, the exposure time and then I tap into your computer history. . . . It comes back pulsing stars. This doesn't mean anything is going to happen to you as such, at least not today or tomorrow. It just means you are the sum total of your data. No man escapes that."

Such a projected or simulated death seems somehow superior to the subject's own living reality. Jack reflects, 'It makes you feel like a stranger in your own dying' (p. 142). Death and environmental disaster, which might seem to exemplify the real, are subordinated to the order of simulation in which every narrative of threat and resolution is hackneyed and insincere. As Richard Kerridge argues:

> *White Noise* positions its reader outside all the available narratives which could process environmental disaster and stabilise it, leaving an impasse, a condition of passive waiting. This novel dramatizes, more unsparingly than any other I know, the impasse between environmental consciousness and the inability of a culture to change.
>
> (1998: 139)

Postmodernist theories of representation may provide accurate diagnoses of environmental crises in the media, but they simulaneously disable the possibility of activism. Baudrillard's notion of simulation, as represented in *White Noise*, tends towards a kind of hyperbolic paranoia, or as he calls it, a 'vertigo of interpretation' (p. 178). Such implacable scepticism towards stable truth claims must be antithetical to an ecocriticism that attends to problems of representation, but is founded ultimately in the assumption of real environmental problems. We must distinguish between an enervating scepticism towards truth in general, as typified by Baudrillard's postmodernist theory, and a revitalising scepticism towards certain supposed 'truths' of popular ecological discourse, exemplified by postmodern ecology.

Crucially, both Baudrillard's enthusiasm for a simulated Earth and deep ecological despair remain entranced by the failed promise of authenticity. Orientated toward practical problems of responsibility, we need not accept the dichotomy between backpacking in the Adirondacks and a cyborg existence on a simulated Earth. The Baudrillardian perspective implies the implosion of meaning in contexts of postmodern ecological risk, but Ulrich Beck's engagement with the same problem yields a quite different conclusion:

> Global ecological dangers, far from intensifying a general lack of meaning in the modern world, create a meaning-filled horizon of avoidance, protection and assistance, a moral climate that grows sharper with the scale of the perceived danger, and in which a new political significance attaches to the roles of hero and villain.
>
> (1999: 45)

The operative myth is not necessarily paranoid apocalypticism, but more like the boy David's pragmatism faced with the giant Goliath. As Beck points out, inflecting the planet through global risk generates new political strategies as well as actors, such as the 'judo politics' of Greenpeace, 'designed to mobilize the superior strength of environmental sinners against themselves'. Such politics, moreover, can mobilise their own virtual inflections of the Earth.

GAIA

It was the novelist William Golding who suggested the name 'Gaia', the ancient Greek Earth-goddess, for the inflection of the Earth developed by his friend James Lovelock (see Chapter 5). It is now used by deep ecologists and ecofeminists to counter the inflection of the Earth as a technologically and economically enframed globe. Lovelock's work began in the science of planetary ecology. His hypothesis was that the Earth could be described as a self-regulating system, analogous to a living organism. It has been known since the discovery of plant photosynthesis that living organisms produce the atmosphere they need to inhabit, but Lovelock took the argument a stage further, asserting that the planet has been so thoroughly altered physically and chemically by living things that the Earth itself has to be seen as kind of super-organism. Rather than merely being a rock in space with life clinging to it, the non-living parts of the planet are as much a part of the whole as the non-living heartwood of a living tree.

According to Lovelock, the sun has been getting hotter as life on Earth has evolved, but our planet has stayed cool to the point of experiencing ice ages. This shows that Gaia has maintained a fairly stable global surface temperature throughout its history. Solar radiation passes through the Earth's atmosphere just as it passes through glass, and warms the surface. The heat produced would be lost to outer space but for the atmospheric gases that absorb it on the way out, trapping it as though under a blanket. Allowing light in, but stopping heat from getting out, is called the greenhouse effect. It is enhanced by high proportions of carbon dioxide. For Gaia to support life, the greenhouse effect must be regulated, since either too much or too little would be lethal. 'Global warming' involves an unacceptable degree of *anthropogenic* greenhouse effect, in addition to what the biosphere naturally provides.

Lovelock pointed out that marine organisms use some of the carbon dioxide dissolved in seawater to make their shells, which are then laid down in vast numbers in sedimentary rocks such as limestone. Some carbon dioxide is removed when dead plants decompose incompletely, forming coal, oil and other sediments. By these means, living things regulate atmospheric carbon dioxide in order to maintain a congenial surface temperature. Michael Allaby's *Guide to Gaia* (1990) explains how analogous mechanisms sustain water, sulphur and iodine cycles, regulate the salinity of the oceans and, perhaps, even affect continental drift. A benign and wholly unconscious conspiracy of millions of species keeps Gaia alive and stable, although the specific organisms and processes have changed considerably during its history and may be expected to continue to do so. Gaia is dynamic and unpredictable, not static and harmonious, although the hypothesis claims that it tends towards a geophysiological balance of energy and chemical elements analogous to the physiological balance of an organism.

Since Lovelock put forward the hypothesis, it has been strongly disputed by other scientists (see Schneider and Boston 1993). Brewer calls it a mere 'charming metaphor' (1994: 372). The debate may be difficult to follow in detail, but the key issues are not forbidding for non-scientists. Gaia has been attractive to deep ecologists and eco-spiritualists as well as climatologists, hydrologists and philosophers of science. Ascribing organismic unity to the planet and giving it the name of an Earth-goddess allows Gaia to be appropriated as the object of global environmental consciousness, and perhaps veneration too. But as Ernest Callenbach asserts: 'Gaia is not a conscious entity with a purpose or special concern for humans. Those who think of it as a stand-in for a Supreme Being or God are misinformed' (1998: 62). Kate Rawles argues that the ethical consequences of Gaia are not at all clear-cut. For example, it has been assumed that Gaia proves our interdependent 'oneness' with the biosphere, and should therefore promote care of it, but Rawles observes that 'while we are indeed inclined to look after ourselves up to a point, we are also notorious for risking long-term damage to our own health for short-term gains, or when the causal mechanisms of the damage are abstract or obscure' (1996: 318).

There are also political disputes concerning Gaia. Ecofeminist critic Patrick Murphy has criticised Lovelock for 'sex-typing the planet'. He acknowledges that 'Gaia has become an immediately recognized, acceptable term for Earth' and that the scientific hypothesis 'works well for changing consciousness' (Murphy 1995: 61, 68), but he nevertheless criticises Lovelock for remaining bound by patriarchal habits of language and thought. Murphy argues that, by adopting a feminine stereotype, Lovelock, in common with radical and Goddess-worshipping ecofeminists (see Chapter 2), 'reinscribes . . . patriarchal sex-typing' because 'the conception of the fertile female as enchanting, sacred, and mysterious is a perception that hinders the very healing they seek' (pp. 62–3). Like Plumwood, Murphy enjoins a non-hierarchical, or 'heterarchical', differentiation of gender that accepts biological differences without forcing them into hierarchical valuations. Gaia, he argues, elevates a specific valuation of the female to a planetary level. Nevertheless, while Murphy subjects Lovelock's hypothesis to ecofeminist critique, his own normative rhetoric remains conspicuously resistant to critique from a truly ecological perspective. He repeatedly measures writers against a yardstick of commitment to 'balance' and 'harmony' that, as we have seen, has little to do with modern ecology, and asserts wrongly (citing a theologian rather than an ecologist) a 'basic ecological principle that diversity is a key component of systemic health' (p. 67). Murphy is an important figure in ecocriticism, having fostered ASLE, ecofeminism, internationalism and greater literary theoretical sophistication, but his basic ecological vocabulary is increasingly anachronistic.

Gaia is, in any case, not simply identical with the Earth. It is a hypothetical construct of Lovelock's theory, a simile for the planet grasped 'as if' it were an organism. As the theory is refined, Gaia ought to come increasingly to resemble the Earth that we know and inhabit, but it will remain indefinitely open to falsification by scientists. One way to test Gaia is to try various computer models of its regulatory mechanisms, such as Lovelock's own Daisyworld simulation, versions of which are available on the Internet (e.g. DaisyBall is at <http://www.gingerbooth.com/course ware/daisy.html>). Simulations can show how Gaia works if it works at all, but on their own they cannot prove its worth as a theory. By comparison with Baudrillard's hyperbolic paranoia, such sensible pragmatism will seem dull, but understanding the responsible use of ecological modelling is essential for understanding the nature of scientific 'prediction' in the age of global ecology. Moreover, although I have analysed only its scientific formulation, Gaian simulation might also provide a basis for attempts to imagine the whole Earth in the literary and other media more usually addressed by ecocritics.

THE FUTURE OF ECOCRITICISM: BETWEEN TWO SIMULATIONS OF EARTH

This book has moved from the ancient trope of pastoral to the contemporary contestation of the figure of the Earth, from Romanticism to postmodernism. The Bible and Graeco-Roman narratives were important sources for the earlier tropes, and we saw that the notion of a pristine original space lost by human misdemeanour runs through pastoral, wilderness and some versions of dwelling, while the hope or fear of some final destination for human struggles with nature saturates apocalyptic

LIVERPOOL JOHN MOORES UNIVERSITY
LEARNING SERVICES

visions. However, Christian tropes are problematic for ecocritics, originating in an other-worldly religion that legitimises environmental destruction. The underlying narrative structure of Christian mythology claims a coherence for the history of Creation that is utterly at odds with evolutionary and ecological processes. Such ancient tropes, as adapted by environmental discourse, have the advantage of deep roots in our culture, but the liability of anachronism in the postmodern era. Only the relatively novel constructions of the human animal and the whole Earth, both profoundly shaped by scientific thought, seem to offer metaphors adequate to the novelty of our predicament, and even these may be inflected quite differently in different contexts.

Much ecocriticism has taken for granted that its task is to overcome anthropocentrism, just as feminism seeks to overcome androcentrism. The metaphysical argument for biocentrism is meant to sustain moral claims about the intrinsic value of the natural world, which will in turn affect our attitudes and behaviour towards nature. Wilderness experiences, or apocalyptic threats, or Native American ways of life, are supposed to provide the impetus or the example by which individuals come to an authentic selfhood orientated toward right environmental action. Whilst the importance of changing the minds and lives of individuals is undeniable, this book has aimed to show the political dimension that this moralistic emphasis may occlude. However, the politicisation of ecocriticism does pose its own problems. Dwelling on the troubling example of Heidegger (Chapter 6), who espoused both Nazism and a kind of deep ecology, Jonathan Bate asserts in *The Song of the Earth* that 'The dilemma of Green reading is that it must, yet it cannot, separate ecopoetics from ecopolitics' (2000: 266). Environmentalism is compatible with most political positions, and while we have seen possible dangers inherent in this, it might also give us a clear argument for better, not less, political attunement in ecocriticism. Bate rightly points out that poets are not the engineers of the world, and that literature cannot provide specific solutions, which means that ecocriticism must continue to adopt and adapt theories from feminist and Marxist traditions, enabling positive engagement in cultural politics.

I would argue that the promise of ecofeminist literary and cultural theory has yet to be realised. With important exceptions such as Haraway, Armbruster, Westling and Murphy, such criticism has been held back by the overstated anti-rationalism and gynocentric dualism of radical ecofeminism. The work of Australian philosopher Val Plumwood offers ecofeminism a sound basis for a much-needed critique of the dynamics of domination as they operate in a range of cultural contexts. A monolithically conceived root cause of environmental destruction, be it labelled anthropocentrism or androcentrism is bound to misrepresent the complexity of causation in the real world. Ecofeminism, modified by dialogue with social ecological positions, can provide insight into the cultural operations of environmental injustice. In this way, the fusion of environmental and social development agendas that has occurred so strikingly within and between global NGOs might come to ecocriticism; *Beyond Nature Writing* (2001), edited by Karla Armbruster and Kathleen Wallace, includes several essays in this emergent field of enquiry.

Ecocritics therefore continue to experiment with hybridised reading practices, drawing on various philosophical and literary theoretical sources. Bennett and Teague's *The Nature of Cities* (1999) reveals a new emphasis on bringing cultural theorists such as Cronon, Ross, Luke and Haraway into dialogue with literary ecocritics, thereby consolidating the field around a critical encounter between genres, perspectives and politics. The work of Richard Kerridge is exemplary in this respect: he writes with as much insight about postmodern risk as he does about Thomas Hardy. Harrison's eclectic *Forests* (1993), which ranges from Grimm fairy tales to the architecture of Frank Lloyd Wright, fosters the making of connections between disparate cultural phenomena without eliminating their peculiarities. Bate and Buell first published books that identified a single 'environmental tradition' in Britain and the USA, stemming from Wordsworth and Thoreau respectively. In later works, however, they favour an explicitly dialectical approach. In *The Song of the Earth*, Wordsworth's piety is leavened with Byron's wit, and Heidegger's portentousness gets a learned sneer from Theodor Adorno. For Buell, *Writing for an Endangered World* involves juxtaposing urbanites like Theodor Dreiser and Gwendolyn Brooks with the more obvious candidates for ecocritical treatment, Jeffers and Berry. Drawing upon such diverse resources of hope enables ecocriticism to connect with the urban and suburban places in which most of us will continue to live, and will add depth to the ecological critique of modernity; material and economic progress is no more the root of all evils than it is an unalloyed benefit to people or the natural world. By such means the risk of fostering reactionary politics might be minimised.

There are two key challenges for the future. One is the relationship between globalisation and ecocriticism, which has barely been broached. Sustained attention to the idea of place as locale has provided us with no sense of the place of the whole Earth in contemporary culture. The second is the difficulty of developing constructive relations between the green humanities and the environmental sciences. This is especially problematic in the light of developments in ecology that expose the rhetoric of balance and harmony as, in effect, versions of pastoral. This notion of nature's wisdom is so deeply ingrained in environmentalist discourse and eco-criticism that only sustained research at the borders of the humanities and the new postmodern biological sciences can disentangle it from our systems of basic presuppositions. As Daniel Botkin observes:

> As long as we could believe that nature undisturbed was constant, we were provided with a simple standard against which to judge our actions, a reflection from a windless pond in which our place was both apparent and fixed, providing us with a sense of continuity and permanence that was comforting. Abandoning these beliefs leaves us on an extreme existential position: we are like small boats without anchors in a sea of time; how we long for a safe harbor on a shore.
>
> (1992: 188–9)

Gaia, for example, implies unpredictability and dynamism rather than predetermined harmony, but also comfortingly reasserts the tendency of life to maintain equilibrium or balance. Botkin's ecology places rather less faith in the harmonious regulatory functions of living organisms. In both cases, the inflection of Earth as a static, fixed image is shown to be terribly misleading. The Earth is perhaps better seen as a process rather than an object.

Postmodern ecology neither returns us to the ancient myth of the Earth Mother, whose loss some ecocritics lament, nor supplies us with evidence that 'nature knows best'. The irony is that a future Earth-orientated system of values and tropes will have to acknowledge contingency and indeterminacy at a fundamental level, but this only *increases* the scope and extent of our liability as the most powerful species on the planet. The poetics of authenticity assumes, against the evidence of ecology, that there is a fixed external standard we ought to try and meet. The poetics of responsibility recognises that every inflection of Earth is our inflection, every standard our standard, and we should not disguise political decisions about the kind of world we want in either the discredited objectivity of natural order nor the subjective mystification of spiritual intuition. Ecocriticism is essentially about the demarcation between nature and culture, its construction and reconstruction. The ultimate logic of pastoral would be the hope that culture might be subsumed within nature, but we have seen the limitations of such idealism. The opposite extreme would be the technological sublimity of simulation, in which nature is no more than a cultural construct, but this world of pervasive representation is a misrepresentation. Ecocriticism, I would argue, will have to work with the shifting, pragmatic sense of the relationship of culture and nature suggested in this book.

Ecophilosophers often criticise the arrogance of anthropocentrism, sometimes using the Ancient Greek term 'hubris' for this fatal flaw of overweening self-righteousness and wilful misuse of power. The history of the world in the last 200 years, and especially the history of the developed world in the last 50 years, supplies ample evidence of such hubris. Yet the solution need not be, as deep ecologists would have it, self-abnegating humility and submission to the presumed natural order. The Ancient Greeks proposed a virtue that combined the proper pride of a clever, resourceful animal with reasonable acceptance of the human place in a world we can neither wholly predict nor control. They called it 'megalopsuche', which translates roughly as 'greatness of soul', and I would suggest this as a worthy aspiration. We can understand the distinction by contrasting two attempts to simulate planetary ecology.

In September 1991, eight people, called 'bionauts', were sealed into an enormous structure in the Arizona desert. For the next two years, they attempted to live and work in 'Biosphere 2', a simulation of the Earth's environment, the original Biosphere. Architecturally, Biosphere 2 is dominated by two stepped tetrahedral pyramids, reminiscent of Meso-American ruins, but built out of steel and glass like corporate buildings. Inside these and associated buildings, there are seven biomes that bring selected plants and animals from around the world together into a supposedly integrated, self-sustaining, total environment. Five 'natural' biomes – ocean, savannah, desert, tropical rainforest and marsh – sustain two 'artificial' ones, including a microcity for the human bionauts and an area for intensive agriculture. Outside the Biosphere itself, the site includes control rooms, conference facilities, exhibition spaces, gift shops and tourist conveniences. The initiative was supposed to provide a functioning model of 'Spaceship Earth' that might not only serve as a testbed for environmental engineering technologies, but also as an example of the eco-simulation technologies we might need for eventual space exploration beyond the limits of food, energy and oxygen supplies brought from Earth.

The original Biosphere 2 mission failed dramatically. Technical problems caused crop failures and elevated levels of carbon dioxide that would have killed the bionauts were it not for external intervention. Few worthwhile scientific results were achieved, and it largely failed as an advertisement or laboratory for self-sustaining life support systems. The second mission in 1994 was cut short, and Biosphere 2 has since had a new lease of life without bionauts or extravagant 'missions' as a research and educational facility of Columbia University. In its original incarnation, Biosphere 2 seems a good example of tragic hubris, occasionally bordering farce. Its 3.2 acres, whilst impressive in terms of large glasshouses, were a ludicrously small compass for such grandiose ambitions. Moreover, as Luke observes, the very basis of the project was disingenuous; while human life and its 'technosphere' depends on the sustaining 'ecosphere' out here in Biosphere 1, the simulated Earth reverses this priority. Underneath the great structures, complex, hidden mechanisms are needed to regulate environmental factors such as temperature or air composition. The ecosphere, in other words, comes to depend upon the technosphere. The biomes themselves are composed of entirely artificial associations of plants loosely associated with particular nations or regions, with a tiny selection of insects and animals included. This makes Biosphere 2 an excellent example of an ecological simulacrum:

> Here, 'Nature' is not Nature, but rather something that has been digitally sampled, botanically colorized, zoologically compressed, and ecologically scanned into a biospheric simulation of itself that could not

and would not exist without the engineering needed to stage this odd
ecological experiment.

(Luke 1997: 102)

On 15 May 2000, the world's largest greenhouses opened to the public
in Cornwall. The Eden Project, as it is called, is presently striving to cope
with its own extraordinary success as a tourist attraction. Superficially, the
Project resembles Biosphere 2: it incorporates two gigantic indoor biomes,
simulating humid tropic and warm temperate conditions with regional
botanical zones. It is brilliantly designed as a tourist attraction, seeming
to hide at the bottom of its enormous claypit until the paying customer
emerges onto the first viewing platform for an impressive panorama of its
eight geodesic domes surrounded by landscaped parkland, outdoor crops
and tourist services. The merchandise is of high quality, the Eden Project
brand name is everywhere and the designers have clearly learned a lot from
theme parks and similar leisure facilities.

Tim Smit, author of *Eden* (2001) and prime mover in the Project, is
candid about its commercial needs but deplores the theme park analogy.
He traces the laborious construction process, and explains that the
philosophy behind it was not to simulate ecosystems in the sense of
pretending to recreate them, but 'to represent and interpret climate zones
which exhibited the maximum impact of man on the environment, thus
providing a canvas on which to explore the widest range of issues' (Smit
2001: 129). Its ambition is not intergalactic and technophilic, but
resolutely terrestrial and educational, emphasising human dependence on
plants for aesthetic and spiritual sustenance as well as food, medicine and
industrial processes. Sculptures litter the inner and outer spaces, and the
site is patrolled by both scientists and performing artists. Technosphere
and ecosphere are constantly and explicitly interrelated, with service pipes
externally mounted on the domes, while within the biomes both creative
and destructive interrelations between culture and nature are explored:

Eden would be dedicated to inspiring people to reflect on the vital role
of plants and come to understand the need for balance between, on the
one hand, husbandry – growing them for our use – and, on the other,
stewardship – taking care of them on behalf of all living things.

(2001: 174)

Perhaps ironically, then, the 'Eden' Project is anything but an exercise in pastoral nostalgia, or a dualistic projection of humans in opposition to, or exile from, the Earth. It is an experiment in imaginary human ecology that flirts with utopianism, but ultimately epitomises something like global georgic:

> Eden isn't about the environment; that's like saying life is about air. It is concerned, in partnership with others, with exploring development in the fullest sense of the word: the sustainable development of human potential and the achievement of the optimum quality of life for all, across economic, social and cultural boundaries.
>
> (2001: 302)

It ought not to be too pious, or too implausible, to associate the ecocriticism of the future with Eden's inflection of the Earth: attuned to environmental justice, but not dismissive of the claims of commerce and technology; shaped by knowledge of long-term environmental problems, but wary of apocalypticism; informed by artistic as well as scientific ecological insight; and committed to the preservation of the biological diversity of the planet for all its inhabitants. It is a long way from the pastoral we started with, and it is a great-souled vision with its feet planted solidly on the ground.

Glossary

Androcentric   system of beliefs and practices that favours men over women.

Animism   belief that natural objects and phenomena have spirits.

Anthropocentrism   system of beliefs and practices that favours humans over other organisms.

Anthropogenic   caused by humans.

Carrying capacity   maximum number of organisms of a certain kind that an ecosystem can support. Sometimes dubiously applied to human populations, e.g. Callenbach 1998: 22–5.

Constructionism   belief that apparently natural phenomena, such as gender characteristics, are mainly or wholly enculturated or 'socially constructed'.

Cyborg   hybrid organism incorporating biological and electro-mechanical elements.

Dialectic   analysis pursued by means of incorporation of opposed arguments or perspectives.

Dualism   explanation of the world in terms of two opposed terms, e.g. mind vs. matter, nature vs. culture.

Ecocide   destruction of entire habitats, rather than just individual organisms or species.

Instrumental value   possessing value only in relation to human interests, usually narrowly economic.

Intraspecies   operating within, rather than between, species.

Intrinsic value   possessing value in its own right, without reference to human interests.

Jeremiad   a discourse of warning or discouragement, often prophetic in tone.

Matrifocal   social system centred on mothers as possessors of wisdom and creativity. Compatible with some forms of patriarchy.

Mechanism   belief that the world is explicable in terms of mechanical physical laws.

Monism   explanation of the world using a single, all-encompassing term.

Normative   proposing or maintaining a standard or norm.

Prolepsis   narratological term for anticipation of future events.

Reductionism   belief that phenomena can be explained in simple, or (by implication) simplistic, terms.

Speciesism   prejudice in favour of one's own species.

Synecdoche   figure of speech in which a part stands for the whole, e.g. 'hand' instead of 'worker', or 'hungry mouth' instead of 'poor person'.

Therianthropic   representation of humans and animals in a single image, usually as a form of caricature.

Theriomorphic   representation of humans as animals, usually with satirical purpose.

Theriophobia   irrational fear of animals.

Trope   any figure of speech, e.g. metaphor, metonymy, irony. Used in this book to name large-scale, underlying cultural metaphors of nature.

Vitalism   largely discredited scientific belief that phenomena possess a vital spirit over and above qualities that may be described mechanistically.

FURTHER READING

The ASLE website is an excellent, growing source of theoretical, bibliographic and pedagogical material, with an especially interesting section that includes twelve different definitions of 'ecocriticism': <http://www.asle.umn.edu/conf/other_conf/wla/1994.html>. This would be a good starting point for further research, as are the following:

K. Armbruster and K.R. Wallace (eds) (2001) *Beyond Nature Writing: Expanding the Boundaries of Ecocriticism*, London: University Press of Virginia. Examines a wide variety of authors and periods, with a broadly social ecological and ecofeminist perspective.

J. Bate (2000) *The Song of the Earth*, London: Picador. A dialectical reading of canonical literature, mainly British, using Heideggerean concepts.

M. Bennett and D.W. Teague (eds) (1999) *The Nature of Cities: Ecocriticism and Urban Environments*, Tucson, AZ: University of Arizona Press. Not only a new terrain for ecocriticism, but also a politically progressive theoretical framework.

D. Botkin (1992) *Discordant Harmonies: a New Ecology for the Twenty-First Century*, Oxford: Oxford University Press. An accessible and thought-provoking introduction to recent ecological theory that recognises the importance of tropes.

L. Buell (2001) *Writing for an Endangered World: Literature, Culture, and Environment in the U.S. and Beyond*, London: Belknap Press. Together with Buell's earlier Thoreau book, constitutes a thorough basis for American ecocriticism.

W. Cronon (ed.) (1996) *Uncommon Ground: Rethinking the Human Place in Nature*, London: Norton. An excellent collection of work by writers from a variety of disciplinary backgrounds.

C. Glotfelty and H. Fromm (eds) (1996) *The Ecocriticism Reader: Landmarks in Literary Ecology*, London: University of Georgia Press. Canonical anthology with a broadly deep ecological approach and exclusively American focus.

R. Kerridge and N. Sammells (eds) (1998) *Writing the Environment*, London: Zed Books. Important anthology containing essays on children's literature, wildlife programming and Oscar Wilde as well as canonical literature.

D. Quammen (1996) *The Song of the Dodo: Island Biogeography in an Age of Extinctions*, London: Pimlico. Excellent example of popular scientific writing that explains one of our most pressing ecological problems.

K. Soper (1998) *What is Nature?* Oxford: Blackwell. An uniquely accessible and insightful discussion of ecophilosophy and politics.

L.H. Westling (1996) *The Green Breast of the New World: Landscape, Gender, and American Fiction*, Athens, GA: University of Georgia Press. A persuasive ecofeminist reading of canonical American literature.

A. Wilson (1992) *The Culture of Nature: North American Landscape from Disney to the Exxon Valdez*, Oxford: Blackwell. A witty and combative contribution to green cultural studies.

BIBLIOGRAPHY

Abbey, E. (1992) *Desert Solitaire: a Season in the Wilderness*, London: Robin Clark. First published in 1968.

Aberley, D. (1999) 'Interpreting bioregionalism: a story from many voices', in M.V. McGinnis (ed.) *Bioregionalism*, London: Routledge.

Adamson, J. (2001) *American Indian Literature, Environmental Justice, and Ecocriticism: the Middle Place* Tucson, AZ: University of Arizona Press.

Allaby, M. (1990) *Guide to Gaia*, London: Optima.

Allen, P.G. (1996) 'The Sacred Hoop: A Contemporary Perspective', in C. Glotfelty and H. Fromm (eds) *The Ecocriticism Reader: Landmarks in Literary Ecology*, London: University of Georgia Press.

Alpers, P (1996) *What is Pastoral?* Chicago: University of Chicago Press.

Armbruster, K. (1998) 'Creating the world we must save: the paradox of television nature documentaries', in R. Kerridge and N. Sammells (eds) *Writing the Environment*, London: Zed Books.

—— (2001) 'Can a book protect a valley?: Rick Bass and the dilemma of environmental advocacy', in O.A. Weltzein (ed.) *The Literary Art and Activism of Rick Bass*, Salt Lake City,UT: University of Utah Press.

Attfield, R. (1983) 'Western traditions and environmental ethics', in R. Elliott and A. Gare (eds) *Environmental Philosophy*, Milton Keynes: Open University Press.

Atwood, M. (1991) *Wilderness Tips*, London: Virago.

—— (1992) *Surfacing*, London: Virago.

Austin, M. (1996) *The Land of Little Rain*, New York: Dover. First published in 1903.

Baarschers, W.H. (1996) *Eco-facts and Eco-fiction*, London: Routledge.

Baker, S. (1993) *Picturing the Beast: Animals, Identity and Representation*, Manchester: Manchester University Press.

Barrell, J. and Bull, J. (1982) *The Penguin Book of English Pastoral Verse*, London: Penguin.

Barry, P. (2002) *Beginning Theory: an Introduction to Literary and Cultural Theory*, Manchester: Manchester University Press.

Bass, R. (1998) *Fiber*, London: University of Georgia Press.

Bate, J. (1991) *Romantic Ecology: Wordsworth and the Environmental Tradition*, London: Routledge.

—— (2000) *The Song of the Earth*, London: Picador.

Baudrillard, J. (2001) *Selected Writings* (2nd edn), ed. M. Poster, Cambridge: Polity.

Beck, U. (1999) *World Risk Society*, Cambridge: Polity.

Beckerman, W. (1995) *Small Is Stupid: Blowing the Whistle on the Greens*, London: Duckworth.

Bennett, M. (2001) 'Jeremiad, elegy and the Yaak: Rick Bass and the aesthetics of anger and grief', in O.A. Weltzein (ed.) *The Literary Art and Activism of Rick Bass*, Salt Lake City, UT: University of Utah Press.

Bennett, M. and Teague, D.W. (eds) (1999) *The Nature of Cities: Ecocriticism and Urban Environments*, Tucson, AZ: University of Arizona Press.

Berger, J. (1979) *Pig Earth*, London: Bloomsbury.

—— (1980) 'Why look at animals?', in *About Looking*, London: Penguin.

Bergon, F. (2000) '"Sensitive to the verge of the horizon": the environmentalism of John Burroughs', in C.Z. Walker (ed.) *Sharp Eyes: John Burroughs and American Nature Writing*, Syracuse, NY: Syracuse University Press.

Berry, W. (1980) *A Part*, San Francisco: North Point Press.

—— (1990) *What Are People For?* San Francisco: North Point Press.

Biehl, J. (1991) *Finding Our Way: Rethinking Ecofeminist Politics*, Montreal: Black Rose Books.

Biehl, J. and Staudenmeier, P. (1995) *Ecofascism: Lessons from the German Experience*, Edinburgh: AK Press.

Biggs, S. (1998) 'The biodiversity convention and global sustainable development', in R. Kiely and P. Marfleet (eds) *Globalisation and the Third World*, London: Routledge.

Botkin, D. (1992) *Discordant Harmonies: a New Ecology for the Twenty-First Century*, Oxford: Oxford University Press.

Brain, T. (1998) 'Or shall I bring you the sound of poisons?', in R. Kerridge and N. Sammells (eds) *Writing the Environment*, London: Zed Books.

Bramwell, A. (1965) *Blood and Soil: Walther Darré and Hitler's 'Green' Party*, Bourne End, Bucks.: Kensal Press.

—— (1989) *Ecology in the Twentieth Century: a History*, London: Yale University Press.

Brennan, A. (1995) 'Ecological theory and value in nature', in R. Elliot (ed.) *Environmental Ethics*, Oxford: Oxford University Press.

Brewer, R. (1994) *The Science of Ecology* (2nd edn.) London: Saunders College.

Branch, M.P. (1999) 'Cosmology in the Casino: Simulacra of Nature in the Interiorized Wilderness', in M. Bennett and D.W. Teague (eds) *The Nature of Cities: Ecocriticism and Urban Environments*, Tuscon, AZ: University of Arizona Press.

Brooks, P. (1980) *Speaking for Nature: How Literary Naturalists from Henry Thoreau to Rachel Carson Have Shaped America*, San Francisco: Sierra Club Books.

Buell, L. (1995) *The Environmental Imagination: Thoreau, Nature Writing and the Formation of American Culture*, London: Princeton University Press.

—— (2001) *Writing for an Endangered World: Literature, Culture, and Environment in the U.S. and Beyond*, London: Belknap Press.

Bunce, M. (1994) *The Countryside Ideal: Anglo-American Images of Landscape*, London: Routledge.

Burke, E. (1990) *A Philosophical Enquiry into the Origin of Our Ideas of the Sublime and the Beautiful*, Oxford: Oxford University Press.

Callenbach, E. (1998) *Ecology: a Pocket Guide*, London: University of California Press.

Callicott, J.B. (1983) 'Traditional American Indian and traditional Western European attitudes towards nature: an overview', in R. Elliot and A. Gare (eds) *Environmental Philosophy*, Milton Keynes: Open University Press.

—— (1995) 'Animal liberation: a triangular affair', in R. Elliot (ed.) *Environmental Ethics*, Oxford: Oxford University Press.

Campbell, S. (1998) 'Magpie', in R. Kerridge and N. Sammells (eds) (1998) *Writing the Environment*, London: Zed Books.

Carson, R. (1999) *Silent Spring*, London: Penguin. First published in 1962.

Cather, W. (2000) *Oh Pioneers!* London: Virago.

Clare, J. (1986) *John Clare: Selected Poetry and Prose*, ed. M. Williams and R. Williams, London: Methuen.

Clark, J. (1990) 'What is social ecology?', in J. Clark (ed.) *Renewing the Earth: the Promise of Social Ecology*, London: Green Print.

Clark, S.R.L. (1998) 'Pantheism', in D. Cooper and J. Palmer (eds) *Spirit of the Environment: Religion, Value and Environmental Concern*, London: Routledge.

Clements, C.D. (1995) 'Stasis: the unnatural value', in R. Elliot (ed.) *Environmental Ethics*, Oxford: Oxford University Press.

Coates, P. (1998) *Nature: Western Attitudes since Ancient Times*, Cambridge: Polity.

Cooper, D. and Palmer, J. (eds) (1992) *The Environment in Question: Ethics and Global Issues*, London: Routledge.

Coupe, L. (ed.) (2000) *The Green Studies Reader: from Romanticism to Ecocriticism*, London: Routledge.

Cronon, W. (1996) 'The trouble with wilderness; or, Getting back to the wrong nature', in W. Cronon (ed.) *Uncommon Ground: Rethinking the Human Place in Nature*, London: Norton.

Crosby, A.W. (1995) *Ecological Imperialism: the Biological Expansion of Europe, 900–1900*, Cambridge: Cambridge University Press.

Cuomo, C.J. (1994) 'Ecofeminism, deep ecology and human population', in K. Warren (ed.) *Ecological Feminism*, London: Routledge.

Daly, M. (1979) *Gyn/Ecology*, London: Women's Press.

Davion, V. (1994) 'Is ecofeminism feminist?', in K. Warren (ed.) *Ecological Feminism*, London: Routledge.

Day, A. (1996) *Romanticism*, London: Routledge.

DeLillo, D. (1986) *White Noise*, London: Picador.

Descartes, R. (1986) '*A Discourse on Method*', '*Meditations on the First Philosophy*', and '*Principles of Philosophy*', London: Dent. 'Discourse on method' first published in 1637.

Dick, P.K. (1997) *Do Androids Dream of Electric Sheep?* London: Voyager. First published in 1968.

Doubiago, S. (1989) 'Mama Coyote talks to the boys', in J. Plant (ed.) *Healing the Wounds: the Promise of Ecofeminism*, London: Green Print.

Eagleton, T. (1996) *Literary Theory: an Introduction*, Oxford: Basil Blackwell.

Ehrlich, P. (1972) *The Population Bomb*, London: Pan/Ballantine.

Ehrlich, P. and Ehrlich, A. (1998) *Betrayal of Science and Reason: How Anti-Environmental Rhetoric Threatens Our Future*, Washington, DC: Island.

Elliot, R. (ed.) (1995) *Environmental Ethics*, Oxford: Oxford University Press.

Elliot, R. and Gare, A. (eds) (1983) *Environmental Philosophy*, Milton Keynes: Open University Press.

Erdrich, L. (1994a) *Love Medicine* (2nd edn), London: Flamingo. First published in 1984.

—— (1994b) *Tracks*, London: Flamingo. First published in 1988.

Ferry, L. (1995) *The New Ecological Order*, trans. C. Volk, London: University of Chicago Press. First published in 1992.

Fitter, C. (1996) *Poetry, Space, Landscape: Towards a New Theory*, Cambridge: Cambridge University Press.

Foltz, B. (1995) *Inhabiting the Earth: Heidegger, Environmental Ethics, and the Metaphysics of Nature*, Atlantic Highlands, NJ: Humanities Press.

Fudge, E. (2000) *Perceiving Animals: Humans and Beasts in Early Modern English Culture*, London: Macmillan.

Fuller, B. (1969) 'Spaceship Earth: An Operating Manual', from <http://www.bfi.org/operating_manual.htm> Accessed 6 December 2003.

Gaard, G. (1998) 'Hiking without a map: reflections on teaching ecofeminist literary criticism', in G. Gaard and P.D. Murphy (eds), *Ecofeminist Literary Criticism: Theory, Interpretation, Pedagogy*, Urbana and Chicago: University of Illinois Press.

Gaard, G. and Murphy, P.D. (eds) (1998), *Ecofeminist Literary Criticism: Theory, Interpretation, Pedagogy*, Urbana and Chicago: University of Illinois Press.

Garrard, G. (1996) 'Radical pastoral?', *Studies in Romanticism* 35(3): 451–65.

—— (1998) 'Heidegger, Heaney and the problem of dwelling', in Kerridge, R. and Sammells, N. (eds) *Writing the Environment*, London: Zed Books.

—— (2000) 'Wordsworth and Thoreau: two versions of pastoral', in R.J. Schneider (ed.) *Thoreau's Sense of Place: Essays in American Environmental Writing*, Iowa City, IA: University of Iowa Press.

Giblett, R. (1996) *Postmodern Wetlands: Culture, History, Ecology*, Edinburgh: Edinburgh University Press.

Gifford, T. (1999) *Pastoral*, London: Routledge.

Glotfelty, C. (1996) 'Introduction', in C. Glotfelty and H. Fromm (eds), *The Ecocriticism Reader: Landmarks in Literary Ecology*, London: University of Georgia Press.

Glotfelty, C. and Fromm, H. (eds) (1996) *The Ecocriticism Reader: Landmarks in Literary Ecology*, London: University of Georgia Press.

Gore, A. (1992) *Earth in the Balance: Forging a New Common Purpose*, London: Earthscan.

Gray, C.H. (1995) *The Cyborg Handbook*, London: Routledge.

Griffin, S. (1978) *Woman and Nature: the Roaring Inside Her*, London: Women's Press.

Hannigan, J.A. (1995) *Environmental Sociology: a Social Constructionist Perspective*, London: Routledge.

Haraway, D. (1991) *Simians, Cyborgs and Women: the Reinvention of Nature*, London: Free Association.

Harris, R. (2000) 'Other-words in *Silent Spring*', in C. Waddell (ed.), *And No Birds Sing: Rhetorical Analyses of Rachel Carson's Silent Spring*, Carbondale and Edwardsville, IL: Southern Illinois University Press.

Harrison, R.P. (1992) *Forests: the Shadow of Civilization*, London: University of Chicago Press.

Harvey, G. (1997) *The Killing of the Countryside*, London: Vintage.

Hayles, N.K. (1996) 'Simulated natures and natural simulations', in W. Cronon (ed.) *Uncommon Ground: Rethinking the Human Place in Nature*, London: Norton.

Hayward, T. (1995) *Ecological Thought: an Introduction*, London: Polity.

Heidegger, M. (1993) *Basic Writings*, ed. D.F. Krell, London: Routledge.

Hochman, J. (1998) *Green Cultural Studies: Nature in Film, Novel, and Theory*, Moscow: University of Idaho Press.

Hughes, J.D. (1996a) *Pan's Travail: Environmental Problems of the Ancient Greeks and Romans*, London: Johns Hopkins University Press.

—— (1996b) *North American Indian Ecology*, El Paso, TX: Texas Western Press.

Ingram, D. (2000) *Green Screen: Environmentalism and Hollywood Cinema*, Exeter: University of Exeter Press.

Janik, D.I. (1995) 'Environmental consciousness in modern literature: four representative examples', in G. Sessions (ed.) *Deep Ecology for the Twenty-First Century: Readings on the Philosophy and Practice of the New Environmentalism*, London: Shambhala.

Jeffers, R. (1987) *Selected Poems*, Manchester: Carcanet.

Kay, J. (1998) 'Concepts of nature in the Hebrew Bible', in R.G. Botzler and S.J. Armstrong (eds), *Environmental Ethics: Divergence and Convergence*, Boston, MA: McGraw-Hill.

Kerridge, R. (1998) 'Small rooms and the ecosystem: environmentalism and DeLillo's *White Noise*', in Kerridge, R. and Sammells, N. (eds) *Writing the Environment*, London: Zed Books.

—— (1999) 'BSE stories', *Key Words: a Journal of Cultural Materialism* 2: 111–21.

—— (2000) 'Ecothrillers: environmental cliffhangers', in L. Coupe (ed.) *The Green Studies Reader: from Romanticism to Ecocriticism*, London: Routledge.

—— (2002) 'Narratives of resignation: environmentalism in recent fiction', in J. Parham (ed.) *The Environmental Tradition in English Literature*, Aldershot, Hants.: Ashgate.

Kerridge, R. and Sammells, N. (eds) (1998) *Writing the Environment*, London: Zed Books.

Kheel, M. (1989) 'From healing herbs to deadly drugs: western medicine's war against the natural world', in J. Plant (ed.) *Healing the Wounds: the Promise of Ecofeminism*, London: Green Print.

Killingsworth, M.J. and Palmer, J.S. (1996) 'Millennial ecology: the apocalyptic narrative from *Silent Spring* to *Global Warming*', in C.G. Herndl and S.C. Brown (eds), *Green Culture: Environmental Rhetoric in Contemporary America*, Madison, WI: University of Wisconsin Press.

—— (1998) 'Ecopolitics and the literature of the borderlands: the frontiers of environmental justice in Latina and Native American writing', in R. Kerridge and N. Sammells (eds) *Writing the environment*, London: Zed Books.

—— (2000) '*Silent Spring* and science fiction: an essay in the history and rhetoric of narrative', in C. Waddell (ed.), *And No Birds Sing: Rhetorical Analyses of Rachel Carson's Silent Spring*, Carbondale and Edwardsville, IL: Southern Illinois University Press.

King, T. (ed.) (1990) *All My Relations: an Anthology of Contemporary Canadian Native Fiction*, London: University of Oklahoma Press.

King, Y. (1989) 'The ecology of feminism and the feminism of ecology' in J. Plant (ed.) *Healing the Wounds: the Promise of Ecofeminism*, London: Green Print.

Kolodny, A. (1975) *The Lay of the Land: Metaphor as History and Experience in American Life and Letters*, Chapel Hill, NC: University of North Carolina Press.

Krech III, S. (1999) *The Ecological Indian: Myth and History*, London: Norton.

Kroeber, K. (1994) *Ecological Literary Criticism: Romantic Imagining and the Biology of Mind*, New York: Columbia University Press.

LaChappelle, D. (1996) *D.H. Lawrence: Future Primitive*, Denton, TX: University of North Texas Press.

Lawrence, D.H. (1988) *The Rainbow*, London: Penguin. First published in 1915.

—— (1989) *Women in Love*, London: Penguin. First published in 1920.

Leahy, M.P.T. (1994) *Against Liberation: Putting Animals in Perspective*, London: Routledge.

Lee, M.F. (1997) 'Environmental apocalypse: the millennial ideology of "Earth first!"', in T. Robbins and S.J. Palmer (eds) *Millennium, Messiahs and Mayhem: Contemporary Apocalyptic Movements* London: Routledge.

Legler, G. (2000) '"I am a transparent eyeball": the politics of vision in American nature writing', in J. Tallmadge and H. Harrington (eds) *Reading Under the Sign of Nature: New Essays in Ecocriticism*, Salt Lake City, UT: University of Utah Press.

Leigh, J. (2000) *The Hunter*, London: Faber and Faber.

Leopold, A. (1968) *A Sand County Almanac and Sketches Here and There*, Oxford: Oxford University Press.

Levinson, M. (1986) *Wordsworth's Great Period Poems: Four Essays*, Cambridge: Cambridge University Press.

Lewis, M.W. (1992) *Green Delusions: an Environmentalist Critique of Radical Environmentalism*, London: Duke University Press.

Littlejohn, B. and Pearce, J. (1973) *Marked by the Wild: an Anthology of Literature Shaped by the Canadian Wilderness*, Toronto: McLelland and Stewart.

Lovelock, J. (1982) *Gaia: a New Look at Life on Earth*, Oxford: Oxford University Press. First published in 1979.

Lukes, T.M. (1997) *Ecocritique: Contesting the Politics of Nature, Economy and Culture*, London: University of Minneapolis Press.

Lutts, R.H. (2000) 'Chemical fallout: *Silent Spring*, radioactive fallout and the environmental movement', in C. Waddell (ed.), *And No Birds Sing: Rhetorical Analyses of Rachel Carson's Silent Spring*, Carbondale and Edwardsville, IL: Southern Illinois University Press.

McGinnis, M.V. (ed.) (1999) *Bioregionalism*, London: Routledge.

McKibben, B. (1990) *The End of Nature*, London: Penguin.

—— (1992) *The Age of Missing Information*, London: Penguin.

—— (2000) 'The call of the not so wild', in C.Z. Walker (ed.) *Sharp Eyes: John Burroughs and American Nature Writing*, Syracuse, NY: Syracuse University Press.

Malamud, R. (1998) *Reading Zoos: Representations of Animals and Captivity*, London: Macmillan.

Malthus, T.R. (1970) *An Essay on the Principle of Population*, Harmondsworth: Penguin.

Marx, L. (1964) *The Machine in the Garden: Technology and the Pastoral Ideal in America*, London: Oxford University Press.

Masson, J. and McCarthy, S. (1996) *When Elephants Weep: the Emotional Lives of Animals*, London: Vintage.

Merchant, C. (1990) *The Death of Nature: Women, Ecology and the Scientific Revolution*, San Francisco: Harper and Row. Originally published in 1980.

Midgley, M. (1983) *Animals and Why They Matter: a Journey Around the Species Barrier*, Harmondsworth, Middx.: Penguin.

Muir, J. (1992) *The Eight Wilderness-Discovery Books*, London: Diadem Books.

Murphy, P.D. (1995) *Literature, Nature, and Other: Ecofeminist Critiques*, Albany, NY: State University of New York Press.

Myers, N. and Simon, J. (1994) *Scarcity or Abundance: a Debate on the Environment*, London: Norton.

Nelson, B. (2000) *The Wild and the Domestic: Animal Representation, Ecocriticism, and Western American Literature*, Reno and Las Vegas: University of Nevada Press.

Nietzsche, F.W. (1974) *The Gay Science*, trans. W. Kaufman, New York: Vintage.

—— (1982) *The Portable Nietzsche*, ed. and trans. W. Kaufman, Harmondsworth, Middx.: Penguin Viking.

North, R.D. (1995) *Life on a Modern Planet: a Manifesto for Progress*, Manchester: Manchester University Press.

Norwood, V. (1996) 'Heroines of nature: four women respond to the American landscape', in C. Glotfelty and H. Fromm (eds) *The Ecocriticism Reader: Landmarks in Literary Ecology*, London: University of Georgia Press.

Oelschlaeger, M. (1991) *The Idea of Wilderness: from Prehistory to the Age of Ecology*, London: Yale University Press.

O'Leary, S.D. (1994) *Arguing the Apocalypse: a Theory of Millennial Rhetoric*, Oxford: Oxford University Press.

Padget, M. (2001) 'Native American Fiction', in H. Grice, C. Hepworth *et al.* (eds) *Beginning Ethnic American Literatures*, Manchester University Press.

Passmore, J. (1974) *Man's Responsibility for Nature*, London: Duckworth.

Payne, D. (1996) *Voices in the Wilderness: American Nature Writing and Environmental Politics*, London: University Press of New England.

Pepper, D. (1993) *Eco-Socialism: From Deep Ecology to Social Justice*, London: Routledge.

Plato (1920) 'Critias', in *The Dialogues of Plato*, vol. II, trans. B. Jowett, New York: Random House.

Plumwood, V. (1993) *Feminism and the Mastery of Nature*, London: Routledge.

—— (2001) *Environmental Culture*, London: Routledge.

Pollan, M. (2002) *Second Nature: A Gardener's Education*, London: Bloomsbury.

Ponting, C. (1992) *A Green History of the World*, London: Penguin.

Quammen, D. (1996) *The Song of the Dodo: Island Biogeography in an Age of Extinctions*, London: Pimplico.

Rackham, O. (1994) *The Illustrated History of the Countryside*, London: Phoenix.

Rawles, K. (1996) 'Ethical Implications of the Gaia Thesis', in P. Bunyard (ed.) *Gaia in Action: Science of the Living Earth*, Edinburgh: Floris.

Rigby, K. (2002) 'Ecocriticism', in J. Wolfreys (ed.) *Introducing Criticism at the 21st Century*, Edinburgh: Edinburgh University Press.

Robinson, D.M. (1999) 'Wilderness and the agrarian principle: Gary Snyder, Wendell Berry, and the ethical definition of the "wild"', *Interdisciplinary Studies in Literature and Environment* 6(1): 15–28.

Ross, A. (1994) *The Chicago Gangster Theory of Life: Nature's Debt to Society*, London: Verso.

Sale, K. (1985) *Dwellers in the Land: the Bioregional Vision*, San Francisco: Sierra Club Books.

Schama, S. (1995) *Landscape and Memory*, London: HarperCollins.

Scheese, D. (1996) '*Desert Solitaire*: Counter-friction to the Machine in the Garden', in C. Glotfelty and H. Fromm (eds) *The Ecocriticism Reader: Landmarks in Literary Ecology*, London: University of Georgia Press.

Schiller, F.W. (1985) 'On Naïve and Sentimental Poetry', trans. J.A. Elias, in H.B. Nisbet (ed.) *German Aesthetic and Literary Criticism: Winckelmann, Lessing, Hamann, Herder, Schiller, Goethe*, Cambridge: Cambridge University Press.

Schneider, R.J. (ed.) (2000) *Thoreau's Sense of Place: Essays in American Environmental Writing*, Iowa City, IA: University of Iowa Press.

Schneider, S.H. and Boston, P.J. (eds) (1993) *Scientists on Gaia*, London: MIT Press.

[Chief] Seathl (1994) *The Great Chief Sends Word: Chief Seathl's Testament*, Coalville, Leics.: Saint Bernard Press.

Sessions, G. (ed.) (1995) *Deep Ecology for the Twenty-First Century: Readings on the Philosophy and Practice of the New Environmentalism*, London: Shambhala.

Shapiro, M.J. (1993) '"Manning" the frontiers: the politics of (human) nature in *Blade Runner*', in J. Bennett and W. Chaloupka (eds) *In the Nature of Things: Language, Politics and the Environment*, London: University of Minnesota Press.

Shelley, P. (1977) *Shelley's Poetry and Prose*, ed. D.H. Reiman and S.B. Powers, London: Norton.

Shiva, V. (1989) 'Development, ecology and women', in J. Plant (ed.), *Healing the Wounds: the Promise of Ecofeminism*, London: Green Print.

—— (1998) *Biopiracy: the Plunder of Nature and Knowledge*, Totnes, Devon: Green Books.

Silko, L.M. (1986) *Ceremony*, London: Penguin. First published in 1977.

Singer, P. (1983) *Animal Liberation: Towards an End to Man's Inhumanity to Animals*, Wellingborough, Northants.: Thorsons. First published in 1975.

Slater, C. (1996) 'Amazonia as Edenic Narrative', in W. Cronon (ed.) *Uncommon Ground: Rethinking the Human Place in Nature*, London: Norton.

Slovic, S. (1992) *Seeking Awareness in American Nature Writing*, Salt Lake City, UT: University of Utah Press.

—— (1996) 'Epistemology and politics in American nature writing: embedded rhetoric and Discrete Rhetoric', in C.G. Herndl and S.C. Brown (eds), *Green Culture: Environmental Rhetoric in Contemporary America*, Madison, WI: University of Wisconsin Press.

Smit, T. (2001) *Eden*, London: Transworld.

Snyder, G. (1999) *The Gary Snyder Reader: Prose, Poetry and Translations 1952–1998*, Washington, DC: Counterpoint.

Sober, E. (1995) 'Philosophical problems for environmentalists', in R. Elliot (ed.) *Environmental Ethics*, Oxford: Oxford University Press.

Soper, K. (1998) *What is Nature?* Oxford: Blackwell.

Spretnak, C. (1989) 'Towards an ecofeminist spirituality', in J. Plant (ed.) *Healing the Wounds: the Promise of Ecofeminism*, London: Green Print.

Sweeting, A. and Crochunis, T.C. (2001) 'Performing the wild: rethinking wilderness and theater spaces', in K. Armbruster and K.R. Wallace (eds) *Beyond Nature Writing: Expanding the Boundaries of Ecocriticism*, London: University Press of Virginia.

Theocritus (1978) *The Poems of Theocritus*, trans. A. Rist, Chapel Hill, NC: University of North Carolina Press.

Thomas, K. (1984) *Man and the Natural World: Changing Attitudes in England 1500–1800*, Harmondsworth, Middx.: Penguin.

Thomashow, M. (1999) 'Toward a cosmopolitan bioregionalism', in M.V. McGinnis (ed.) *Bioregionalism*, London: Routledge.

Thompson, D. (1997) *The End of Time: Faith and Fear in the Shadow of the Millennium*, London: Minerva.

Thoreau, H.D. (1983) *The Maine Woods*, Princeton, N.J.: Princeton University Press. First published in 1864.

—— (1992) *Walden*, London: Dent. First published in 1854.

—— (2003) 'Walking' from <http://eserver.org/thoreau/walking.html> Accessed 25 July 2003. First published in 1862.

Trafzer, C.E. (1993) *Earth Song, Sky Spirit: Short Stories of the Contemporary Native American Experience*, London: Anchor.

Virgil (1984) *The Eclogues*, trans. G. Lee, London: Penguin.

—— (2002) *The Georgics* from <http://www.tonykline.free-online.co.uk/Virgilhome.htm> Accessed 25 July 2003.

Warren, K. (1990) 'The power and the promise of ecological feminism', *Environmental Ethics* 12(2): 124–46.

Warren, K. (ed.) (1994) *Ecological Feminism*, London: Routledge.

Welch, J. (1986) *Fools Crow*, London: Penguin.

Westling, L.H. (1996) *The Green Breast of the New World: Landscape, Gender, and American Fiction*, Athens, GA: University of Georgia Press.

White, L., Jr. (1996) 'The historical roots of our ecologic crisis', in C. Glotfelty and H. Fromm (eds) *The Ecocriticism Reader: Landmarks in Literary Ecology*, Athens, GA: University of Georgia Press.

Wheeler, M. (ed.) (1995) *Ruskin and Environment: the Storm-Cloud of the Nineteenth Century*, Manchester: Manchester University Press.

Williams, J. (1993) *Wordsworth: Contemporary Critical Essays*, London: Macmillan.

Williams, R. (1989) 'Socialism and ecology', in *Resources of Hope*, London: Verso.

—— (1993) *The Country and the City*, London: Hogarth. First published in 1973.

Willis, R. (1974) *Man and Beast*, London: Hart-Davis, MacGibbon.

Wilson, A. (1992) *The Culture of Nature: North American Landscape from Disney to the Exxon Valdez*, Oxford: Blackwell.

Wilson, J. (1998) *The Earth Shall Weep: A History of Native America* London: Picador.

Wollstonecraft, M. and Godwin, W. (1987) 'A Short Residence in Sweden' and 'Memoirs of the Author of "The Rights of Woman"', London: Penguin .

Wordsworth, W. (1977) *A Complete Guide to the Lakes . . .* , ed. E. de Selincourt, Oxford: Oxford University Press.

—— (1979) *The Prelude: 1799, 1805, 1850*, ed. J. Wordsworth, M.H. Abrams and S. Gill, London: W.W. Norton.

—— (1969) *Poetical Works*, ed. T. Hutchinson and E. De Selincourt, Oxford: Oxford University Press.

Yearley, S. (1996) *Sociology, Environmentalism, Globalization: Reinventing the Globe*, London: Sage.

Zimmerman, M.E. (1990) *Heidegger's Confrontation with Modernity: Technology, Politics and Art*, Indianapolis, IN: Indiana University Press.

—— (1993) 'Rethinking the Heidegger–Deep Ecology Relationship', *Environmental Ethics* 15 (Fall): 195–224.

Index

eBooks – at www.eBookstore.tandf.co.uk

A library at your fingertips!

eBooks are electronic versions of printed books. You can store them on your PC/laptop or browse them online.

They have advantages for anyone needing rapid access to a wide variety of published, copyright information.

eBooks can help your research by enabling you to bookmark chapters, annotate text and use instant searches to find specific words or phrases. Several eBook files would fit on even a small laptop or PDA.

NEW: Save money by eSubscribing: cheap, online access to any eBook for as long as you need it.

Annual subscription packages

We now offer special low-cost bulk subscriptions to packages of eBooks in certain subject areas. These are available to libraries or to individuals.

For more information please contact webmaster.ebooks@tandf.co.uk

We're continually developing the eBook concept, so keep up to date by visiting the website.

www.eBookstore.tandf.co.uk